Timepass

TIMEPASS

*Youth, Class, and the
Politics of Waiting
in India*

CRAIG JEFFREY

STANFORD UNIVERSITY PRESS
Stanford, California

Stanford University Press
Stanford, California
© 2010 by the Board of Trustees of the
Leland Stanford Junior University

Library of Congress Cataloging-in-Publication Data

Jeffrey, Craig.
  Timepass : Youth, class, and the politics of waiting in India / Craig
Jeffrey.
      p. cm.
  Includes bibliographical references and index.
    ISBN 978-0-8047-7073-6 (cloth : alk. paper) —
    ISBN 978-0-8047-7074-3 (pbk. : alk. paper)
    1. Young men—India—Meerut—Social conditions. 2. Unemployed
youth—India—Meerut. 3. College students—Political activity—India—
Meerut. 4. Middle class—India—Meerut. I. Title.
HQ799.8.I42J44 2010
305.242'108694109542—dc22

                                                        2010011335

Printed in the United States of America on acid-free, archival-quality
paper

Typeset at Stanford University Press in 10.5/15 Garamond

Contents

Acknowledgments

I am very grateful to the villagers and students in Uttar Pradesh who feature in this book for their time and friendship. I will always remember the hospitality and warmth of many of the people with whom I worked. I am also most grateful to Dr. OP Bohra for his assistance in the field in 1996 and 1997. OP's wisdom and energy contributed a great deal to the research. The fieldwork upon which this book is based was primarily funded by the Economic and Social Research Council (R000200573).

In India I am indebted to a host of people for their advice and guidance, especially Amita Baviskar, Radhika Chopra, Prem Chowdhry, Krishna Kumar, Satendra Kumar, Satish Kumar, Jagpal Singh, Kanchan Singh, Rajni Palriwala, Saraswathi Raju, Nandini Sundar and Patricia Uberoi. Thank you, too, Katrine Danielsen in Delhi and Uncle and Auntie Verma in Meerut for your generosity and kindness.

I have benefited a great deal from conversations with colleagues and friends in Cambridge, Edinburgh, Seattle and Oxford since 1995 as well as from discussions with other scholars at conferences and seminar events. I would particularly like to thank the following people for their ideas, assistance and encouragement: in the UK, Harriet Bulkeley, Sharad Chari, Shana Cohen, Nandini Gooptu, Thomas Hansen, Barbara Harriss-White, Patricia Jeffery, Roger Jeffery, Alex Jeffrey, Jens Lerche, Emma Mawdsley, Fiona McConnell, Linda McDowell, Filippo Osella, James Sidaway and Philippa Williams; in the US: Paul Brass, Dipesh Chakrabarty, Lawrence Cohen, Veena Das, Vinay Gidwani, Ann Grodzins Gold, Patrick Heller, Victoria Lawson, Katharyne Mitchell, Anand Pandian, Sarah Pinto, Priti Ramamurthy, Paul Robbins, "Shivi" Sivaramakrishnan, Mathew Sparke, Susan Wadley, Steven Wilkinson, Kathleen Woodward and Anand Yang. I would also like to thank Dena Aufseeser, Colin McFarlane, Jane Dyson, Deborah Durham, Rowan Ellis, John Harriss, David Jeffrey and Stephen Young for their close readings of draft versions of the manuscript and for discussing the ideas in the book. Jennifer Hele and Stacy Wagner at Stanford University Press helped a great deal in the preparation of the manuscript. It was a great privilege to have been guided by Stuart Corbridge for my doctoral dissertation in Cambridge in the 1990s.

This book would not have been written without the love and kindness of my family, especially my wife, Jane Dyson. The book is dedicated to our two children, Florence and Finn.

Timepass

1   India Waiting

In 2004 I spent time with a student named Jaipal in Meerut College, Uttar Pradesh (UP). Jaipal was in his late twenties at that time and came from a lower middle class, rural background. He had failed to obtain a salaried job; Jaipal described himself as "unemployed," someone "just waiting." Politics was Jaipal's métier. He was often at the forefront of collective student demonstrations against the Meerut College bureaucracy. A typical morning might find him leading protests against the corruption of university officials or lambasting a government official for neglecting student issues. Curiously, however, Jaipal often spent his evenings at the homes of university administrators and government bureaucrats colluding over how to make money from illegal admissions. It was an open secret in Meerut that many student leaders (*netās*) protested alongside other students against corruption while also making money from their political influence.

How common is it for young men in Meerut to imagine themselves as "just waiting"? Why and how do young men like Jaipal engage in such contradictory forms of politics? And what might answers to these questions tell us about class, politics and "waiting"? This book addresses these questions with reference to field research conducted in the North-Western part of Uttar Pradesh (UP) State. I focus on educated unemployed young men and rich farmers from a threatened middle class in order to engage with three main areas of scholarly inquiry. First, I contribute to emerging debates on postcolonial middle classes. Second, I examine the micro-politics of class and caste dominance in UP. Third, I reflect on how different forms of "waiting" are implicated in processes of social change.

I consider issues of class, politics and waiting through telling the story of a lower middle class of Jats in Meerut district, especially students from this caste studying in Meerut. A prosperous, socially confident and politically influential set of rich Jat farmers emerged in North-Western UP in the first four decades after Indian Independence, partly as a result of improvements in agricultural production. During the 1990s they faced new threats to their power associated with the rise of lower castes. They addressed these threats by trying to influence the operations of local government and by investing in their children's education—strategies which farmers imagined as forms of "waiting" (see Chapter Two of this book). Yet only a few of the sons of these rich farmers were able to obtain the salaried jobs that they had been led to expect and many had come to imagine themselves as people who had no option but to wait. I examine cultures of limbo among educated unemployed young men. Unemployed young men were advertising their aimlessness through a self-conscious strategy of hanging out—a masculine youth culture that challenged the dominant temporal logics of their parents and the state (Chapter Three). This culture of masculine waiting was precipitating collective youth protest in Meerut, especially around issues of corruption, students' progression through academic institutions, educational mismanagement and government officials' harassment of students. In Meerut young men from a wide variety of social backgrounds sometimes came together to orchestrate agitations against the state and university (Chapter Four). Yet class and caste inequalities fractured collective protest around unemployment and corruption. In particular, among unemployed students a set of Jat "leaders," who also called themselves "fixers" (*kām karānewale*), used their social contacts to monopolize local networks of "corruption"—practices that undermined young people's collective action (Chapter Five). Through documenting these different forms of youth cultural and political action, alongside an analysis of the strategies of rich farmers in rural areas, the book highlights the micro-politics of class power in north India and the importance of waiting as a basis for mobilization.

This chapter locates my study with reference to broader literatures on time, middle-class unemployed youth and everyday politics in India. In the next section, I introduce recent literature on waiting and the Indian middle classes. I then focus on the experiences of educated unemployed young men within the lower middle classes, especially their temporal anxieties and political responses to waiting. This is followed by a consideration of how the politics of lower middle-class young men in India might be theorized. Finally, I outline my research strategy and the structure and argument of the book.

Waiting and Middle India

We all wait. Waiting has always been a characteristic feature of human life. Waiting for rain, harvests, birth and death are important components of the social organization of non-industrialized societies. Waiting is also a key dimension of modernity; during the twentieth century the increasing regimentation and bureaucratization of time in the West created multiple settings—such as traffic jams, offices and clinics—in which people waited (see Corbridge 2004; Moran 2004; Bissell 2007). But what of long-term waiting? What of situations in which people have been compelled to wait for years, generations or whole lifetimes, not as the result of their voluntary movement through modern spaces but because they are durably unable to realize their goals?

There is a growing literature based in different parts of the world on forms of "waiting" wherein people have been incited by powerful institutions to believe in particular visions of the future yet lack the means to realize their aspirations. Of course, there is nothing new about such chronic, fruitless waiting, which characterized the experiences of colonized populations (Chakrabarty 2000) and the lives of Europe's large *population flottante* in the eighteenth and nineteenth centuries (Darnton 1999), for example. From a rather different perspective, Siegfried Kracauer (1995 [1963]) argued that many professionals in urban Germany in the 1920s had a profound sense of "just waiting." Kracauer described upper middle classes *horror vacui* (fear of empty time and space) in the context of a decline in religious faith.

Yet in a recent book, Jean-Francois Bayart (2007) has argued that long-term experiences of "waiting" became a more prominent feature of the experiences of populations, especially subaltern people, across the world after the 1960s (see also Bourdieu 2000). Bayart cites as evidence: an increase in

reasons for waiting

the numbers of international migrants occupying detention centers on the edge of industrial states; the rising prison population in the US and parts of Europe; and people forced to move between countries in the global south in the aftermath of war or economic collapse. Bayart also suggests that there are whole nations, such as Zimbabwe in 2008, effectively waiting for a future and great swathes of the world's population, for example in Sub-Saharan Africa and north India, who have written into their minds certain hopes but for whom social goods are elusive and, who, as a result, define themselves as people in wait (see Ferguson 2006). Much recent scholarship supports the tenor of Bayart's argument. Ethnographic research on asylum seekers (Conlon 2007), refugees (Wong 1991; Stepputat 1992), urban slum dwellers (Appadurai 2002), the unemployed (Mains 2007) and rural poor (Corbridge et al. 2005), for example, is full of references to people waiting and their associated feelings of boredom and lost time. Moreover, these waiting populations are often subjected to discourses that stigmatize people as "surplus to requirements" or "loitering" (Mbembe 2004).

During my fieldwork I met large numbers of unemployed young men in north India who were engaged in forms of waiting characterized by aimlessness and ennui. Unemployed young men in Meerut commonly spoke of being lost in time and they imagined many of their activities as simply ways to pass the time ("timepass," as it is often described in India). This waiting was not wholly purposeless, however: it offered opportunities to acquire skills, fashion new cultural styles and mobilize politically.

I also discuss another form of "waiting" in this book. Several scholars have referred to how situations of rapid change in the contemporary world may persuade people to readjust their temporal horizons. In particular, they may come to prioritize long-term over short-term goals: they choose to wait. For example, the anthropologist Arjun Appadurai (2002) has described how activist organizations in Mumbai improved the living conditions of the urban poor by deliberately adopting a "long-term political horizon." These organizations encouraged their members to disregard the near-term development targets of foreign NGOs in favor of pursuing longer range goals. Such deliberate forms of investment have also been discussed in studies of household decision-making. In many situations, and perhaps especially during periods of rapid

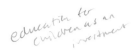
education for children as an investment

socio-economic change, people forego a desire for immediate consumption in favor of investing in the future of their families (Berry 1985). In the north Indian case I examine in this book, rich farmers made an explicit decision in the mid-1990s to prioritize their children's education and they imagined this strategy as a form of "investment" that entailed "waiting."

In elaborating on these two different forms of waiting—relatively purposeless youth timepass and more strategic investment on the part of rich farmers—my aim is not to construct a meta-narrative about the significance of waiting in India or across the world. I adopt instead an ethnographic approach that discusses the nature and social implications of waiting from the perspective of a struggling lower middle class, especially educated unemployed young men.

Middle classes of different types are highly visible social and political actors in many parts of the postcolonial world. Middle classes in Latin America, Africa and Asia often include struggling indigenous elites created through colonialism (e.g. Scheper-Hughes 1992), class fractions seeking to protect their access to state largesse in the face of the downsizing of the state (e.g. Harriss-White 2003) and entrepreneurs who have taken advantage of nation-building projects, economic restructuring and projects of international development to separate themselves from the poor (e.g. Berry 1985; Mawdsley 2004; Robison and Goodman 1996; Fernandes 2006). What tends to unite these disparate classes is a shared anxiety about the possibility of downward mobility and a determination to use their economic and social resources to shore up their position vis-à-vis the poor (e.g. Barr-Melej 2001; Cohen 2004).

India offers an example of how middle classes in postcolonial contexts are reshaping social and political life. The much vaunted emergence of Information Technology (IT) allied to the rapid economic growth rate in India since the early 1990s are often said to have raised increasing numbers of Indians into the middle class. There is considerable debate over the size of the Indian middle class; estimates vary from 50 million to 350 million (see Deshpande 2003; Nijman 2006), in large part because of disagreement over what combination of factors—lifestyle, income levels, consumption patterns and employment status, for example—should be used to delineate classes. For example, Deshpande (2003: 138) reports that if ownership of consumer goods is a key criterion for defining the Indian middle class, this segment of society was small in the mid-1990s: less than 8 percent of Indian households possessed a color television in 1995–96. If we examine the middle class as a social category actually used by people on the ground it may be even smaller than Deshpande suggests; Sheth (1999) argues that people tend to define themselves as "middle class" in India only when they possess a suite of consumer goods, education, a brick-built house and white-collar occupation. There is nevertheless a consensus that a reasonably substantial, moderately prosperous stratum now exists in India that does not herald from traditional elites but which exerts a profound influence over the politics, culture and social organization of the country (Fernandes 2006; Fernandes and Heller 2006; Varma 2006; see Milanovic 2005 for a dissenting view).

Fernandes and Heller (2006) identify three tiers within the Indian middle classes: first, senior professionals, higher bureaucrats and others with advanced professional credentials; second, a petit bourgeoisie that seeks to emulate the upper tier and which is comprised of rich farmers, merchants and small-business owners; and third, those with some educational capital who nevertheless occupy positions low-down within bureaucratic hierarchies. Fernandes and Heller stress that class and caste tend to overlap: middle classes tend to be from higher castes.

There is an important strand of research that has focused on the contemporary social and political practices of the highest tier in Fernandes and Heller's schema: the upper middle classes usually residing in urban India, and especially in the metropolises of Delhi, Mumbai, Kolkata and Chennai (e.g. Favero 2005; Harriss 2006; Nijman 2006; Fuller and Narasimhan 2007; Van Wessel 2007). This research suggests that upper middle classes benefited from the liberalization of the Indian economy from the early 1990s onwards. Rich urbanites were able to use their social connections and accumulated cultural capital, especially their mastery of English, to capture the most lucrative and secure positions that emerged in IT and allied industries in India or to expand their own businesses. Fuller and Narasimhan (2007), in a study of IT workers in Chennai, write of a mood of "prevailing optimism" and a sense among IT professionals of the multiple benefits wrought by the opening up of the Indian economy since the early 1990s (see also Favero 2005).

There is rather less research examining the second and third tiers of the middle classes in Fernandes and Heller's categorization: the assortment of "lower middle classes," including rich farmers, merchants, small-business owners, low-ranking bureaucrats and also sections of organized labor (see Harriss-White 2003; Gooptu 2007). The expansion of the Indian state bureaucracy, democratization of access to education and capital intensification within agriculture between 1947 and the late 1980s expanded the size and power of these middle-class fractions. For example, in many parts of the Indian countryside, a stratum of rich farmers emerged in the 1960s and 1970s, largely as a result of government subsidies for farming and technological changes in agriculture (e.g. Harriss 1982; Upadhya 1988; Rutten 1995; Gidwani 2008). Capitalist intensification and increased state expenditure on agriculture and business also heightened the importance of a wide range of merchants and entrepreneurs in India, who Harriss-White (2003), following Kalecki (1972), terms the "intermediate classes" (see also Chari 2004). The expansion of Indian state bureaucracies also swelled the ranks of the middle class, especially in urban areas (Fernandes 2000).

Economic reform threatened the accumulation strategies of many sections of this heterogeneous lower middle class, who typically came from middle-ranking castes. Between 1947 and the mid-1980s, India's approach to macroeconomic planning combined a leading role for the private sector in economic decision-making with state intervention aimed at accelerating growth and redistributing social opportunities (Chandrashekhar and Ghosh 2002). In the face of a growing fiscal crisis, however, and under pressure from multilateral lenders, the Indian state began a program of economic liberalization in the mid-1980s which intensified in the early 1990s (see Corbridge and Harriss 2000). Economic reforms, while benefiting some sections of the lower middle classes (Chari 2004), often threatened middle classes' access to state subsidies, reduced the supply of government jobs and undermined state services, such as educational and health facilities. By the late 1990s a gulf was emerging between an upper middle class in metropolitan India, the apparent beneficiaries of liberalization, and the lower middle classes, who typically found their jobs, educational strategies and access to state goods under threat. The rise of lower castes within formal politics in many parts of India and the related emergence of a small Dalit (ex-untouchable) and lower caste elite in the 1980s and 1990s unsettled middle classes still further (Jaffrelot 2003).

Leela Fernandes (2004, 2006) has shown how these economic and political threats to lower middle classes in India coincided with the circulation of new images of rapid social mobility. In particular, the onset of liberalization was accompanied by intense efforts on the part of sections of the state, business interests and media organizations to promote images of "new middle-class" success. Depictions of prosperous urban Indians occupying expensive sub-urban homes equipped with all modern conveniences became prominent at almost the precise moment at which lower middle classes were struggling to maintain their standard of living. This disjuncture between image and reality generated a feeling among some lower middle classes of being somehow "in limbo" and of their "waiting" for development (Favero 2005; Fernandes 2006). For Fernandes it was such a sense of waiting that staved off more radical protest among the middle classes: "anticipation of future benefits mediates the immediacy of political opposition to the economic disruptions or deterioration produced by reforms" (Fernandes 2006: xx).

Such lower middle-class anxiety is obviously not limited to India. Solvay Gerke (2000) has argued that a threatened Indonesian middle class in the 1990s were forced to resort to a form of "virtual consumption," a set of strategies designed to display standards of living that they could not afford. Shana Cohen (2004) has described the emergence of middle classes in Morocco in the 1970s and 1980s, who saw similar a gap opening up between their aspirations and social realities. As in Fernandes (2006) work, Gerke and Cohen argue that middle classes increasingly imagined their individual mobility to involve participating in the drama of Western social progress, either through migrating or via the consumption of consumer goods and education.

Neither Gerke nor Cohen discusses in detail the politics of the middle class. But in India lower middle classes have devoted considerable energy to preventing downward mobility and expressing anxieties within political spheres. Several studies describe middle-class involvement in Hindu nationalist political organizations as a response to social frustration (Corbridge and Harriss 2000; Hansen 2001; Fernandes and Heller 2006). Others refer to politicking outside the realms of formal political organizations (Rutten 1995;

Harriss-White 2003; Fernandes and Heller 2006). For example, Harriss-White (2003) shows that intermediate classes in Tamil Nadu reacted to economic liberalization through intensifying efforts to collude with local government officials within dense webs of "corrupt" and violent local-level practice. Similarly, Fernandes and Heller (2006) emphasize the "opportunity hoarding" of India's lower middle classes within local networks of political relations.

Educated Unemployed Young Men

Threats to middle-class power in India are often especially keenly felt by educated young men excluded from secure employment. Indeed, such unemployed men may be key political actors in contemporary India. The scale of the employment crisis in India meant that some of the country's bourgeoisie and upper middle classes experienced unemployment in the 1990s and early 2000s (see Favero 2005). Increasing education among formerly marginalized communities in India, such as Dalits and Muslims, also exacerbated problems of educated unemployment among historically poor sections of society (see Parry 1999; Jeffrey et al. 2008). Yet educated unemployment in India is often a particular problem for lower middle-class young men, who commonly possess the financial backing to obtain education and engage in a prolonged job search, but lack the funds, social networking resources and cultural capital to succeed within fiercely competitive markets for government jobs and positions in the new economy (see Fernandes 2000).

Official figures collected at employment exchanges and by the National Sample Survey (NSS) are poor indicators of joblessness because few people in India register themselves as unemployed (Ul Haq 2003). Nevertheless, according to NSS data, 12 million people were openly unemployed in 2004–5. Desai (2007) suggests that in the same year, about 150 million were in low-quality employment, many of them young people with high school and college qualifications. Rates of employment in India's organized sector of the economy were stagnant in the late 1990s and early 2000s despite rapid economic growth. Industrial and service-sector growth in India was skill- and capital-intensive during this period and therefore tended not to generate employment. Sharp projected increases in the young adult population in the next ten years are likely to aggravate this problem. Joshi (2009) states the situation succinctly in a discussion of one of India's apparently vibrant new sectors: "The IT sector currently employs 1 million people; in five years, it may employ 3 million. But in five years India's labour force will grow by around 65 million and much of the rise will occur in backward states."

Educated unemployment is not new in India. The colonial state often encouraged large numbers of young people to enter formal education, and not all of these men acquired salaried work (see Coleman 1965). Complaints about "semi-educated" young men "hanging about" around government offices surface in the reports of colonial officials at least as far back as the mid-1850s in India (Dore 1976: 53). Moreover, Robert Dore (1976) argued over thirty years ago that a combination of population growth, a lack of expansion in manufacturing and service industries and increased enrollment in education had created a large cohort of unemployed young people in many parts of India. Yet educated unemployment has become especially pronounced since the 1970s.

Similar contradictions have been noted in other postcolonial settings, as well as in the West (see Kaplinsky 2005). A recent rise in the visibility of unemployment or underemployment among educated youth has been discussed in places as diverse as Papua New Guinea (Leavitt 1998; Demerath 1999), Ethiopia (Mains 2007), Morocco (Cohen 2004) and Peru (Stepputat 2002). Substantial numbers of people in Asia, Africa and Latin America, especially those from lower middle classes, have looked to formal schooling as a means of social mobility since 1970, and they have been exposed via this education, the media or development institutions to images of progress through education and entry into white-collar work (e.g. Silberschmidt 2001). At the same time, global economic changes since 1970 have failed to generate large numbers of permanent white-collar jobs within manufacturing or service. The result has been the emergence of a global surplus population, which, unlike the "reserve army of labor" discussed by Marx in the nineteenth century, possess educational qualifications and are sometimes highly skilled (see Kaplinsky 2005). Indeed, many in this group perceive themselves to be "underemployed" rather than wholly without work. They are dependent on involuntary part-time work, engaged in intermittent unemployment, and/or involved in poorly remunerated labor (Prause and Dooley 1997: 245). I therefore use the term "educated unemployed" to refer both to people who are unemployed and underemployed.

Emerging work on joblessness in the global south suggests that educated unemployment bears most pressingly on men in their twenties or early thirties. This is not to deny the importance of unemployment for older people (see Breman 2000; McDowell 2003) or for young women, who comprise a substantial section of the educated unemployed in some regions of the global south, such as the Middle East (Miles 2002) and parts of South America (Miles 1998). But the prevalence of male breadwinner norms in the global south often means that educated unemployment has especially direct negative consequences for young men.

Scholars employing ethnographic methods have started to uncover the anxieties of educated unemployed youth in the 1990s and 2000s within and outside India.* Educated unemployed young men are often unable to marry (see Masquelier 2005; Chowdhry 2009). They frequently find it difficult to leave home and purchase or rent independent living space (Hansen 2005). Educated unemployed young men are also commonly dogged by a sense of not having achieved locally salient norms of masculine success (Osella and Osella 2000; Cole 2004); they might conform by dint of their education to a particular vision of successful masculinity but lack the resources necessary to assume the role of male adult provider (Cole 2004, 2005). Public discourses of educated unemployed young men as "louts" (McDowell 2003) or hyper-masculine and violent "threats" to the state and civil society exacerbate this gendered crisis (Stambach 1998; Roitman 2004).

An intriguing aspect of recent work on youth unemployment is scholars' tendency to mention young men's anxieties about time. Educated unemployed young men may feel that they need to pass time in new ways in

---

*My focus on educated unemployed young men should not obscure the importance of examining the strategies of uneducated young people. On this point see some of the comments on my blog on The Guardian's website: http://www.guardian.co.uk/profile/craig-jeffrey. See also my Rethinking Democracy blog: http://rethinkingdemocracy.wordpress.com/.

the face of their joblessness (e.g. Corrigan 1979). Indeed, time may become a central social preoccupation, as Michael Ralph (2008) argues in a recent essay on young men "killing time" in urban Nigeria and as Mains (2007) also suggests in research among youth in Ethiopia. This dimension of educated unemployed young men's experiences must be contextualized with reference to changes in how time has been imagined and experienced over the past two hundred years. The onset of modernity in Europe and North America was associated with the institutionalization of chronological time (see Thompson 1967; Zerubavel 1985; Thrift 1996). Rather than operating according to seasonal rhythms, people began to measure their lives and activities more closely with respect to abstract units of time, such as days, weeks, years and decades. From at least the nineteenth century onwards, and via development institutions in the postcolonial period, national governments and large capitalist organizations often imposed Western ideas of linear time in the global south (Postone 1993), and young people were often exposed to such visions of time through their schooling. In addition, the colonial and postcolonial project of "development" reconfigured notions of linear time in an especially ideologically potent manner (see Gidwani 2008). As Raymond Williams (1985) has argued, powerful institutions in the West combined the biological notion of development (the life-cycle of an organism) with evolutionary ideas to present a vision of social and economic development as a linear unfolding of progress (see also Cowen and Shenton 1996). Western nations were presented as the mature form of development for other countries to emulate—Walter Rostow's *Stages of Growth* (2008 [1959]) model of modernizing development became a well-known example of this ideological drive. Reflecting the weight of such ideas, countries in the global south were frequently perceived as occupying the "waiting room of history" (Chakrabarty 2000: 256): a permanent state of "not now, not yet."

For young people in postcolonial countries the force of such dominant visions of time has another dimension. In the nineteenth and twentieth centuries in Euro-America, there was a formalization of how societies imagined people should move through their biological lives and increased emphasis placed on distinct life "stages" (Johnson-Hanks 2002). Particular models of how social lives should be mapped onto chronological time became enshrined in new laws and public institutions (Cole and Durham 2008: 6): childhood, youth, adulthood and old age were institutionalized as distinct phases of life (e.g. Aries 1962). In addition, the notion of school trajectories and adult (usually male) working careers became ubiquitous (Wiener 1981). During the colonial and postcolonial periods, dominant institutions promoted these visions of maturation, which often replaced older models of how people mature or lent a new force to indigenous life-stage models (Osella and Osella 2007). In so doing, Western models frequently exerted a type of symbolic violence on people, such as educated unemployed young men, unable to "transition" between various "stages of life" (see Johnson-Hanks 2002; Ruddick 2003; Cole and Durham 2008).

In the face of these multiple pressures, educated unemployed young men in the global south commonly experience their exclusion from secure salaried work as a triple temporal hardship. First, they are unable to conform to dominant visions of how people should comport themselves with respect to linear, clock time—they "miss years" or have "gaps" on their resumes, for example (Øian 2004). Second, they are unable to obtain the social goods, such as a secure white-collar job, which connote "development" as this is articulated by Western governments and international organizations (e.g. Heuzé 1996). Third, they are incapable of moving into gendered age-based categories, especially male adulthood, such that they come to be labeled or label themselves as "drop outs," "failures" or people "on the shelf" (Mbembe 2004; Argenti 2005; Ralph 2008).

The theme of waiting emerges strongly in recent research on unemployed young men in India. The author Pankaj Mishra (2006) has written evocatively of towns in north India where young men appear to be "waiting," and his novel on youth politics in Benares is saturated with images of young men in limbo (Mishra 2004; see also Myrdal 1967 on waiting in India). Gerard Heuzé's work in provincial central India brings out these themes even more clearly. Heuzé describes a population of lower middle-class young men who spent long periods in education but who were unable to acquire government work or marry and spent most of their time simply "hanging around" at major road intersections. Heuzé (1996: 105) concludes that "waiting has become an art and may become a profession for the majority of India's youth." The

cultural and political importance of unemployed young men haunted by boredom and a sense of being left behind is also well attested in Indian cinema.
Ranjani Mazumdar (2007) has traced a move in Bollywood films from depictions of "angry young men" in the 1970s, typified by Amitabh Bachchan, to
representations of unemployed young men as disorientated loafers (*tapori*)
in the 1990s (see especially the movie Rangeela (2004). The educated unemployed young man, wandering about, flirting or simply "waiting for something
to happen," was a central motif in some of the popular comedies produced
by Hrishikesh Mukherjee (see the film *Gol Mal*, 1979) and Sai Paranjape (for
example *Chashme Buddoor*, 1981) in the 1970s and 1980s. But in the 1990s and
2000s the *tapori* became a staple of popular Indian cinema.

Recent research within and outside India has chronicled educated unemployed young men's political responses to situations of uncertainty. R. Harriss
(2003), for example, has described the role of educated unemployed young
men in political demonstrations in Argentina in the early 2000s. Following
the collapse of the Argentine economy in 2001, educated young men joined
union members, indigenous leaders, women and younger children in a nation-
wide network of picketers and popular assemblies. In his account of "pavement politics" in Cape Town in the mid-1980s, Bundy (1987) emphasizes the
often covert and micro-political manner in which unemployed youth challenged Apartheid. In Bundy's account, it was educated unemployed young
men who possessed the educational training, time and motivation to work as
provocateurs. At a more everyday level, De Vries's (2002) study of political
brokerage in Mexico suggests that educated unemployed young men, including those from middle-class backgrounds, often use their educated skills to
assist the poor in their negotiations with the state. Similarly, Demerath (1999)
documents the emergence of a set of educated unemployed youth in Papua
New Guinea who occupied positions in local government organizations, circulated radical political discourses and acted as mediators between the poor
and urban state bureaucrats (see also Weiss 2002).

Jennifer Cole (2004, 2005) argues for the capacity of threatened youth to
challenge and transform dominant structures of power, and she does so with
especial attention to the changing lives of underemployed young men and
young women in urban Madagascar. Cole observes that whereas many edu-

cated young men in a Madagascan city had been forced to enter poorly paid criminal activity, young women were often able to earn substantial amounts of money through engaging in transactional sex with foreign visitors to the country. These dynamics led to a change in the regional politics of gender relations wherein young men (*jaombilos*) relied on their female partners for money and in return provided sex, companionship and the image of a youthful style. Cole argues that youth in Madagascar had responded to economic uncertainties through rethinking the gendered structures framing their lives.

Recent research in India offers a vibrant picture of the often informal nature of the politics of educated unemployed young men and their engagement in politicized and gendered cultural practices (Hansen 1996, 2001; Pai and Singh 1997; Krishna 2002; Nisbett 2007; Rogers 2008). Some accounts emphasize the reactionary, self-serving nature of educated unemployed young men's cultural and political action. For example, Hansen (1996) describes how widespread exclusion from secure employment led lower middle-class young men in Bombay in the 1990s to craft identities as Hindu nationalist political bosses. These men reconstructed a sense of masculine prowess through assuming roles as brokers between the urban poor and government officials. They also acted as provocateurs during anti-Muslim agitations and "hard men" capable of intervening violently to assist their friends (see also Heuzé 1992). Hansen emphasizes the capacity of lower middle classes to mobilize through local politicking to defend their narrow class, caste and religious interests. Paralleling Hansen's account, Prem Chowdhry (2009) has studied unemployed young men in Haryana, north India, who channeled frustration into work in all-male caste *panchāyats* (caste associations). These young men used the *panchāyats* to engage in illegal reactionary political practices, for example violently punishing those who marry across caste boundaries.

Other work highlights the democratic activity of lower middle-class young men in India. Where educated unemployed young men come from formerly subordinated communities they may act as political entrepreneurs, assisting their communities in matters of everyday social and political endeavor. Richer educated unemployed young men also sometimes become spokespeople for the poor, forging links across caste and class boundaries. Krishna (2002) argues that educated unemployed young men from lower middle-class backgrounds in rural western India in the 1990s often used their schooling to assist impoverished villagers in their negotiations with the state, circulate political discourses and intercede in local disputes (see also Kamat 2002). In a similar vein, Gooptu (2007) has described relatively wealthy young men from families historically associated with organized labor in West Bengal who engaged in "social service" (*samāj sewā*). Studies of educated unemployed young men in India therefore resonate with other scholarship on the educated unemployed by highlighting the importance of mundane forms of mobilization. Educated unemployed young men often advance their goals—be they reactionary or progressive—along relatively hidden pathways, in everyday spaces of social life and through cultivating relationships with diverse representatives of the state.

Theorizing the Politics of Unemployed Young Men

The varied, informal nature of the political practices of unemployed young men, and their concern with cultural forms of political action, points to a need for a flexible, fine-grained approach to theorizing politics, one that examines micro-tactics and everyday endeavor as well as institutions, social movements, electoral politics and major epochal events. In the 1950s, 1960s and 1970s, there was a rich vein of political anthropological work that addressed questions of quotidian political action in India, including Frederick Bailey's (1957, 1963) multiple studies of local politics in Orissa, Paul Brass's (1965) work on Congress politics and Anthony Carter's (1974) detailed analysis of the political strategies of elites in south India. With notable exceptions (e.g. Wade 1985, 1988; Robinson 1988), political science research on South Asia in the 1980s and 1990s shifted to a certain extent towards analysis of elections and the construction of large-scale models of political behavior.

Recent anthropological research on the relationship between state and society within and outside India suggests a renaissance of interest in ethnographic approaches to politics and offers a useful starting point for thinking about the political strategies of educated unemployed young men (e.g. Gupta 1995; Das and Poole 2004; Ferguson 2006). Drawing on Foucault, scholarship on the anthropology of the state has exposed the subtle discursive and material apparatus through which the state and other powerful institutions constitute people as subjects of rule (e.g. Fuller and Bénéï 2001; Hansen and Stepputat 2001). This emphasis on governmentality, understood as the micro-political processes through which state power conditions people to act in specific ways, demonstrates how visions of moral and social behavior disseminated by dominant institutions come to shape the practices of people on the ground. A governmentality perspective encourages reflection on the mechanisms through which powerful organizations persuade or compel unemployed young men to remain in situations of "limbo" or "waiting," for example through the social production of visions of hope and development (see also Verdery 1996; Spivak 2004).

Building on these ideas of how power operates, scholars have begun to rework Foucault in order to show how threatened young people and other liminal social actors inhabit, manipulate and contest broader governmentalizing logics (e.g. Gupta 1995; Appadurai 2002; Ferguson and Gupta 2002; Chatterjee 2004; Li 2005). Many authors have described how subordinated populations negotiate governmental power in the global south, including, for example, Tania Li's (2005, 2007) research on the politics of Indonesian development and Akhil Gupta's (1995) account of discourses of anti-corruption in north India. These studies usefully highlight the importance of what Li (2005) calls "metis": messy, contextualized forms of knowledge and practice that lie outside the purview of state planners and tend to be ignored in mainstream political science (see also Moore 2005).

At the same time, however, studies of governmentality in the postcolonial world sometimes emerge from an engagement with Foucault presenting a somewhat unhelpful binary picture of political practice wherein the state and urban bourgeoisie is pitted against a local "political society" (Chatterjee 2004) or "public culture" (Gupta 1995). The search for some broad arena of radical non-state action—the politics of "the masses"—takes precedence over analysis of how ordinary society is divided, for example between relatively prosperous people and the very poor. One of the effects of this de-emphasis on class divisions at the local level is to distract attention from the often crucial role played by lower middle classes, including youth from this section of society, in political dynamics on the ground.

This argument can be drawn out through reference to the influential recent work of Partha Chatterjee. Chatterjee (1998: 59) makes a distinction between "civil society" and "political society" in India. In Chatterjee's model, civil society refers to institutions originating in Western societies which are founded on legal norms and moral ideas of fair play. "Civil society in India today, peopled largely by the urban middle classes, is the sphere that seeks to be congruent with the normative models of bourgeois civil society" (Chatterjee 2008: 57). For Chatterjee, political society refers to a zone of political action in which the urban poor and the majority of those living in rural areas bargain with the state. "Those in political society make their claims on government, and in turn are governed, not within the framework of stable constitutionally defined rights and laws, but rather through temporary, contextual and unstable arrangements arrived at through direct political negotiations" (ibid.) These "contextual and unstable arrangements"—often illegal and sometimes violent—typically involve the members of political society developing their own moral claims to resources based on particular notions of community. The denizens of political society rarely make reference to bourgeois norms of liberal government: they hustle, negotiate and break the law.

In his elaboration of how political society works in practice, Chatterjee frequently emphasizes broad-based political mobilizations in which "the masses" obtain resources from the state. Chatterjee therefore tends to see political society as a democratizing force. Moreover, Chatterjee foregrounds instances in which different lower middle classes, such as party workers or schoolteachers, have assisted the poor within political society.

Chatterjee's emphasis on informal political practice occurring mainly outside of elections is useful for an understanding of the politics of unemployed young men in India. And his conceptualization of how lower middle classes, such as teachers and local-level party workers, may assist the poor in negotiations with, or campaigns against, the state and bourgeoisie is important. But Chatterjee overplays the distinction between civil and political society, ignoring how civil and legal practices often characterize the politics of ordinary people in India—a point I will demonstrate in a discussion of student politics in Meerut. More importantly, in emphasizing the democratic potential of political society, Chatterjee distracts from destructive forms of lower middle-class politics. Barbara Harriss-White (2003) has demonstrated how

threatened lower middle classes in India are crucially important in reproducing geographies of social exclusion and privilege within a sphere analogous to
Chatterjee's "political society." Yet the accumulative tactics of these middling
sections of society are rarely the explicit object of discussion in Chatterjee's
analyses or, indeed, the work of many anthropologists concerned with the
everyday relationship between the state and society in India (e.g. Gupta 1995,
1998; Appadurai 2002). One of the principal contributions of this book is
therefore to highlight the importance of a lower middle class in the constitu-
tion of politics on the ground and to show how such micro-politics might be
theorized. I argue in particular for examining the multiple "fields" in which
middle classes and poorer groups compete for social advantage.

In developing a conceptualization of the everyday politics of social reproduction in North-Western UP, I build especially on the work of Pierre
Bourdieu. Drawing on an analysis of French society, Bourdieu (1984; 1986) argued that people are differentiated according to their possession of economic
capital, social capital—which he defines as useful social connections accruing
to individuals or class fractions—and cultural capital: a range of goods, titles
and forms of behavior that provide distinction in social situations. Bourdieu
was especially interested in the practices through which class advantage is
communicated and reinforced, and he stressed the manner in which power is
contained within the "habitus": internalized orientations to action inscribed
in people's demeanor, reflexes and tastes that both reflect people's histories
and shape their futures. Bourdieu (2001: 38) refers to the operation of the
habitus as a type of "magic," which works "on the basis of the dispositions
deposited, like springs, at the deepest level of the body."

Bourdieu has stressed that the habitus must be understood in relation to the
concept of "field." He viewed society as comprised of distinct fields of social
competition in which people with greater economic, social and cultural capital
and with a habitus attuned to possibilities for gain tend to outwit poorer groups.
Bourdieu often used the analogy of the game to express what he meant by
field. Like the game, the field has stakes (*enjeux*). Similarly game-like is people's
tendency to invest in competing within different fields based on their shared
appreciation of the value of the goods at stake: "Each field calls forth and gives
life to a specific form of interest, a specific illusion, a tacit recognition of the

value of the stakes of the game" (Bourdieu and Wacquant 1992: 117). Bourdieu stresses that the value of a particular form of social capital, such as connection in a government bureaucracy, or cultural capital, such as an educational qualification, varies within different fields. "Just as the relative value of cards changes with each game, the hierarchy of the different species of capital (economic, social, and cultural) varies across the various fields" (ibid.).

Bourdieu's theoretical schema is valuable in highlighting inequalities within a population of educated unemployed young men. Bourdieu's practical application of the concepts of habitus and field pointed to the ability of those from advantaged backgrounds to negotiate markets for social goods with relative confidence and ease. Bourdieu also focuses on the type of confidence that comes with being able to succeed routinely within multiple spheres of social competition. Middle classes habituated to being able to acquire the right schooling for their children, negotiate with state agents and obtain favors and subsidies from the state are liable over time to acquire a sense of entitlement and privilege that is itself a form of capital and is communicated in people's everyday demeanor, movements and speech. Bourdieu stressed especially powerful people's "feel for the game" and a corresponding lack of gamesmanship among the poor (see especially Bourdieu and Wacquant 1992: 356ff).

Time is also important in this analysis. At the micro scale, Bourdieu wrote of how temporality is woven into people's ability to navigate fields of power on an everyday basis. The skilled footballer passes the ball into the space into which a teammate will run, rather than directly to the teammate. In a similar way, advantaged classes typically have an excellent sense of how to micromanage complex fields so that they act in a timely way. Bourdieu also emphasizes that routine success across a number of fields instills in people an ability to project their lives into the future. Like a chess grandmaster plotting tactics eight moves ahead, advantaged classes have an ability to imagine alternative futures and plot their hypothetical responses. In this account the poor are at the very least doubly subordinated: they lack the assets that confer advantage in everyday struggles and the spatio-temporal acuity that comes with routine success (see also Appadurai 2004).

Social class in this Bourdieuian analysis is not defined, as it is in Marx's work, in terms of a person's position with respect to the social relations of production. Rather, class refers to people with a similar volume of social, economic and cultural capital and thus with a similar capacity to navigate fields, plan futures and embody success in their habitus. As Mike Savage et al. (2005: 40) argue, class in this Bourdieuian apprehension does not emerge out of a person's location within a structural hierarchy but is the emergent product of individuals' agency. Similarly, "politics" for Bourdieu does not refer only to elections, political parties and large-scale social movements but also to the daily business of gaining advantage over others in different spheres of competition, for example for school places, good jobs and government assistance.

In sum, Bourdieu highlights the durability of class power, the multidimensionality of dominance and the importance of understanding the mechanisms through which class attributes are stored in people's bodily comportment and transferred across generations (Savage 2003). Bourdieu's emphasis on social reproduction as a set of complex games and his reference to the importance of timing and a feel for the game are especially instructive for an analysis of how middle-class Jats in western UP negotiate socio-economic threats.

Bourdieu has defended himself against the charge that his vision of social life is deterministic and that it does not allow for human creativity and change. Bourdieu emphasizes that fields do not transparently reproduce dominant structures of power within broader society but "refracts" them. He also suggests that people are capable, often through a type of "warrening from within" (Thompson 1963), of transforming the operation of fields. Through describing fields as games, Bourdieu demonstrates his openness to people's improvisations: for example he points out that "[my model] does not imply that all small capital holders are necessarily revolutionaries and all big capital holders are automatically conservatives" (Bourdieu and Wacquant 1992: 109). Yet much of Bourdieu's work does suggest that narrow class-based interests usually determine the social and political strategies of relatively powerful actors within a field, and thus that people's activities within different fields are patterned in predictable ways according to their social class (e.g. Cloke et al. 1995; see also Savage 2003). Bourdieu's writing does not fully anticipate the possibility that lower middle classes may in certain circumstances seek common cause with the poor, for example in coordinated protests against the state and bourgeoisie, in ways that partially escape class logics. It is therefore useful to set alongside Bourdieu's framework the emphasis of other scholars on agency and resistance (e.g. Chatterjee 2004), and especially the agency of youth (Gramsci 1971; Willis 1982; Hall 1985; Butler 1997).

The British sociologist, Paul Willis, a lead figure in the Centre for Contemporary Cultural Studies (CCCS) or "Birmingham School" of the 1970s and 1980s, offers concepts that are more open than Bourdieu's notions of habitus and field to the creativity of young people. Willis conducted research with working-class young men but his arguments are relevant to understanding the politics of educated unemployed young men belonging to the lower middle classes. Willis (1977) built on his analysis of the everyday social practices of young men in a Midlands school to stress young people's "cultural production": the active and creative use of available symbolic materials in ways shaped by people's structural position (see also Hebdige 1979). Willis also used his fieldwork to show that working-class young men in the school engaged in "partial penetrations" of dominant structures. On the one hand, the young men with whom Willis worked were capable of critiquing the class-based philosophies peddled in school; for example they realized that it would take more than good results in their examinations to obtain a white-collar job. On the other hand, however, working-class young men's rebellious practices within school—"having a laff" and "wagging off," for example—involved them in reproducing aggressive forms of heterosexual masculinity. Recent post-structuralist writing is often said to have moved beyond Willis by questioning the notion that youth cultural practices can be traced to underlying class interests (Butler 1990; Arnot 2003; Blackman 2005). But Willis's (1977) notion of cultural production and partial penetrations anticipated many of the themes of more recent post-structuralist inspired work, for example by showing that practices do not always cohere into "identities" (Butler 1990), emphasizing ironic and mischievous dimensions of politics (Demerath 2003; cf. Foucault 1988; Bakhtin 1986) and extending analysis of the political into intimate arenas of feeling, bodily practice and demeanor (e.g. Yon 2000; see also Blackman 2005). Willis's work encourages a search for youth practices that are orthogonal to class or that undermine class power in addition to those that perpetuate inequalities.

I therefore offer a critically minded Bourdieuian approach to a study of middle-class power in India. This approach relies centrally on Bourdieu's insights with respect to how advantages of strata in society perpetuate privilege. At the same time, my Bourdieuian analysis is tempered by sensitivity to instances in which people do not straightforwardly pursue their material interests as these are defined by their class position. This is precisely what the example of Jaipal's double-dealing at the beginning of this chapter appears to require: attention to middle-class micro-strategies that serve narrow goals and to middle-class actions that are contrary to, or removed from, class "interests."

Field Research

This book examines middle classes, micro-politics and waiting with reference to research I have conducted in UP since 1995. My research in India began with an interest in rural social transformation. One of the most pressing questions of agrarian development in the early 1990s concerned how a burgeoning rural middle class of "rich farmers" in the Indian countryside was investing their agricultural surplus. Were rich farmers reinvesting in the local economy in such a way as to promote local growth? Or were their investments and consumption practices being channeled in other directions? Reflecting my interest in these issues, I carried out doctoral research on the social and political strategies of rich farmers in 1996 and 1997. This book draws on this work and, to a greater extent, on more recent research I conducted in 2004 and 2005 in Meerut City, North-Western UP.

My focus on Meerut district reflects my interest in agrarian change in the early 1990s. When I first arrived in India in March 1996, scholars in Delhi advised me to base myself in North-Western UP, a region often grouped with Punjab and Haryana as part of the heartland of India's "Green Revolution." I ultimately worked in a large village on the main road north of Meerut, called Daurala, and two moderately sized villages in other parts of rural Meerut district, one, Masuri, which Meerut academics said was a "typical prosperous village" and one, Khanpur, in which farmers had begun to grow mangoes, as they had done in large parts of south-western Meerut district. Members of the middle-ranking Jat caste dominated the agricultural and social lives of these three villages, and in this respect Daurala, Masuri and Khanpur were similar to many other villages in rural Meerut district (see Singh 1992).

Dr. OP Bohra worked as research assistant in 1996–97. OP was in his early forties and comes from an upper middle-class Brahmin family with roots in Rajasthan. In 1997, he worked for a government public policy organization in New Delhi. OP acted as a facilitator and rapporteur during interviews; he was a superb communicator and was frequently able to draw out our respondents on sensitive topics. We worked in Daurala, Khanpur and Masuri between December 1996 and December 1997 and interviewed male farmers. We focused on farmers possessing more than 4 hectares of agricultural land, which corresponded to local definitions of a "rich farmer." We worked with local genealogists (bāt) to construct ten-generation lineages of Jats in each settlement—two lineages in Daurala and one each in Masuri and Khanpur. These served as a basis for mapping processes of economic accumulation. The lineages offered a comparative framework wherein we could ask rich farmers as well as those possessing less than 4 hectares about the fluctuating fortunes of varied members of their extended family (see Jeffrey 1999).

In each village, we conducted semi-structured interviews regarding farmers' assets and production; off-farm business and employment; education and fertility; relationship with in-laws, marriage and dowry; and political activity and affiliations. We memorized topics and questions that could be discussed under each of these subject areas, and we usually interviewed each farmer twice, in his home, for about an hour or two hours. I recorded responses in a notebook and wrote up my notes on a computer within the next few days.

As the research progressed, I became less concerned with farmers' economic investments and more interested in how they were investing in their families, through education and dowry, and in political networks centered on government. I became aware of the significance of social networking in farmers' efforts to navigate multiple "fields" of social competition, especially in their attempts to protect land, market crops and obtain a good education and public-sector employment for their sons. Investigating these issues entailed becoming more peripatetic. We moved out from the three villages to discuss the politics of multiple fields of practice. We spoke to land revenue officials, police officers, lawyers and politicians in small towns and in Meerut and Delhi. In all we conducted 290 interviews with 125 rich Jat farmers in Daurala, Masuri and Khanpur, as well as interviews with 20 of the wives of rich farmers, 25 Dalits (former untouchables) across the three villages, and 76 government officials or politicians. The Dalit households were selected using a snowball sample (see Harper 1992) whereby an initial low-caste contact in each village provided an introduction to another household. The interview work was interspersed with substantial periods of unplanned non-participant observation. Before or after interviews, we were often involved in tours of sugar mills and long sojourns in offices and tea stalls. OP and I were frequently included in social events, group debates and trips to fields, industrial units and local towns.

In the three villages in which we were mainly based, at least two Jats had obtained PhDs and there were tens of MAs. Rich Jat farmers were able to understand why I was interested in conducting research and they often volunteered advice on interview questions and asked for my conclusions. Indeed, some of the rich farmers with whom I worked acted as mentors and guides during the research process, introducing me to key contacts, offering meals in the village and collecting useful newspaper reports. I often felt less that I was conducting research "on" rich farmers and more that I had entered a type of interpretative community. This is neither to deny the inequalities that existed between me and many of my informants nor to downplay the mistakes associated with fieldwork. But in many situations I was able to find ways of building alliances with Jat farmers, who became research interlocutors, mentors and friends. Moreover, I was often able to use the obvious differences that existed between myself and rich farmers as a basis for generating conversations, for example about the nature of education in Meerut district as compared to other parts of the world or the impact of colonialism on policing, schooling and the operations of the state in UP.

In 2000–2002 I carried out fourteen months of intensive field research with Patricia Jeffery and Roger Jeffery, professors at the University of Edinburgh, on educational transformation and the reproduction of social inequalities in rural Bijnor district, which lies immediately to the east of Meerut district. One of the products of this research was a monograph on the social and political strategies of educated unemployed young men in rural Bijnor district (Jeffrey et al. 2008). In this book we use an account of the strategies of young men, including youth from Dalit and Muslim backgrounds, to critique Amartya Sen's (1999) notion that education is an unproblematic social good. We argue instead that education is a contradictory resource: providing certain economic and political opportunities while also drawing people more tightly into systems of inequality.

During the Bijnor research, I became aware of the salience of student politics in North-Western UP. I was also intrigued by the apparently increasing number of bored unemployed young men in rural areas of Bijnor district and in Bijnor Town, men who discussed themselves as just doing timepass. In 2004 I decided to conduct a project on student politics and youth activism in Meerut. This project allowed me to take forward my interest in educated unemployed young men by focusing on their political strategies within the particular context of a large regional education center. It also allowed me to focus more specifically than had been possible during the Bijnor research on unemployment among lower middle-class young men. Building on my 1996–97 research with rich Jat farmers, I decided to focus on the political practices of educated unemployed Jats in Meerut. The new research on student politics also offered a means to think through the importance of young male "idleness" in processes of social change.

When embarking on research into student politics in Meerut, I decided not to conduct a straightforward intergenerational research project wherein I would seek out the sons of men I had interviewed in 1996 and 1997. This strategy would not have allowed me to build up a large sample of student politicians active in Meerut in 2004 and 2005. Thus, I did not undertake a "longitudinal" study of the type conducted by Patricia and Roger Jeffery (1997) for two villages close to Bijnor (see also Lanjouw and Stern 1998). Instead I concentrated on interviewing Jats from rural backgrounds who were involved in politics and a sample of Jats and other students not involved in politics studying in two Meerut higher educational institutions. Initial interviews suggested that it would be useful to work in both Meerut College (MC), a government-funded institution, and the institution to which it is affiliated, Chaudhry Charan Singh University (CCSU).

In the Indian system of higher education, universities assume responsibility for postgraduate education and the coordination of syllabi; semi-autonomous colleges cater mainly for undergraduates. Universities are supported by State governments but also receive recognition and grants from a central authority, the University Grants Commission (UGC). In 1950–51, there were 6 universities and 40 colleges in UP enrolling roughly 50,000 students. In 1999–2000, there were 27 universities and 763 colleges in the State and 1.3 million students in higher education (Kingdon and Muzammil 2003). CCSU was founded in 1966 and caters for postgraduate students. Between the early 1990s and mid-2000s, CCSU vastly expanded its educational operations through establishing privately funded departments on its home campus and granting affiliation to other educational institutions scattered across North-Western UP. MC, which is affiliated with CCSU, was founded in 1892 and enrolls undergraduates and postgraduates. There are ways in which CCSU and MC differ from higher educational institutions in some other areas of UP. But analysis of CCSU and MC may offer insights into processes of student mobilization in urban UP more widely: the pattern of a new, highly privatized affiliating university existing alongside an older government college is repeated in many cities across the State.

I conducted 38 interviews with student politicians, 18 in MC and 20 in CCSU, and 44 with students who did not identify themselves as politicians, 24 in MC and 20 in CCSU. In total, I conducted 160 interviews with 62 men and 20 women. Of these 82, 38 were Jat, 15 Dalits, 11 Muslim and 18 from other Hindu castes. I also interviewed a range of people who interacted with student politicians: thirteen teachers in MC and CCSU, four politicians, five ex-student leaders, three journalists, two lawyers, two police officers, two district magistrates, the Vice-Chancellor of CCSU and Principal of MC. These interviews improved my understanding of issues raised by students and also offered valuable perspectives on the representation of students in public discourse.

The semi-structured student interviews varied from arranged meetings to opportunistic discussions. They focused on students' biography, political practices, opinions of higher education and cultural styles. Non-student interviews commonly concerned the person's views on student politics and youth cultures. I conducted interviews in classrooms, tea stalls, offices and on the street, as well as in people's homes and hostel rooms. Students and other interlocutors were usually uncomfortable with interviews being recorded. Instead, I took detailed notes and wrote up descriptions of the interviews on a computer within 24 hours. I analyzed these interviews using Atlas Ti data analysis package. I carried out the interviews alone; the variety in the social backgrounds of interviewees and the need to work flexible hours made it impossible to conduct interviews with a full-time research assistant. Ninety percent of interviews were carried out in the local forms of Hindi or Urdu spoken in Meerut and the others were in English.

Beyond interviewing students, in 2004 and 2005 I engaged in participant observation during political rallies, demonstrations and visits to government offices; I collected over 2,000 newspaper cuttings related to higher education in Meerut from two regional Hindi newspapers, *Dainik Jagran* and *Amar Ujala*, from March 2000 to March 2005; acquired data on student enrollment, staff numbers, faculty/department structure and teaching facilities in MC and CCSU; and, using a questionnaire, I obtained information about the background of hostel students. I also organized eight workshops to discuss political issues with students and six more informal "tea-shop conferences," which did not follow a regular schedule and occurred in relatively private areas of the campus. The students formulated a list of rules for the tea-shop conferences whereby we agreed not to disclose personal opinions aired in the meetings and encouraged those usually silent in seminars to participate. These conferences frequently resulted in debates on sensitive issues such as student violence and corruption.

To a greater extent than during my fieldwork in rural Meerut district, students in Meerut were eager to guide, even sometimes direct, my research: introducing me to key figures, steering conversations towards hot topics, warning me against particular interviews and assisting with logistics in the city. Richa Nagar, currently a professor at the University of Minnesota, and colleagues based in eastern UP have recently engaged in a collaborative form of research practice in which the boundaries between the Western-based researcher and north Indian research subjects are problematized and reworked. Nagar and six women based in UP formed an intimate collective and wrote a book about their experiences of childhood, gendered social relations and development praxis (Sangtin Writers and Nagar 2006). Such an approach would not have enabled me to collect broad information on the varied cultural and political activity in which young men engaged. But I did often feel part of an interpretative community of young people interested in social and political change. Many of my informants said that they valued our discussions as opportunities to vent frustration and reflect on their socio-political position. It also became clear early on in the research that for many students I was a resource: a source of information on what was happening outside UP and a sounding board for students' own ideas about how north Indian society was changing. That I had been conducting research in UP for a decade, spoke Hindi fluently and knew a large number of the senior students in the two educational institutions, was crucial in terms of building up trust and facilitating exchange of information and views.

I nevertheless faced multiple dilemmas and frustrations in the field (see also Jeffrey 1999; Jeffrey et al. 2008). First, I was often preoccupied with the question of my productivity. I often experienced fieldwork not as the steady accretion of perspectives and information but as long periods of relative inertia interrupted by moments of tremendous excitement. Most of the time I was either travelling to meet someone, dealing with practical aspects of the research process, waiting for an interview or talking to an informant who had little interest in my questions. But at other moments, the research seemed to move forward at breakneck speed, for example when an informant poured forth on topics central to my interests; the research almost seemed to be doing itself during these moments. My fieldwork sometimes felt like a species of waiting in the double sense that I had to spend long periods in enforced idleness and in that my research seemed slow relative to that of many colleagues in the UK and US who are not carrying out long-term ethnographic studies. These points were not lost on many of my student friends, who often joked that I, like them, spent substantial periods of the day "doing very little" and asked me several times, "Was your previous research so unsuccessful that you had to return?"

Another set of tensions were moral and political. During research on student activism and cultures of unemployment it was difficult not to become too closely associated with particular social groups, a problem that OP had done much to anticipate and address in 1996 and 1997. Students at CCSU and MC commonly tried to persuade me to support their political campaigns, for example by giving speeches at political events or appearing at cultural functions that they had organized for students. I had to walk a difficult line between "giving back" some of my time and energy while not becoming too closely associated with any one faction. I found that living off campus at the home of a friend on the outskirts of Meerut helped in this respect, but I sometimes felt that my work with Dalits was compromised by my being too closely associated with the Jats. I was also aware of the possibility that my work might put some of my informants at risk. Reflecting these concerns, I avoided alluding to other conversations when I interviewed students. It should also be noted in this context that I have used pseudonyms when referring to individual people throughout this book and have also changed details of people's background and activities to prevent their being identified.

A further set of concerns I had in the field related to my position as a university teacher. In 1996, when I lived for a few weeks in Meerut College, I was perceived as one of the students, younger than many of the men with whom I was living. But in 2004 and 2005 I had a job at the University of Edinburgh, and some students regarded me as a symbol of authority and as embodying aspects of a dominant higher educational culture from which they were excluded. I managed this in part by stressing my close interest in student life and by becoming involved in jokes, games and protests on campus. I also tried to use the gap between my structural situation and that of many long-time students in Meerut as a basis for opening up discussion on issues such as unemployment, mobility and aspirations. But these efforts were constantly being unpicked in practice, through my own mistakes, because I lacked the time to get to know informants better, and as a result of being enrolled in the social projects of professors and administrators. The last point is especially notable: on two occasions university teachers invited me to classes and proceeded to pillory students for their apathy in a way that implied that I would agree with their views.

Dilemmas and tensions continued when I returned from the field; questions of power and representation remain crucially important during the writing up of research, as many feminist scholars have pointed out (Mohanty 2003; Madison 2005). Some have accused ethnographers of ventriloquizing others by setting out accounts that purport to be true representations of "subaltern voice" but which always reflect the proclivities and will of the author (Spivak 1988). There is no gainsaying these arguments, except to point out, as have others (Scheper-Hughes 1992, 1995; Gold and Gujar 2002; Tarlo 2003), that ethnographers have typically devoted substantial time to trying to understand and represent particular social situations. I continue to believe in the possibility and importance of spending long periods attempting to appreciate people's social practice and of presenting the resulting findings in a way that others, including my informants, find meaningful. Moreover, I am committed to developing ways of interacting with and learning from my interlocutors in North-Western UP that are not founded on the assumption that certain modes of political and social practice, for example those characteristic of the US, are inevitably superior to those prevalent in UP. My focus in this book on storytelling, long-term learning and reciprocal exchange is broadly consistent with Spivak's own position as articulated in some recent writing (see Spivak 2004: 577 n.66). Making these points should certainly not obscure the manner in which this book is a form of cultural capital that bolsters my position in the academy while inevitably doing less to address the pressing concerns of my interlocutors (see also Gidwani 2008 on this point). This is a persistent and troubling aspect of ethnography crafted in part for a Western audience.

There are three other important points that I want to draw out on the topic of the process and presentation of my research. First, I found detailed note taking to be crucial in terms of building up an understanding of everyday politics in north India. I typically spent only two or three hours "in the field" every day and six to eight hours writing field notes in my room. These notes recorded in micro-detail aspects of people's dress, speech and comportment and I found these non-verbal minutiae to be highly important as I wrote this book. Second, the capacity to improvise was a key skill that I developed through the research process. In Chapter Six of this book I describe a north Indian notion of improvisation (*jugāṛ*) that stresses the value of creative ingenuity and opportunism. During the total of 38 months I have spent conducting ethnographic research in north India since 1995, I have found *jugāṛ* to be crucial. On numerous occasions I discovered that the person I had hoped to interview was unavailable and I had to revise my plans or sit for several hours waiting. But it was often these detours and holdups that yielded the richest ethnographic material. Indeed, such moments sometimes compelled me to examine aspects of rural or urban life that I would otherwise have taken for granted. Third, I believe that a constant attention to various forms of reciprocity is crucial to successful ethnographic fieldwork. Although my research sometimes felt highly "extractive" (cf. Gutmann 1996; Sangtin Writers and Nagar 2006), it involved constant back and forth with my informants as we debated striking contrasts and unexpected similarities between politics and society in the UK and India and repeated efforts to share my emerging results via seminars and articles that I wrote in local newspapers. One of my lasting memories of conducting research in UP is of the willingness of farmers and young people to debate my work and involve me in local events.

Argument and Structure of the Book

This book uses a focus on the strategies of rich farmers and unemployed young men to reflect on middle classes, micro-politics and waiting. A central aim is to rethink how middle classes reproduce their power. I argue that a lower middle class of Jats defended class advantage through a dual strategy. First, Jats invested in cultural capital and social networking. Other studies of middle classes in the global south stress their enthusiasm for "global" and "Western" symbols and social networks (e.g. Cohen 2004; Fernandes 2006). What was perhaps remarkable about Jats' social networking and cultural capital accumulation in the 1990s and early 2000s was their tendency to concentrate on maintaining local power, for example through monopolizing access to relatively good schooling opportunities within and around the village, in the case of rich farmers, or dominating campus politics in Meerut, in the instance of student politicians. At the same time, Jats were stretching "the local" via their rural-urban practices in North-Western UP, bringing together villages, urban offices, schools and universities in a tight weave.

The second prong of Jats' reproductive strategies was to co-opt and colonize the local state. Some recent research on the middle classes, most notably Cohen's (2004) work in Morocco, stresses middle classes' disengagement from the state and nation in favor of cultivating a global identity. In Meerut district the state remained crucially important, materially and ideologically. Jats looked to the state as a provider of resources and believed in the ideal of the nation-state. And yet I will suggest that Jats were primarily interested in shaping local, informal incarnations of "the state." Rich Jat farmers in the mid-1990s and Jat student leaders in 2004 and 2005 tended to eschew intensive investment in party politics and formal civic associations in favor of a politics oriented around the pursuit of leverage in varied informal fields of local state practice: networks built around influencing the police, agricultural marketing and government education, for example.

I use these points about cultural capital, social capital and fields—as they become important in the telling of the story of the Jats—to argue for the continued salience of Bourdieuian theorizing for an understanding of social change in India. The notion of field is especially helpful for apprehending the micro-politics of class advantage in India. Yet I also acknowledge the limits of Bourdieuian theory. In Meerut in 2004 and 2005 there was a prominent set of Jat young men social reformers, who worked alongside poorer Dalit and Muslim students and avoided using their power to advance their material interests. The existence of these reformers points to the dangers of assuming that lower middle classes inevitably exhibit an aggressive individualism. Moreover, a spirit of irreverence characterized youth cultural and political activity in Meerut which is difficult to understand through a Bourdieuian lens.

I make two somewhat different arguments about "waiting." First, threaded through the book is a concern with how middle classes maintain their power in part through a strategy of deliberate "waiting": they invest in specific futures based on their knowledge of likely "returns." The ability to wait patiently before cashing in on a social connection or wait for sons to acquire urban jobs depends on people's knowledge of how fields operate. At the same time, this "waiting" strategy is not always successful, as evident in the increasing numbers of unemployed youth in Meerut, men like Jaipal who were forced to engage in a form of unplanned, comparatively aimless waiting. I argue that it is precisely young men's sense of being somehow "in limbo" in Meerut in the 2000s that generated cross-class action. Standing around, self-consciously unemployed on street corners in Meerut, young men struck up friendships across caste and class lines and engaged in political protests together: limbo can be a crucial context for novel cultural and political practice.

Chapter Two describes the rise of Jat power in North-Western UP. Rural Jats historically engaged in farming, and this caste became locally dominant in large parts of North-Western UP in the second half of the twentieth century. But rich Jat farmers faced two new threats to their power from the early 1990s onwards. First, the emergence of the pro-Dalit Bahujan Samaj Party (BSP) in the 1990s presented a new political challenge. Second, economic liberalization since the early 1990s had a negative impact on agricultural production, reduced opportunities for government work in UP and tended to undermine state welfare provision. I examine how Jats were responding to these threats using fieldwork that I conducted in the mid-1990s in rural Meerut district. I show that Jat farmers were channeling resources into influencing the local state and investing in the education of their children. These social networking and educational strategies required farmers to adjust their mental horizons: long-term goals were prioritized over short-term gains. These "waiting" strategies were largely successful in bolstering Jat power.

At the same time, however, Jat strategies were creating a new cohort of self-consciously "unemployed" youth. Indeed, one of the most important outcomes of rural parental strategies in North-Western UP in the 1980s and 1990s was the formation of a large and visible generation of young men who had spent long periods in formal education but who had failed to acquire secure salaried work.

Chapters Three, Four and Five examine the cultural and political strategies of these educated young men through reference to research conducted in 2004 and 2005 among students in Meerut City. In Chapter Three, I document the emergence of a sense of limbo among unemployed students in Meerut. Young men were often engaged in an unfulfilling wait for secure employment. They felt bored and disoriented in time and space. Indeed, many of these men said that they spend much of their days doing timepass, for example standing about at street corners and tea stalls. At first blush, this form of apparently "purposeless" waiting presents a stark contrast to the "purposeful" waiting of Jat parents. Youth waiting in Meerut was not wholly fruitless, however: timepass provided opportunities to acquire educational qualifications and knowledge about local politics and the informal economy. Moreover, young men used their time in Meerut to develop a shared youth culture based around hanging out. Street corners, tea stalls, bus stops and other nodes within the city provided a site for the development of a distinctive culture of masculine waiting that included Jats, Dalits and Muslims. At the same time, timepass cultures further entrenched pernicious gender norms. In addition, class, caste and religious divides sometimes became apparent among young men hanging out, especially in fights over young women.

A sense of relatively purposeless waiting among young men not only created opportunities for relatively novel cultural practice but was also a foundation for political action. In Chapter Four I consider the extent to which a culture of urban waiting had precipitated collective political protest on university and college campuses in Meerut. I argue that waiting had generated a poorly institutionalized but vibrant form of politics built around informal demonstrations and networking. In particular, unemployed young men mobilized around the issues of the costs of education, corruption, young people's stalled progress through university and the harassment of students. A set of Jat "social reformers" was at the forefront of these protests, but the agitations involved young men from a variety of caste, class and religious backgrounds and sometimes also young women.

Chapter Five considers how class and caste inequalities fractured a collective youth politics with reference to the political work of Jat student leaders or "fixers" in Meerut. Unemployed Jat students from relatively prosperous backgrounds publicly sought to articulate the demands of unemployed young men as a whole. But after winning a student union post, middle-caste leaders capitalized on their power to make large personal incomes, mainly through acting as intermediaries between private educational entrepreneurs and the state educational bureaucracy. In addition to offering cash, a position on a university student union provided student leaders with a sense of spatial and temporal security and belonging. Other students often viewed student leaders' "corrupt" practices as a betrayal. Yet Jat fixers had a range of justificatory tactics at their disposal to shore up their reputation, including euphemism, denial and obfuscation. More than this, I show that Jat student leaders had used the "guilty secret" of their double-dealing as a basis for solidifying friendships with other middle castes and generating an image of accomplished masculinity oriented around notions of shrewd improvisation (*jugār*). The capacity of a small set of lower middle-class politicos to perpetuate power was therefore founded in large part, and to a greater extent than was the case with rich Jat farmers in the 1990s, on energetic cultural production.

The conclusion highlights the relevance of my account for thinking about the Indian middle classes, micro-politics and waiting. A focus on the reproductive strategies of rich Jat farmers and educated unemployed young men offers something of a counterpoint to broader work on Indian and postcolonial middle classes, laying emphasis on the local, state-centric means through which a class perpetuates power. My ethnographic work also offers an opportunity to rethink everyday politics in India with reference to fields. Finally, I throw light on waiting as a basis for counterintuitive forms of cultural and political practice.

2 Cultivating Fields: The Rise and Resilience of a Rural Middle Class

This chapter considers the strategies of "rich farmers": agriculturalists who own the means of production, hire in labor for most farming tasks and possess between 4 hectares and 10 hectares of land (Patnaik 1976). More specifically, I examine the consolidation of a class of prosperous Jat farmers in North-Western UP, focusing on their political and social practices in the mid-1990s. I argue that a lower middle class of rich Jats had emerged from the ranks of the rich peasantry in the 1970s and 1980s and chart how this section of society defended its privileges in the context of new social and economic threats.

Several scholars have examined the growing visibility of a set of rich farmers in rural India from the late nineteenth century onwards (e.g. Upadhya 1988; Rutten 1995; Gidwani 2008). Much work has linked the recent strength of these agriculturalists to changes in the political economy of India from the mid-1960s onwards. In 1964 the Indian Government shifted the direction of development planning from a model of industrial growth towards a more committed drive to improve agricultural production. C. Subramaniam's appointment as India's Food and Agriculture Minister in 1964, advice from the World Bank, changing US aid policies and concerns over a communist threat in the Indian countryside conspired to effect a move away from the Nehruvian policy of low food prices and institutional reform. The Indian state focused instead on creating incentive prices for producers through the establishment of an Agricultural Prices Commission and the Food Corporation of India in January 1965. This intervention in the food-grain market was harnessed to a drive towards agricultural production increases, principally through encouraging the application of High Yielding Varieties (HYVs) of grain, fertilizers, pesticides and improved irrigation.

Not all rich farmers in the mid-1960s succeeded in increasing their wealth in the following thirty years (see Gidwani 2001). There were marked regional variations in the socio-economic trajectories of prosperous agriculturalists (e.g. Rutten 1995; Harriss-White 1996a; Chari 2004). But many studies suggest that farmers possessing agricultural holdings of between 4 and 10 hectares in the mid-1960s were often able to use their control over land to extend their power in the following three decades. Rich farmers tended to be much more successful than poorer farmers in taking advantage of Green Revolution technologies and in using their agricultural dominance to diversify out of agriculture. Rich farmers had more money, superior access to credit and greater social networking resources and cultural capital (Upadhya 1988; Rutten 1995; Harriss-White 1996a). Studies from a wide array of settings suggest that rich farmers used agricultural profits to move either into trade and small-scale entrepreneurial activity (e.g. Breman 1993; Harriss-White 1996a; Chari 2004) or white-collar, government employment (e.g. Wadley 1994; Jeffery and Jeffery 1997). At the same time, many rich farmers, who typically come from middle-ranking caste backgrounds, used caste solidarities to expand their network of contacts in urban areas (Rutten 1995; see also Upadhya 1988; Chowdhry 1997). Prosperous agriculturalists also commonly tried to raise their social standing, for example by withdrawing themselves and their family members from agricultural cultivation (see Gidwani 2001), acquiring consumer goods (Rutten 1995) and preventing female household members from engaging in paid work outside the home (Chowdhry 1997). These shifts—towards non-agricultural activities, expanding urban influence and acquiring education—suggest that by the 1980s in many parts of India the rich farmers who had benefited from agricultural innovation in the mid-1990s constituted a "middle class" of sorts. But in many areas they remained a "lower middle class": they rarely broke into circles of upper middle-class power in urban areas.

At the same time, rich farmers became more politically powerful in the period between the mid-1960s and late 1980s in many regions of India

(Rudolph and Rudolph 1987). In the 1960s and 1970s the number of MPs from a farming background rose dramatically (Varshney 1995), and political parties representing a rural lobby began to compete effectively with the formerly dominant Congress Party (Byres 1988).

Rich farmers faced important challenges to their power in the late 1980s and 1990s. Most notably, economic reforms threatened to undermine the viability of farming. In 1991, the Indian government embarked on a program of economic liberalization that would—if carried out fully—lead to a marked reduction in subsidies on key agricultural inputs and increased foreign competition within the agricultural sector. Not all rich farmers were threatened by economic liberalization; some of those who had moved into trade and small-scale industry prospered in the 1990s (Chari 2004). Yet even among rich farmers with diverse assets, there was considerable concern in the 1990s about their future access to state resources (Harriss-White 1996b, 2003). Rich farmers also faced a growing political threat from the rise of lower castes. Patterns of low-caste political resistance vary regionally in India; in the south there has been a much longer history of mobilization against upper castes than in many northern states (see Corbridge and Harriss 2000: 223; Heller 2000). But during the 1980s and early 1990s, in disparate regions of India, there were growing tensions between rich farmers and sets of newly mobilized and increasingly confident lower caste political agents (see Samata Sanghatana 1991). This double threat—from economic reforms and low castes—to the historical privileges of diverse lower middle-class fractions affected not only rich farmers, but also members of a lower middle-class salariat, who found their access to government employment curtailed, and merchants and small-business people, whose capacity to extract rental incomes and subsidies from the local state was put in jeopardy (Harriss-White 2003).

A number of scholars have shown that middle classes in many parts of India reacted to new uncertainties in the 1980s and 1990s by engaging in new ways with the state. In many areas, lower middle classes, including rich farmers, joined Hindu nationalist political organizations. By offering images of Hindu reassertion in the face of the "theft" of resources by "outsiders," the forces of the Hindu Right tapped directly into class frustrations (e.g. Heuzé 1992; Hansen 2001; Fernandes and Heller 2006). At the same time, lower middle classes in many parts of India deepened their investment in social networks and local politicking outside the realm of formal politics, for example within formal civil society organizations (e.g. Gooptu 2007), through public interest litigation (Mawdsley 2004; Baviskar 2007) and via social networks oriented around controlling access to government resources (e.g. Hansen 2001; Harriss-White 2003). Most notably, Harriss-White (2003) suggests that intermediate classes in Tamil Nadu reacted to economic liberalization through developing local political networks involving low- and middle-ranking government officials. The merchants and entrepreneurs in Harriss-White's work were engaged in a range of "economic crimes" and forms of "corruption" through these networks, such as tampering with weights and measures, evading tax and extorting money from the poor.

Lower middle classes also responded to threats by seeking cultural distinction. This search for status involved the purchase of urban consumer goods (Chari 2004), negotiation of high-status marriages via the payment of high dowries (Roulet 1996) and reshaping of public space to reflect middle-class interests and ideologies (e.g. Fernandes 2004; Nijman 2006). One of the most remarkable aspects of middle classes' drive for cultural capital in the late 1990s was the energy with which they pursued educational qualifications for their children. Middle-class investment in education obviously predated economic liberalization; the middle class had emerged in the 1960s and 1970s largely through availing of formal schooling. But during the 1980s and especially 1990s, middle classes intensified and diversified their educational investments, and a welter of specialist non-state schools and higher educational institutions emerged to cater for this rising demand. Middle classes sought out schools that enrolled their children at an early age, offered their offspring English competency and extra-curricular skills and inculcated in their sons and daughters the cultural norms of "new middle class" India. Parents were especially keen for their sons to obtain the credentials and skills that would allow them to obtain secure salaried work, either in government, India's new economy or abroad (see Donner 2006; Scrase 2006; Bénéï 2008).

This chapter advances understanding of lower middle-class defensive strategies in India in the 1990s through reference to case material from North-Western UP. I begin by describing the rise of a rural Jat middle class in the twentieth century. I then discuss threats to Jat power. Next I turn to the results of my own fieldwork in UP in the mid-1990s to discuss rich Jat farmers' response to social and economic threats. This discussion supports the emphasis of other scholars on middle-class investment in local politics and cultural distinction as a basis for managing risk. Rich Jat farmers in North-Western UP adopted a dual approach to social reproduction in the 1990s, cultivating local political contacts at the same time as investing in the education of their children. I draw attention to spatial and temporal aspects of this set of strategies.

The Rise of Jat Power in North-Western Uttar Pradesh, 1850–1990

The population of UP can be roughly divided into three social blocs. Upper-caste Hindus—principally Brahmins, Thakurs and Banias—comprise roughly 20 percent of the population. These castes have dominated salaried employment, local government bureaucracies and landownership in many parts of UP (Hasan 1998). A second bloc of households belong to Hindu middle castes and includes the Jats, who are concentrated in western parts of UP, and upper sections of the castes legally identified as "Other Backward Classes" (OBCs), such as the Yadavs (see Michelutti 2007). The Jats and upper-ranking OBCs control access to political and economic power in some rural parts of the State. The remainder of UP's population is mainly comprised of Muslims, who made up 17 percent of UP's population in 2001; Dalits (21 percent); and poorer OBCs, often called Most Backward Classes (MBCs), whose population is difficult to ascertain. There are elites among Muslims and Dalits in UP. But Muslims, Dalits and MBCs typically own few material assets and tend to work in exploitative and insecure conditions.

This book focuses on Jats in North-Western UP, an agro-ecological region comprised of eleven relatively well-irrigated districts chiefly located between the Ganges and Yamuna rivers and supporting mainly sugar cane and wheat agriculture (see Jeffery and Lerche 2003: 24ff). North-Western UP had a population of 28.2 million in 2001 of which Jats comprised 8 percent, Dalits 18 percent and Muslims 36 percent. Of the Dalits, the majority were Chamars (also called Jatavs), who on their own made up 11 percent of the population of these eleven districts. In terms of social development indicators, North-Western UP generally fares better than other regions of the state: literacy rates are slightly higher and infant mortality is lower than in other areas (see Jeffery and Lerche 2003: 34f). Economically, North-Western UP is distinguished from the rest of the State by its relative prosperity, evident in higher levels of industrialization, and by its concentration on sugar cane and wheat agriculture; roughly 27 percent of the agricultural area was sown to sugar cane in North-Western UP in 1991 (Sharma and Poleman 1993).

Jats have dominated landownership in large parts of North-Western UP since at least the mid-nineteenth century. Jats managed their land on a collective basis through a system known as *bhaīachārā* (literally: "brotherly share"). Jat men within a particular village formed into a brotherhood and divided among themselves individual plots that could be worked by separate Jat households under a system of direct cultivation. In practice, during the later nineteenth century, and especially during the twentieth century, this system of land tenure disintegrated, such that most rural Jats began to regard their *bhaīachārā* land as freehold property owned by individual families (Baden Powell 1971: 78–81). As farmers directly cultivating relatively fertile and moderately sized plots of land, rich Jats have been able to take advantage of technological changes in agriculture and associated infrastructural transformation in North-Western UP for at least 150 years. The British undertook a program of engineering in the far west of UP in the second half of the nineteenth century which included the construction of the Eastern Yamuna canal (1871), Ganges canal (1888) and numerous minor water courses (Nevill 1922: 13–14, 50–56; Stone 1984). The British also introduced standardized marketing procedures for key crops, which weakened the power of itinerant local traders and allowed farmers to deal directly with large export buyers. Reflecting these changes, during the late nineteenth century Jats in North-Western UP increasingly moved away from subsistence crops and invested in growing sugar cane, wheat, maize and rice for the market (Joshi 1965).

Jats also began to diversify out of agriculture from the 1850s onwards. The British tended to imagine Jats as loyal, strong and industrious: "a slave to his farm . . . thrifty to the verge of meanness and industrious beyond comparison," as William Crooke (1973 [1889]: 289) put it in his *Guide to North Indian*

Castes. After the 1857 Meerut Revolt, many Jats in North-Western UP were regarded as having "behaved nobly in the support of law and order" (R.H Dunlop, District Magistrate of Meerut, quoted in Stokes 1986: 157). The British rewarded the Jats by giving them positions in the army and local government administration.

The activities of the Arya Samaj religious reform movement acted as a further stimulus to Jat diversification out of agriculture. Dayananda Saraswati, a religious scholar, established the Arya Samaj in 1877 to reform Hindu religious practice by reducing its dependence on Brahmin priests and promoting self-improvement through physical exercise, education and social work. These ideologies resonated with Jats' practical approach to religion and their long-running antagonism towards Brahmins (Datta 1999). Between 1900 and 1930, the Arya Samaj established a host of schools and associations in North-Western UP that catered mainly for Jats and other middle castes and included a Jat newspaper and a Jat *mahāsabhā* (Jat caste society) (Nevill 1922: 82). By the early 1960s, there was a small elite of Jats located in urban areas of North-Western UP which resembled upper-caste urbanites: they were educated, attended urban social functions and often belonged to clubs and associations in the city (cf. Vatuk 1972).

Between the mid-1960s and late 1980s, the introduction of private tube-well irrigation, HYVs of wheat and sugar cane and new chemical fertilizers increased the predictability and profitability of cash crop agriculture in North-Western UP and bolstered the position of the Jats (Singh 1992). Many rich Jat farmers took advantage of this growing wealth by removing themselves and their family members from the physical act of cultivating the soil (Jeffery and Jeffery 1997). Jats often managed the pressures that this withdrawal and agricultural commercialization placed on their farms by arranging piece-rate contracts with local low-caste laborers. In this scheme, a trusted worker was charged with organizing a small gang of laborers to conduct a particular task, such as the weeding or tying of sugar cane (Srivastava 1995; cf. Gidwani 2008). Jats also reinvented forms of customary labor. Under the *jajmānī* system of patron-client relations common in North-Western UP in the first half of the twentieth century, Jats as a landowning caste (*jajmāns*) called upon non-landowning castes to perform specific work related to their household and land. This system was both moral and economic: Jats felt that they had a right to request services from other castes but also made payments in kind to the lower castes (see Raheja 1988). The *jajmānī* system declined in North-Western UP in the 1960s and 1970s, largely as a result of the expansion of off-farm job opportunities for low castes. But Jat farmers were often able to draw on the notion of their role as village patrons to revitalize certain forms of customary labor, for example through compelling laborers to cut sugar cane in return for a portion of the green sugar cane leaves which are used as cattle feed (Lerche 1995).

Off-farm diversification became much more pronounced among Jats in North-Western UP in the three decades after 1965. The absence of large tracts of land upon which to expand agricultural production and the introduction of land ceiling legislation militated against Jat reinvestment in agriculture. At the same time, the expansion of inexpensive government schooling in rural areas of North-Western UP provided rural Jats with an opportunity to educate their children in large numbers. More important still, the growth of the state held out the prospect of white-collar and secure jobs to educated Jats, who had a history of diversifying into government work. Reflecting these considerations, Jat farmers began to limit the size of their families and school their sons (Jeffery and Jeffery 1997). Many prosperous Jat households also started small enterprises which they ran alongside their farms, such as transport firms, cold storage businesses or shops (Sharma and Poleman 1993). Such diversification was often bound up with lifestyle changes; rich Jat men purchased expensive consumer goods and expanded their household's influence through marrying their daughters into wealthy urban Jat families (Singh 1992; D. Gupta 1997). Off-farm diversification was bound up with the production of a new vision of Jat masculinity wherein male power was communicated through control over social networks and cultural capital rather than primarily via physical prowess in the fields.

M. N. Srinivas (1989) has written of processes of "sanskritization" in India, wherein a caste changes its social practices to imitate those of higher ranked castes. Social mobility, however, was limited to only some rural Jats in the 1960s, 1970s and 1980s, and those Jats who were mobile were more interested in their class standing than in their ritual caste status.

The consolidation of a class of rich Jat farmers was also intimately linked to their growing political influence. Rich Jat farmers, represented by the Jat politician Chaudhry Charan Singh, were able to exert some influence over state power, especially between the late 1960s and mid-1980s. As a member of the Congress Party in the 1950s, Charan Singh advanced the notion of a "peasant brotherhood" (*birādiri*) or "farmers' (*kisān*) lobby" comprising Jats, Yadavs, Gujars and Rajputs. As revenue minister in UP after Independence, Singh confiscated the agricultural property of absentee landlords (*zamindārs*) and redistributed land to other villagers, especially farmers cultivating between 4 and 10 hectares (Siddiqui 1999). Charan Singh also played a lead role in the passing of the Consolidation of Holdings Act (1953) which reduced the fragmentation of land, a particular boon for rich farmers concerned to introduce new technology on their holdings (Byres 1988: 154). As Chief Minister of UP in 1967 and later as Minister of Finance in the national government, Singh enacted measures that boosted agricultural prices, reduced the cost of agricultural inputs and extended subsidies on fertilizers and irrigation (see Byres 1988).

Charan Singh also encouraged the large-scale mobilization of rich farmers and poorer villagers on issues such as agricultural subsidies and crop prices, drawing heavily on populist imagery and the slogan of "urban bias" (Byres 1988: 162). This assertion provided the basis for the later rise of the Bharatiya Kisan Union (BKU). The BKU was formed in 1978, but came to prominence in the late 1980s in North-Western UP. Under the leadership of the charismatic Jat, Mahendra Singh Tikait, the BKU undertook its first large-scale agitation in January 1987 in protest against a government-imposed increase in the electricity tariff on irrigation pumps. The BKU subsequently organized a range of rallies, including demonstrations several hundred thousand strong in Meerut and Delhi in 1989 and 1990. The BKU's chief goals were to persuade the central and UP State governments to raise government prices for sugar cane and wheat, improve electricity supply in rural areas and strengthen farmers' access to cheap credit. Rich Jat farmers were at the forefront of BKU mobilization (Bentall 1995; D. Gupta 1997), and Jat ideologies of direct cultivation, plain living and brotherhood figured prominently in BKU rhetoric (Bentall and Corbridge 1996: 39–40; A. Gupta 1997). In many protests, Jats contrasted authentic, honest, rural *Bhārat* (the Hindi word for India) against a vision of inauthentic, corrupt, urban "India," populated by upper castes.

At an everyday level, there is considerable evidence of Jats' capacity to influence and sometimes capture local state agencies in North-Western UP. A nexus between the Jats and local state officials was noted in District Gazetteers as long ago as the 1880s, when Jats are recorded offering the local police bribes of a pig to guarantee their favor (Nesfield 1885: 112). But the protection of Charan Singh and growing wealth of the Jats significantly increased their power to co-opt state officials from the mid-1960s onwards, as evident in G. Kristoffel Lieten's (1996) research on rich Jat dominance over local village councils (*panchāyats*) and Paul Brass's (1997) accounts of dominant castes' relationship with the police in 1980s and early 1990s North-Western UP.

When we place the political studies of Byres, Lieten and Brass alongside evidence of Jats' local economic power in North-Western UP in the 1980s, it is difficult to escape the conclusion that Jats possessed what Srinivas (1955) terms "decisive dominance" at the local level: the capacity to reproduce advantage across a number of connected spheres simultaneously and in mutually reinforcing ways. But Jats were not a dominant caste in the cities of North-Western UP in the 1970s and 1980s, despite having made significant inroads in urban areas (see Vatuk 1972). Moreover, the Jats did not move in large numbers to Delhi in the four decades following Indian Independence (see D. Gupta 1997).

Threats to Jat Power: Economic Reform and the Rise of Low Castes

Economic reforms in India beginning in the mid-1980s and gathering pace in the early 1990s posed a challenge to the accumulation strategies of rich Jat farmers in North-Western UP. Chief among the reforms of the early 1990s were the dismantling of a system of industrial licensing, the introduction of new measures to encourage foreign equity investment in India and the partial removal of tariff and non-tariff barriers to foreign trade (see Corbridge and Harriss 2000: 152f). Economic reform also triggered a decline in government expenditure on education, health care, urban infrastructure and power transmission; capital expenditure as a percentage of India's GDP declined from 2.8

percent in 1990–91 to 1.5 percent in 2000–2001 (Chandreshekhar and Ghosh 2002). Agriculture was not a primary target of the reforms in the 1990s. Rich farmers continued to receive large subsidies on power, water and fertilizers, and they benefited from high government purchasing prices for key crops during the 1990s (McCartney and Harriss-White 2000; Ferro et al. 2004). But economic reforms reduced the availability of institutional credit on favorable terms (Chandreshekhar and Ghosh 2002). Furthermore, government disinvestment in state electricity provision increased problems in rural power supply. Partly as a result of these factors, there was a marked slowdown in the growth of the agricultural area under irrigation, use of electric power, cropping intensity and agricultural productivity in UP in the second half of the 1990s. Even where liberalization did not complicate the livelihood strategies of rich farmers, it often exacerbated their fears regarding access to government subsidies, electricity supply and state protection from foreign competition (Gupta 1998; Madsen 1998).

Liberalization also widened the gap between prosperous states in India and UP, which has consistently ranked as one of the two or three worst performers in terms of key development indicators since the 1950s (Ahluwalia 2001; Harriss-White 2005; World Bank 2006). Economic reforms reduced the capacity of the central state to spread economic investment across the country and thus deepened economic crises in poorer states. In the wake of reform, corporations looking to invest in India tended to bypass UP and direct funds instead to states which had better infrastructural and educational facilities and governance records. UP's Gross State Domestic Product grew by only 1.3 percent per year during the 1990s, less than a third of the national average during this period and less than the growth rate in UP in the 1980s (Ahluwalia 2001). The Gini coefficient of State per capita incomes in India rose from 21 in 1980 to 29 in 2001 (Joshi 2009).

UP's economic crisis in the 1990s and early 2000s, combined with a decline in the central government and UP State's capital expenditure on social services, threatened to restrict the flow of "rents" that rich farmers had previously extracted from the state by colluding with public officials (cf. Harriss-White 2003), although this point must be offset against the increase in spending on populist measures in rural areas in the 1990s (Krishna 2002;

Singh 2007). Important from the perspective of rich farmers seeking to diversify out of agriculture was the negative effect of economic reform on education. Until the early 1990s, the state was expanding its financial support for government schooling. During the 1990s, however, economic reforms undermined government educational provision (Mooij and Dev 2002). The Central Advisory Board of Secondary Education (CABE) in India noted widespread infrastructural and curricular neglect within secondary schooling in UP in the early 2000s (CABE 2004). With the exception of a small number of elite state colleges, government schools and colleges usually lacked teaching aids and equipment, catering facilities and basic amenities (Kingdon and Muzammil 2003; Chopra and Jeffery 2005). Numerous non-state institutions entered the educational sphere to fill this vacuum, but these schools and colleges were, on the whole, poorly regulated, staffed and funded (Jeffery et al. 2005). During the 1990s and early 2000s, a vast gulf opened up in UP between a thin upper stratum of higher educational institutions offering internationally acclaimed qualifications—such as the Indian Institute of Technology (IIT) in Kanpur—and the mass of poorly funded government and private institutions catering for the majority of the population, including most Jats.

UP's fiscal crisis also compromised Jats' attempts to obtain salaried jobs for their sons outside agriculture. The UP State government responded to a rising State fiscal deficit by reducing the number of new positions created within government bureaucracies, especially education, banking and health—all sectors that had been absorbing the sons of rich Jat farmers in North-Western parts of the State. By the late 1990s, the number of government employees was actually declining within education (see Jeffery et al. 2005), and in 2001, the World Bank made an annual 2 percent cut in the size of UP's bureaucracy a condition of continuing aid to the State. Moreover, liberalization failed to generate private sector employment in UP, at least until the early 2000s. UP's long-established industrial base—of textile mills, especially in Kanpur—had almost completely collapsed, and most parts of UP did not witness a growth in the IT industry. The drying up of flows of cheap government credit also reduced opportunities for entrepreneurialism (Chandrashekhar and Ghosh 2002). At the same time, the number of young men entering the labor market in UP rose in the 1990s and early 2000s; in 2001 there were nearly 50 percent more young men (21.9 million) in the age category 15–29 than there were in the age category 30–44 (14.7 million) in India (Registrar General and Census Commissioner of India 2004). This posed particular problems in UP, which was already experiencing high levels of unemployment and underemployment in the 1990s, especially among young people (Visaria 2003). It is therefore unsurprising that unemployment, particularly youth joblessness, was a key electoral issue throughout the 1990s and early 2000s in UP.

Jats also faced powerful political threats to their dominance during the late 1980s and early 1990s. Soon after the death of Charan Singh in 1987, "quota politics"—the politics of reservations in education and government employment—came to trump and fracture the "*kisan* (farmer) politics" formerly championed by Charan Singh (Duncan 1997). In the late 1970s the ruling Janata Party investigated strategies for extending reservations in education and government employment to OBCs by establishing a Second Backward Classes Commission, under the chairmanship of B. P. Mandal (a first commission had reported in 1950). The Mandal Commission Report (1980) outlined a program for reserving seats in educational institutions and government bureaucracies for OBCs. Prime Minister VP Singh acted on these recommendations in August 1990, a decision which provoked a fierce reaction among upper castes and some middle castes (Dirks 2003: 284–85). North-Western UP and Delhi formed an epicentre of anti-Mandal protests, which involved large strikes on the part of university teachers and dramatic acts of violence by students, including self-immolation. The reservations issue drove a wedge between Jats and OBC castes (such as the Yadavs) that had formerly been part of a broader, farming alliance.

The rise of Dalits within UP politics also presented a threat to Jat power. The pro-Dalit Bahujan Samaj Party (BSP) was founded in 1984 by the Dalit Kanshi Ram and emerged out of a Dalit trade union. The BSP formed coalition governments in UP in 1993, 1995, 1997 and 2002. In April 2007 the BSP won a landslide victory in the state elections, capturing power on its own for the first time. Mayawati, a Dalit woman and former schoolteacher, has led the BSP since 1995. Under Mayawati, the BSP has tried to raise the political, economic and social standing of Dalits, especially Chamars. The BSP pursued its goals through transforming the symbolic landscape of UP: it established parks, statues and libraries dedicated to Dr. Bhim Rao Ambedkar and other Dalit heroes. The BSP also reconfigured government bureaucracies and programs to reflect the interests of Dalits. For example, the BSP transferred Dalits into key positions within government and improved Dalits' access to reserved positions in government training and professional courses (Duncan 1999; Frøystad 2005: 230). Additionally, the BSP tried to create a climate of fear among government bureaucrats through disciplinary action and implementing a measure which made discrimination against Dalits punishable with imprisonment (Jaffrelot 2003). Moreover, Mayawati extended an Ambedkar Village Program that allots funds for infrastructural development to villages with large Dalit populations (Pai 2002).

The efforts of the BSP to improve Dalits' access to power interacted with changes in the formal system of Indian government. In 1992, the 73rd Amendment Act was enacted with the goal of increasing the power of local government in India. The Act implemented a three-tier system of local government in all states of India with populations of over 2 million people. Under this new system, *panchāyat* councils would play a central role in the provision of public services, the creation and maintenance of public goods and the planning and implementation of development activities. The Act stipulated that *panchāyat* elections should be held every five years and provided a periodic 33 percent reservation of *panchāyat* seats for women, Scheduled Tribes (STs) and Scheduled Castes (SCs), indigenous peoples and low castes originally listed as socially marginalized on Government "schedules" in the 1930s.

The BSP's political drive was also closely linked to Dalit social mobility. Between 1970 and the early 1990s, most Dalits in rural UP benefited slightly from government development schemes and the introduction of new technologies and marketing arrangements within agriculture, which often increased real wages within farming (Lerche 1999). Most Dalits remained poor, but in UP in the 1970s and 1980s a small Dalit middle class of business entrepreneurs and government employees emerged in rural areas (Dube 1998; Mendelsohn and Vicziany 1998; Ciotti 2006). Sudha Pai (2000) has written of the rise of a "new generation" of educated, securely employed, Dalit young men who were challenging the historical dominance of the Jats in parts of rural North-Western UP in the 1990s.

The emergence of the Hindu rightwing Bharatiya Janata Party (BJP) potentially offered Jats a medium for expressing political goals in the face of a Dalit challenge. The BJP held power in Lucknow three times between 1990 and 2005 and governed India between 1999 and 2004. In particular, the Hindu Right sponsored a series of high profile political campaigns in the 1990s. These included a *rath yatrā* (pilgrimage) undertaken by the BJP politician, Lal Krishan Advani, in 1990, which sparked off riots and pogroms across north India (Basu 1995) and the demolition of the Babri Masjid in Ayodhya in December 1992 (Jaffrelot 1996). Jats were involved in attacks on Muslims in North-Western UP in the early 1990s coordinated by right-wing Hindu organizations (Jeffery and Jeffery 1994). Zoya Hasan (1995) notes a substantial move towards the BJP among Jats in the 1990s. Indeed, the BJP granted OBC status to Jats in UP in 2000, thereby allowing Jats to claim reserved places in educational institutions and government employment. But the BJP gave most visible expression to the ambitions and anxieties of UP's urban classes and the upper castes, with whom rural Jats had little in common. Hindu nationalist political animators were frequently frustrated in their efforts to mobilize Jats around the agenda of the Hindu Right in North-Western UP (D. Gupta 1997: 84). Partly reflecting the influence of the Arya Samaj, Jat religious practice places little emphasis on orthodox Hinduism or Hindu ritualism. In addition, during BKU demonstrations in the 1980s and early 1990s Jats often emphasized their solidarity with Muslim "brothers," and the existence in rural Meerut district of a set of Jat farmers who had converted to Islam further contributed to dissolving religious communal antagonisms (Rana 1994).

By the mid-1990s, then, rich Jat farmers faced threats from the liberalization of the Indian economy and rise of low castes. At the same time, they did not possess a political figurehead capable of galvanizing a farming lobby. In 1996 and 1997 I conducted field research in rural Meerut district that examined how rich Jat farmers were responding to the prospect of blocked mobility.

Meerut district, with a population of 3 million in 2001, lies between the Ganges and Yamuna rivers in North-Western UP. The rich loamy soils and relatively high water table support intensive sugar cane and wheat agriculture in the district. Drawing on the 1931 Census (the last census in which caste was recorded), Singh (1992) estimates that roughly 16 percent of Meerut District's population in the late 1980s was upper caste (Brahmins, Rajputs and Tyagis), 12 percent Jat, 4 percent Gujar and 14 percent Chamar (see also Superintendent of Printing and Stationery, Allahabad 1931). The remaining roughly 54 percent were made up of a wide range of low-caste Hindus and Muslims. Jats act as a dominant caste in many parts of rural Meerut district; at the time of the last settlement in 1940, they cultivated 31 percent of the agricultural land in the district.

Meerut city had a population of 1.07 million in 2001. Meerut has one of the largest army cantonments in north India and a history of the production of sporting goods, textiles, scissors and musical instruments. The city benefited from rapid commercialization as a result of the expansion of capitalist agriculture in the 1970s and 1980s. Meerut also witnessed the emergence of several new industries and services from the 1970s onwards, including automotive repair, private health care and education. The relatively high proportion of Jats in Meerut district and the district's comparatively advanced economic development relative to some other parts in North-Western UP make it especially likely to be a site of Jat mobility.

The economic advancement of Meerut district should not be exaggerated, however. Many industrial units closed in Meerut district in the 1990s and early 2000s, including a large rubber factory that was a major employer in the region. By 2004, there was a substantial gap between the commercial scene in Meerut and processes of economic development closer to Delhi, for example in Ghaziabad and NOIDA (New Okhala Industrial Development Area) districts to the south. In Ghaziabad and NOIDA a large number of multinational firms opened IT centers and companies connected to the automobile industry in the 1990s and early 2000s. By contrast, there were no substantial IT firms located in Meerut in 2004.

Meerut district therefore offers a setting in which we would expect rich Jat farmers to have prospered in the 1970s and 1980s but where economic liberalization and the rise of Dalits might have been unsettling dominant caste accumulation strategies in the 1990s and early 2000s. I argue below that most rich Jat farmers were well-equipped to defend social advantages in Meerut district in the mid-1990s, but that their strategies were exacerbating other social contradictions, especially the problem of youth unemployment.

Responding to Threats I: Intensifying Local Political Investments

In December 1996, I visited a rich Jat farmer named Habir in Masuri. Habir was in his early fifties and belonged to one of the richest ten Jat farming families in the village. As I arrived at the family's large metal gate on the edge of their compound, Habir sprang from his chair, banished a German shepherd dog to the corner of the courtyard and ushered me into his home. Within five minutes he had changed into a white shirt and *pyjāmā* trousers and ordered tea, raisins and salty snacks to be arranged on the low wooden table at the center of an urban-style front room. On hearing that I was interested in the strategies of rich Jat farmers, Habir's brow furrowed. He launched into a description of the difficulties associated with being a farmer in UP: the bureaucratic obstacles to developing a working farm, the constant threat of the withdrawal of government support for farmers and the declining fertility of the soil after three decades of intensive Green Revolution agriculture. But Habir quickly brightened when asked how he was responding to these threats. Habir: "My main strategy is to deepen and extend my political contacts. I want to pass on a strong farm to my sons." Habir proceeded to trace the fine channels of trust, obligation and mutual appreciation that linked him to local politicians, land revenue officers, state marketing agencies and the police. Habir: "Being a successful farmer means cultivating connections as well as cultivating land!"

Habir's typical day offers insights into his political work. In the morning, Habir might visit a politician to keep abreast of local gossip, drop in at a police station to register a complaint about a neighbor encroaching on his land and host lunch for a visiting district-level bureaucrat. The afternoon might find Habir smoking with the *pradhān* (village council leader) or chatting with officials in the Cane Societies responsible for organizing the delivery of sugar cane to government mills. In between these visits, Habir might issue instructions to the farm laborers working his land and check on his agricultural machinery.

Rich Jat farmers in rural Meerut district believed that their livelihood was under threat. They spoke at great length about the rising costs of labor, the problem of the subdivision of land between sons at inheritance and the possibility that the government would withdraw subsidies on fertilizers, insecticides and other farm inputs. Many farmers also complained about government purchasing prices for sugar, which rose by roughly 25 percent between 1992 and 1996, but did not increase relative to inflation in 1997. In addition, there was an abiding sense among rich farmers that their capacity to dominate local political institutions and preside over the village economically was in jeopardy. The following statement from a rich Jat was typical:

> Nowadays the Dalits are wandering about the village listening to Sony Walkmans. Dalits have become the new Brahmins and Jats have become the new Dalits. The world has been turned upside down. Dalits can demand such high wages these days, and they hardly know what to do with the money. And they receive every type of Government support.

These vastly exaggerated tales of Dalit economic success and political power were endlessly repeated in the *baithaks* (male sitting areas) of rich Jat farmers (see also Chowdhry 2009). A type of public culture of lower middle-class anxiety pervaded the village lanes and courtyards that I visited in 1996 and 1997.

It would be problematic to view Jats' micro-political strategies in 1990s rural Meerut district as straightforward responses to economic insecurities and low-caste threat. But my strong sense was that the presumed ascendance of Dalits and fears over the viability of farming were centrally important in Jats' decision to intensify long-standing efforts to obtain local political influence. One means through which Jat farmers tried to promote their goals was via the BKU farmers' movement. BKU activity was piecemeal and scattered in the district by 1996, but roughly three-quarters of the Jat farmers whom I interviewed in 1996–97 had participated in a BKU rally or meeting during the previous year, and they often tried to involve poorer farmers and local Dalit laborers in their protests. For example, in November 1996 and January 1997, Jats organized large demonstrations outside a government sugar mill close to Meerut in protest against a breakdown in the mill's machinery (*Amar Ujala*, 28 January 1997). In May 1997, they staged a roadblock close to Daurala to protest about the failure of Cane Societies to remunerate farmers. Some rich farmers had connections with local newspaper journalists, allowing them to publicize their campaigns and maintain pressure on the state.

Another significant area of political investment for rich Jat farmers was the struggle to control *panchāyats*. Until the early 1990s, Jats dominated the headship (pradhānship) of *panchāyats* in Daurala, Masuri, Khanpur and surrounding villages. The 73rd Amendment Act threatened Jats' control over the *panchāyats* by periodically reserving the position of *pradhān* for Dalits. But Jats responded by arranging for a Dalit to stand as a proxy candidate in the *pradhān* elections. In order to ensure the victory of the Dalit candidate they were sponsoring, Jats organized feasts for villagers in advance of elections, intimidated voters and sometimes seized election booths on polling day. Similarly, where the headship was reserved for a woman, rich Jat farmers arranged for their wives to run for the position of *pradhān*. After winning a post, their wife would defer to her husband on key decisions.

Rich Jats benefited financially from controlling *panchāyats*. The 73rd Amendment increased the flow of resources through the *panchāyat* and boosted opportunities for *pradhān*s to extract rents from their posts. According to some estimates, it was possible for a *pradhān* to make an illegal income of between Rs. 250,000 and Rs. 400,000 in 1997 by appropriating money intended for development initiatives (see also Lieten and Srivastava 1999: 223f). In the three villages in which I worked, there were a total of 46 rich farming families who had colluded with the *pradhān* to ensure that they were qualified to receive development resources as people "Below the Poverty Line" (BPL). Such malpractice is part of a wider phenomenon. A recent report estimated that, of BPL cardholders in UP in 2001, 29 percent were from the richest third of the population (World Bank 2006; cf. Corbridge et al. 2005). The Auditor Reports of the Comptroller General in UP describe similar forms of malfeasance in the administration of development schemes partly organized through *panchāyats* (Comptroller Auditor General 2008).

Making these points should not obscure instances in which Jat *pradhāns* assisted poor villagers. Jat *pradhān*s sometimes empathized with the plight of particular families and used their local political influence to help them. For example, after a poor Dalit boy was crippled in a traffic accident in Khanpur, the Jat *pradhān* went to considerable lengths to ensure that the family received development assistance. But rich Jats typically used the pradhānship to make personal incomes and reward close friends.

More important than Jats' involvement in BKU mobilization and *panchāyat* politics, however, were their everyday political networking. As the case of Habir suggests, Jats made incremental and often illegal attempts to win round a multitude of state officials. They were consciously seeking to intensify their efforts within multiple "fields" of political endeavor (farmers used the English word "field" or the Hindi term *kshetrā*). For Jats, the metaphor of the field did double duty, connoting social conflict in a particular terrain (as in "battlefield") and evoking the idea of cultivating connections: tending to the needs of local notables in the hope of receiving future rewards. Each of these fields had a corresponding geography, not a flat playing field but a moving assemblage of bodies, people, objects and ideas splayed across the Meerut district landscape and influenced by events and processes occurring outside the region.

One of the most important fields of struggle was the marketing of sugar cane (see also Jeffrey 2002). Cane Societies managed the delivery of sugar cane to government sugar mills in UP by periodically issuing permission slips that allowed farmers to deliver fixed quantities of cane to the mills. Farmers relied on the regular arrival of a good supply of permission slips in order to obtain quick profits from their sugar cane and clear their fields. A delay could be costly, preventing farmers from planting winter wheat. Reflecting these concerns farmers spent long periods throughout the year ingratiating themselves with Cane Society officials in the hope of ensuring a smooth supply of slips. Jat farmers often visited the Cane Society offices to drink tea or deliver gifts and sometimes invited key officials to their homes for refreshment. Jats repeatedly emphasized the painstaking, long-term and incremental nature of this aspect of their political activity. They said that guaranteeing that one possesses a "known and trusted figure" (*jān-pehachān*) within a Cane Society office requires constantly "feeding" varied officials with praise, presents and goodwill. Ultimately, Jats hoped that the relationship would become *pukkā* ("fully formed" or perhaps "fully grown"). Of course, Jats also had alternatives to this long-term effort at cultivation: where they were unable to acquire permission slips quickly, they frequently used blackmail, bribery and physical intimidation to convince Cane Society officials to work on their behalf. But it was the theme of steadily building contacts within Cane Societies that dominated my conversations with rich Jats.

In addition to the guarantee of a supply of permission slips, rich Jat farmers could use their influence within Cane Societies to manage the dilemmas associated with marketing sugar cane. During most years, the government price for cane was well above the price farmers received at private crushers. Occasionally, however, the private price rose above the government price, and in these years many farmers sold their crop privately. The government sugar mills, through the Cane Societies, tried to guard against this defection by using the amount of cane supplied by a farmer as a consideration in allocating permission slips in the two subsequent years. A farmer who sold cane to a private crusher might find that in the following year he received very few permission slips. When private prices significantly exceeded the government price, farmers therefore faced a difficult choice: should they sell on the private market and suffer a reduced supply of permission slips for the few next years, when government prices would likely rise above private prices? Or should they play safe and continue to supply to the government mill? Rich Jats could escape this dilemma. They sold their cane to private crushers during years of high private prices and used the good understanding that they had accumulated with Cane Society officials to persuade the officers to ignore their defection. Some rich farmers were even able to sell permission slips to poorer farmers, particularly during the two years following a year of high private prices, when competition for permission slips was intense. Such practices were part of a broader phenomenon. In 1998 the UP government announced "misappropriation and financial irregularities" amounting to 240 million rupees in the State's Cane Societies (*Economic Times*, 18 May 1998).

Jats also tried to build relationships with land revenue officers (*patwārīs*), who were responsible for maintaining agricultural land records, registering plots and facilitating the buying and selling of land. Rich Jat farmers argued that a link with a *patwārī* provides protection against land theft and also offers opportunities to covertly appropriate others' land. I recorded five examples of rich Jat farmers seizing neighbors' land with the help of *patwārīs*.

Outside the agricultural sphere, rich Jat farmers' tried to build rapport and feelings of friendship within the police force by making regular gifts of *ghī* (clarified butter), mangoes or wheat to the local police inspector. Rich Jats also maintained pressure on the local police by establishing close relationships with politicians. Whereas the relationships between rich Jat farmers and local Cane Society officials were fairly equal, politicians were of a higher social standing than the Jats, and flattery was a key tool for cultivating connections with these local notables. Sweet talk is described in the district gazetteer for Meerut in the 1920s (Nevill 1922), but rich Jats said that it had become increasingly important to learn how to flatter politicians in the context of a new atmosphere of economic and political uncertainty. In each village Jats could readily identify peers who had developed a capacity for "buttering" (they also used the Hindi term *chaplūsī*). In addition to sycophancy, Jats could provide politicians with information, a rural base during elections and assistance in canvassing. Politicians could help Jats in their relationship with the police because they exerted some influence over the transfer and promotion of senior police officials in the district. I heard numerous stories in which a well-connected rich Jat whose interests were being threatened by a local police official, phoned a politician friend who then contacted a senior police official to ensure that the local officer was brought into line. Politicians could also help Jats in other arenas of competition for state access. A link with a politician was often conceptualized by the Jats as a type of "trump card" in the game of local politicking. Many rich Jats also referred to politicians as their "political umbrellas."

Where local influence and a link with a politician failed to convince a police officer to act in a rich Jat's interest, farmers sometimes bribed them, using a politician as a broker. If farmers possessed a good link with a politician the MP or Member of the Legislative Assembly (MLA) might act as an intermediary free of charge. In other situations, politicians earned money from working as mediators, as the following explanation, from a former politician living in Meerut, suggests:

> The farmer will approach the MLA with a problem. The MLA will then phone or go to the police station or SP's [Superintendent of Police's] office. The police officer will either say give me this much and I will get your work done or it will work with influence. The MLA will go back [to the farmer] and say "he asked for Rs. 15,000," when in fact he only asked for Rs. 10,000. So politicians have become like commission agents.

Jats emphasized that social connections with a politician and senior police officer were a finite resource; many politicians would think that, once they had helped a rich Jat, they were not obliged to do so again for some time. Much of the skill of the rich farmer therefore lay in deciding upon when and how often to capitalize on their link with a politician or senior police officer. A certain form of patience was woven through Jats' experience of local politicking; they had to slowly cultivate relationships and also wait before drawing on their fund of goodwill.

There were occasions when well-connected Jats assisted poorer caste members or Dalits in their negotiations with state officials. In each village in which I worked, there were between six and twelve rich Jat farmers known as link men who were willing to act—typically without demanding a fee—as intermediaries between poorer members of the village and the state, if they felt that the issue at hand merited their attention. Jats were especially likely to act as go-betweens where they had some kinship connection with the person petitioning them for help. Jats also sometimes interceded in cases where their laborers' security or property was at risk.

But rich Jats' dominance of local political networks usually had negative consequences for other villagers, including poorer Jats, Dalits and women of all caste and class backgrounds. Poorer Jats, Dalits or women who possessed land found it difficult to market their sugar cane successfully. In the 1996–97 sugar cane supply season, when the prices at sugar mills were considerably higher than those available at private crushers, only 56 percent of farmers possessing less than 1 hectare supplied to the government mill compared to 78 percent of farmers possessing more than 5 hectares. Of the 11 Jats possessing less than 1 hectare whom I interviewed, five mentioned problems with the allocation of permission slips, whereas only one of the thirty rich farmers I interviewed regarding this matter complained.

In addition, rich Jat farmers were able to use their contacts with politicians and the local police force to influence local government elections, intimidate opponents and evade punishment for acts of violence perpetrated against lower castes. In certain instances, Jats also used their power to extort money or land from poorer villagers. Between October 1996 and December 1997 I heard of four instances in which rich Jats had seized land from Dalits, three examples of their stealing crops and three cases in which Jats had physically assaulted lower-caste villagers. In each of these incidents, Jats had escaped punishment, and in four of these nine cases they had actively involved the local police in their activities.

Poorer Jats were reluctant to challenge the dominance of their richer, caste peers. But in each of the villages in which I worked, a few Dalit political entrepreneurs, almost all of them Chamars, tried to undermine Jats' influence over the *panchāyats* and local government bureaucracies. These men usually came from richer Dalit backgrounds and maintained contact with BSP politicians in Meerut or Delhi. They typically possessed at least a secondary school qualification and had developed a good working knowledge of the operation of informal political networks. These men engaged in a type of subaltern "politics of patience" (Appadurai 2002) that mirrored the long-term efforts of Jats to cultivate contacts. Dalits focused on developing good relationships with key figures in the police bureaucracy, political parties and the local state more broadly, and they could typically be found traveling to government offices in the local small town or in Meerut, drinking tea with officials, petitioning officers on behalf of other Dalits and keeping abreast of local news.

In a few cases, Dalit politicos successfully challenged Jat dominance. Between June and December 1997 when the BSP was in power in UP, Dalit political entrepreneurs used their links with BSP politicians as leverage in negotiations with local state officials and powerful Jats. For example, in Masuri, two Dalit politicos successfully petitioned a Meerut politician to ensure that their village was labeled an Ambedkar Village. In Khanpur, a Dalit political entrepreneur intervened conclusively in a case in which a Jat farmer had been harassing a Dalit young woman. Most notably, a Dalit named Bed Vir was able to win the position of *pradhān* on the Daurala *panchāyat* without Jat backing in 1996. Bed Vir had a large following in the village and was known as an especially charismatic political operator. He convinced many Jats to vote for him without putting himself in the position of being obliged to dominant castes. Once in post, Bed Vir was able to direct resources flowing from government development schemes towards some of the poorest Dalits in the village.

Yet the successes of Dalit political entrepreneurs tended to be short-lived. In a well-publicized act of violence, rich Jat farmers in Daurala knocked Bed Vir unconscious during a quarrel over the use of *panchāyat* funds—one rich

Jat told me bluntly: "He became cheeky, so we punched out his teeth." Dalits in Daurala failed to bring the perpetrators of this violence to justice, in spite of appealing to the local Sub-Divisional Magistrate (SDM). Although she was a Dalit, the SDM did not feel that she had the power to act against well-connected Jats in Daurala. Jats continued to enjoy privileged access to the police, land revenue officials and marketing opportunities for their sugar cane in rural Meerut district in the 1990s.

The efforts of Dalit politicos to counter Jat power failed in part because of internal divisions among low castes. Dalit political entrepreneurs often headed rival factions of Dalits, and therefore found it difficult to work together. Moreover, mutual suspicion militated against the formation of alliances between Dalits and poor Muslims, MBCs and poorer Jats in the three villages. But the main reason why Dalit politicos were not able to effect a broader social transformation in the three villages relates to the institutionalized nature of Jat social dominance. Jats had a range of social sanctions at their disposal that they could impose on Dalits. On one of my first visits to Masuri, in October 1996, many Jats in the village were boycotting local Dalit labor in response to an effort among Dalits in the village to unionize. Similarly, Jats responded to a dispute with Dalits in Daurala in January 1997 by refusing to pay them for labor performed and blocking Dalits' access to Jat fields.

Jats' continued dominance over political networking possibilities also needs to be understood with reference to the micro-geography of local politics. Space and timing are crucial in negotiations with local officials within various fields, and Jats possessed a large advantage vis-à-vis poorer groups in their access to private transport and telephones. Eighty-five percent of rich Jat households in my sample possessed a motorcycle or jeep, compared to 47 percent of poorer Jat households and just 16 percent of Dalits across the three villages. Similarly 46 percent of rich Jats owned telephones compared to 7 percent of poorer Jats and 1 percent of Dalits. Jat power also rested on their access to the money required to bribe officials, offer them gifts and build expensive rural homes in which to entertain government bureaucrats.

Rich Jats also tended to be more adept at developing the styles of self-presentation valued within local political networks. Rich Jats built solidarities with urban officials through playing on collective appreciation of a shared middle/upper-caste masculine culture of meat eating, alcohol and guns (see also Chowdhry 1994). Chicken and whisky parties, featuring shooting and arm-wrestling, were especially popular and served to reinforce feelings of upper- or middle-caste masculine conviviality. Rich Jat farmers put considerable emphasis on equipping their rural homes to impress visiting guests. Some said that they had developed an intuitive sense of what is "proper" with respect to home organization and decoration, and they could point to fellow villagers, usually from lower castes or poorer backgrounds, whose houses were either too sparsely decorated or inappropriately gaudy. In the context of these social networks and spaces, caste acted as a type of "mooring point" for rural social strategies (cf. Osella and Osella 2000). Rich Jats often spoke of how their caste background influenced their accent, mode of moving about (*chal chalan*) and *ūthnā baithnā*, literally: "manner of getting up and down." As one rich Jat farmer put it, "Being a Jat is like a feeling of power welling up from within."

Several upper-caste politicians in Meerut ridiculed the boorish nature of Jat hospitality and self-presentation. These upper castes, usually Brahmins, said that Jats always retain the patina of "uneducated" behavior, and they recalled jokes about Jat stupidity and rusticity. But rich Jats tended to be much more successful at generating camaraderie among upper-caste notables visiting rural areas than poorer Jats and Dalits, who lacked the money required to make a "good impression."

The continued dominance of Jats posed dilemmas for prosperous members of this caste. Jat farmers depended on other villagers for votes in *panchāyat* elections and assistance in farmers' agitations and therefore did not want to gain a reputation for liaising with local officials and promoting "corruption" (*bhrashtāchār*). Jats often cited increasing tensions between rich Jat farmers, routinely capable of co-opting the local state, and poorer Jats, less adept at negotiating with officials, as one of the main reasons for the lack of BKU activity in Daurala in 1996–97. Madsen and Lindberg (2003) also argue that class-related tensions within the BKU movement were important in its decline. The manner in which Jats addressed resentment about their political work varied according to context. In large mixed caste gatherings, Jats commonly feigned naivety about local state relations. In marked contrast to my first private meeting with Habir, in which he spoke forthrightly of his knowledge of informal political networks, rich Jats often asserted publicly their bewilderment about goings on within local state offices. Among members of their own caste, rich Jats frequently acknowledged that they possessed close links in multiple state agencies, but justified their efforts to construct informal political networks by referring to the upward mobility of Dalits and the support that low castes allegedly received from the Indian state (see also Parry 1999; Anandhi et al. 2002; Chowdhry 2009).

In summary, rich Jat farmers in North-Western UP in the mid-1990s were responding to economic and political threats by dominating multiple "fields" of social competition (Bourdieu 1984). They established good relations with a variety of officials as a means of guaranteeing their capacity to engage in capitalist agriculture and co-opt state power. At the same time, this strategy was creating tensions, especially between poorer and rich Jats and between rich Jats and Dalits.

Responding to Threats II: Rich Jat Diversification Strategies

A second prong of Jats' response to new threats in the 1990s was to seek education and off-farm employment for their sons. Again, it is difficult to establish diversification strategies as a clear-cut reaction to social and economic threats. But there was a gathering sense in rural Meerut district in the mid-1990s that the rise of Dalits and economic reforms were making it much more important to obtain forms of non-agricultural influence and money.

Diversification strategies, like efforts at local political networking, involved Jats in demonstrating a particular form of patience. One Jat farmer explicitly referred to his efforts at expanding his economic interests outside agriculture as a "waiting game." Like many other Jats, he said that he prioritized investing in his children's future mobility over spending large sums on himself. This form of deferred economic and social gratification was founded in part on rich Jat parents' expectation that their sons would support them financially and socially in old age. Farmers said that, in the absence of a state pension, "A son employed outside agriculture is a type of insurance." I also frequently heard Jats repeating the semi-humorous phrase, "A son is capital, a grandson interest, and a great grandson is compound interest" (cf. Berry 1985; Chowdhry 2009). Jat parents imagined the "return" on their investment in their children's education in terms of a dutiful and hard-working son gainfully employed in government service and a daughter married into a well-connected urban family.

My conversations with a rich Jat farmer named Kishanpal brought out these points. Kishanpal was in his late forties in 2004, a prosperous farmer living in the center of Khanpur village. He spent much of his time in a loose fitting *kurtā pyjāmā* relaxing in the *baithak* attached to his large urban-style house and chatting with other farmers and visiting officials. When I first met Kishanpal, he sprang from his chair to greet me, pressed a beaker of buffalo milk into my hand and fetched an enormous silver cup that his son had won at a local English-medium school. "He won first prize in the Math class," Kishanpal told me proudly as he placed the cup on a straw-covered patch of ground between our seats. The rather incongruous brightly polished cup acted as a focal point during the following conversation. Kishanpal repeatedly dodged my questions about agriculture and business to focus on what he said were his "real concerns": getting his three sons (aged between 12 and 18 in 2004) employed in government service and his 20-year-old daughter married into a "good family" in Meerut. In a phrase I heard repeated in the male sitting areas of rich farmers across Meerut, Kishanpal said that he wanted to raise the "value" (*qīmat*, literally: price) of his sons and daughter via education so that they could "become something" (*kuch banenge*).

Kishanpal said that education was of utmost importance for his sons and his daughter. He claimed that he had spent lavishly on the education of his children: "I gave them nursery schooling then sent them to the best English-medium school in the area." Kishanpal's wife, Simmi, spoke of the unremitting work associated with her children's education: "From pre-nursery onwards, I had to supervise homework, prepare their uniforms, check on their appearance and provide tuition." Both parents referred to a need to keep their children "on the right path [*rastā*]," and Kishanpal emphasized how quickly his children had moved along the "road" of education: "my son passed out of Tenth Class at age fourteen!"

Kishanpal and Simmi's ideas of what their children should do with their education were strongly gendered. For their sons, the talk was only of acquiring educational qualifications and leverage in government employment competitions. Kishanpal had been to Delhi to meet a friend of his cousin who worked in the Delhi police. The policemen instructed him on the niceties of obtaining a police job in the capital; Kishanpal said, "At the very minimum, my sons need a Tenth Class pass, a recommendation letter from a politician and Rs. 100,000 in bribe money." Kishanpal and Simmi focused on the value of education in raising the standing of their daughter in regional marriage markets; they did not expect her to enter paid employment outside the home. Kishanpal said that, if his daughter acquired the right qualifications and embodied traits, he might be able to marry her into a well-connected family in Meerut. Not only would this mean that their daughter was "well placed" but such an alliance might open up employment opportunities for Kishanpal and Simmi's sons. Seeking such an alliance would almost inevitably entail Kishanpal paying a large dowry to the urban family concerned: "A farming family marrying into a service family would probably have to pay at least Rs. 500,000, and that is assuming there is no shortcoming [*kamī*] with the bride."

Kishanpal and Simmi's story points to three key dimensions of rich Jat farmers' diversification strategies in rural Meerut district in the mid-1990s. First, their example underlines the emphasis rich Jats placed on education as a basis for social mobility. Rich Jats said that for both boys and girls, education is important in providing confidence, social awareness and good manners. They also claimed that the educated have better habits, tastes and impulses than the uneducated. Reflecting gendered conceptions of schooling, Jat parents guided their sons towards courses that would directly improve their chances of paid employment and their daughters towards instruction in extra-curricular activities associated with home-making and "feminine" work. For example, a rich Jat farmer said that he chose a particular English-medium school for his daughter because it offered a "training in motherhood," and he proceeded to read approvingly from the school's advertising brochure: "Our school offers cleanliness of surroundings for girls, as well as oil and fabric painting, first aid, cooking, needlework, paper cutting, bread and flower making, bouquet making and flower decoration."

Second, the example of Kishanpal and Simmi points to rich Jats' move into private schooling. In the 1950s, 1960s and 1970s, rich Jat farmers tended to enroll their children in rural government schools—they had often been influential in ensuring that the state established these institutions in their villages after Independence. But by the 1980s, a large number of Dalits and poorer Jat families were sending their children to government schools in rural Meerut district, and in the 1990s the quality of the educational infrastructure in these schools began to decline rapidly (see also Singh 1995). Rich Jat farmers responded by scaling up their educational investment and sending their children to private, usually English-medium schools, often located in peri-urban Meerut district. Educational commercialization in Meerut also offered richer rural parents an ever-expanding array of non-school goods and services devoted to the project of developing the mental and bodily quality of youth. For example, tuition, coaching classes and "personality centers" were all available. In addition, a lively shadow market in private tuition had emerged in rural Meerut district oriented around exam training, the inculcation of embodied traits (such as the ability do embroidery) and instruction in English. These tuitions often occurred in rich Jat farmers' own homes, and they were conducted in the mornings before school or late in the evening.

Rich Jat farmers frequently relied on urban kin for assistance in managing their children's attendance at urban private schools. Rich Jats asked brothers or cousins who had settled in urban areas to house their children during school terms. In some cases large satellite households were comprised of cousins and second cousins residing in a single large urban household. Rich Jat farmers frequently asked urban in-laws, often their wife's parents, to put up rural children during school time, supervise their studies, arrange tutorials and even plan aspects of their educational career. In many instances maternal grandparents had become important figures in the education of middle-class children (see also Epstein 1973; Jeffrey 1999; Donner 2006).

Jats were keen to avoid delays in their children's search for credentials, qualifications and urbanity: they wanted their children to move speedily through classes, obtain an inside track on examination processes and quickly acquire the rudiments of English. In the early 2000s several principals and teachers in Meerut private schools described Jat parents petitioning them to move their children as rapidly as possible through school, and the idea that their children might have to repeat a year was anathema to my rich farmer informants. The rise of nursery education testifies to this enthusiasm for speed. Many nursery schools boasted of their capacity to be able to provide children with a "head-start" in life. Rich Jat parents' concern with quickly acquiring educational capital also came across in their determination to ensure that their children's days were filled with life-enhancing activities. Children's daily routine often began as early as 5 AM with a tutorial and might not finish until 7 PM after the completion of an English-language class. As in other parts of middle-class India (e.g. Fernandes 2006; Scrase 2006), children's lives were increasingly "curricularized" (Ennew 1994).

A third theme to emerge from the case of Kishanpal is the importance of seeking off-farm employment in rich Jat strategies. Since the early 1970s, roughly a third of the rich Jat households in my sample had moved into some form of business, mainly agriculturally related enterprises such as the refrig-eration of farm produce, running private sugar cane crushers or transport-ing agricultural goods. The richest families managing the largest businesses employed *munshīs* (fixers) to supervise labor and negotiate with government bureaucrats. Others treated their operations as "side-businesses" which they oversaw whenever there were gaps in their political and agricultural work.

Despite emerging evidence of such activity, however, Jats said that they lacked the social contacts required to invest further in business and also the knowledge and experience necessary to enter agricultural trade (cf. Rutten 1995). Instead, the majority of rich Jats were responding to a sense of eco-nomic threat in the early 1990s by investing in efforts to secure government employment for the next generation. A government job, especially one high up in the Indian Administrative Service (IAS), was regarded as a major prize.

The rapid expansion in the number of people with secondary education meant that often several hundred people applied for a single low- or mid-dle-ranking government post in the mid-1990s. In this context, jobs tended to go to candidates who had well-developed social contacts within govern-ment employment or who possessed a connection with a local politician. Rich Jat farmers tended to be better placed than poorer Jats and Dalits to compete effectively within these markets for work. Rich Jat farmers went to great lengths to manufacture good relations with politicians perceived to have influence over appointments to local government bureaucracies. Jat farmers also sought to develop friendly relations with a set of "brokers" (*dalāl*) who toured rural areas advertising their capacity—for a fee—to negotiate government jobs for rural hopefuls.

Rich Jat farmers also used the prevailing system of arranged marriages to obtain leverage in the market for government jobs. Rich Jats commonly tried to persuade influential Jat families living in urban areas to accept their daughter as a bride. Aware of class snobberies that might make urbanites wary of welcoming a rural young woman into the family, Jat rich farmers were prepared to pay very large dowries: the average dowry of Jat rich farmers in the period 1992–97 was Rs. 300,000—three to four times these households' annual income. Where this strategy worked, rich Jat farming families could request their in-laws' assistance in finding government employment. Of the eight stories I was able to investigate in detail in which young men obtained work through social connections or bribes, three used in-laws to obtain a job.

Jats' educational and employment strategies were tightly bound up with the reproduction of class, caste and gender inequalities in rural Meerut district. There was a sharp rise in the educational qualifications of rich Jats in the 1980s and 1990s. For example, while 45 percent of Jats (57 percent of men and 32 percent of women) born between 1922 and 1946 in rich Jat households in my sample possessed a Twelfth Class, this figure increased to 88 percent (95 percent of men and 83 percent of women) for those born after 1946. Jat children entered school at an earlier age than children from poorer Jat and Dalit backgrounds, they moved more quickly through school and they remained in formal education for longer. For example, 74 percent of children brought up in rich households and born between 1947 and 1972 had obtained a Twelfth Class pass, compared to 43 percent of those born in poorer Jat households and just 9 percent of Dalits. Whereas 55 percent of rich Jat children in my sample were studying in private schools in 1997, the equivalent figures for poorer Jats and Dalits were only 31 percent and 15 percent.

Rich Jats' efforts to acquire employment also bore fruit. The proportion of Jats moving out of agriculture increased in the 1960s and 1970s. Of the 63 male Jats born between 1922 and 1946 in rich households, 72 percent remained in agriculture, 8 percent entered business and 20 percent obtained service employment, mainly government jobs as teacher, lawyers, agricultural officers or doctors (see Jeffrey 1999 for details). Of the 80 born after 1946, the equivalent figures were 46 percent (agriculture), 15 percent (business) and 37 percent (service). Only one man born after 1946 had entered manual laboring work. Poorer Jats, for whom the threat of land subdivision was more pressing, had been similarly successful in entering service employment. But poorer Jats were more concentrated in relatively insecure private service work and in lower-ranking government jobs, such as employment as drivers on UP State buses or work as land revenue officers. Dalits had been much less adept at acquiring service employment than had rich Jats: only 4 percent of Dalit men in my sample born between 1922 and 1946 had acquired a government post.

Rich Jat strategies were not wholly successful, however. By the mid-1990s there was a small cohort of young men from rich Jat farming families, fourteen in my sample in Daurala and eight each in the other two villages, who had been unable to capitalize on their education in the field of employment. These men had often spent twenty or even twenty-five years in formal education, but found that, despite their best efforts, they were out-maneuvered in increasingly competitive employment markets, often by better-connected and richer upper castes living in urban areas.

Conclusions

During the twentieth century a self-confident set of prosperous Jat cultivators emerged in North-Western UP. The social and economic strategies of these men in the post-Independence period were similar in many respects to those of rich farmers in many other parts of India. They invested in capitalist agriculture, began to seek ways of broadening their economic portfolio outside farming and tried to raise the social standing of their households. In the late 1980s and early 1990s they faced new threats, from economic liberalization and from the political rise of Dalits. Research in three villages in rural Meerut district in the mid-1990s suggests that rich Jat sugar cane farmers were successfully maintaining their dominant position within rural society in the face of these threats.

Jats adopted two interconnected sets of strategies to perpetuate their power. First, they intensified pre-existing efforts to influence the local state. This conclusion tallies with the research of Harriss-White on how "intermediate classes" managed social threats in an area of South India in the wake of economic liberalization. But my analysis presents an interesting contrast to some studies with urban Indian middle classes (cf. Harriss 2003; Scrase and Ganguly-Scrase 2008). For example, John Harriss (2003: 334–35) has shown that an upper middle class of business entrepreneurs in India frequently responded to economic liberalization by disentangling themselves from local state networks in favor of new managerial styles that emphasized corporate transparency. Harriss refers to this process as a "disembedding," drawing on the work of Anthony Giddens (1990). By contrast, Jats engaged in a type of "re-embedding" in response to rapid change: they aggressively cultivated links with local officials in an attempt to extract money, protection and favors.

Jats imagined these engagements with the state as occurring across a range of "fields," sometimes using the English term and sometimes employing the Hindi word "*kshetrā*." Not only do Bourdieu's concepts of social capital, cultural capital, habitus and field, help us understand the mechanics of middle-class reproduction in North-Western UP. In addition, the very terms that Bourdieu uses to politicize our understanding of class reproduction are deployed by people on the ground to explain their capacity to perpetuate power.

The second strategy of the Jats which I have described is that of rapidly deepening and extending their investment in their children's education with a view to their sons obtaining off-farm employment. Again, this investment was a continuation of past practices. But Jats' efforts to school their children had a new sense of urgency in the mid-1990s: they sought a greater range of educational opportunities, started to give their children extra-school tutorials and used schools outside the immediate vicinity.

Throughout the chapter I have emphasized the importance of understanding spatial and temporal dimensions of middle-class power. Investing in political contacts and education involved Jats in developing new geographies of class accumulation. Most notably, they fashioned novel links to UP's towns and cities, for example through the formation of "satellite" urban households for the purposes of schooling. Jats' focus on cultivating connections and improving children's education also entailed extending their mental horizons. In rural Meerut district in the mid-1990s I encountered strong moral discourses in which investing in the long-term future of one's household was accorded priority over short-term spending. Whether this amounted to a form of "waiting" was not always clear; but some Jat farmers commonly referred to being in a state of relative "limbo" while they waited to reap the benefits of their investments. As one Jat put it, "We are betting on our sons."

But have these bets paid off? The next chapter examines the fate of those who in a sense embodied the strategies of rich Jat farmers in the 1990s. A set of prosperous, but increasingly disillusioned young men existed in Meerut in 2004 and 2005—men who had grown up with the notion that they would obtain middle-class jobs but crucially lacked the means to realize their goals.

3   Life at the Crossroads: Timepass

In November 2004 I posed for a photograph with young men at a street intersection close to Meerut College. One of the students present said that the picture should be put on the college website. "What would be the caption?" I asked. "Life at the crossroads" he replied. This chapter examines a set of young men who were at several crossroads: between childhood and adulthood, the lower middle class and urban upper middle classes and rural UP and metropolitan India.

The young men described in this chapter were also often literally "living at the crossroads": they spent much of their days standing at major street intersections, socializing, joking or simply passing time (timepass karna). One of the unintended consequences of the strategies of rich farmers in the 1990s was to create a cohort of Jat young men in higher education in Meerut in the 2000s, and many of these men felt somewhat lost in time and space.

This chapter examines the experiences and practices of young men studying in two colleges in Meerut. I discuss the sense of temporal and social suffering of young men, with particular reference to students who had failed to acquire government employment and remained in higher education for long periods. I also show how young men used the idea and practice of timepass to fashion distinctive masculinities.

It is important to point out what this chapter is not. I did not collect much information from young men in Meerut on love and marriage. Nor was I able to conduct research on how young men's relationship to their parents and siblings changed as a result of their remaining in higher education for long periods (but see Jeffrey et al. 2008: chapter 7). This chapter and the subsequent two refer instead to aspects of the educational, cultural and political strategies of young men. This approach allows for detailed comment on the fortunes of Jats from prosperous rural backgrounds as they negotiated particular "fields." But it inevitably distracts attention from the diverse motivations of young men and from some of the fields in which they operate, notably that of marriage.

In investigating aspects of young men's social and cultural lives in 2004 and 2005, I worked especially with male students living in hostels in Chaudhry Charan Singh University (CCSU) and Meerut College (MC), Meerut. CCSU was established as a postgraduate university in 1966 on the outskirts of the city. Until the mid-1990s, CCSU had three divisions: Plant Science, Physical Science and Behavioral Science. In 1995 CCSU began a program of rapid growth, and, during the subsequent ten years, 29 "self-financing" courses were established at CCSU, mainly offering applied or business-oriented Master's Degrees to students willing to pay.

In 2004, 72 academic staff worked at CCSU, of whom eleven were women and ten Dalit. The student population was just over 2,600, of which 36 percent were women. Jat students have historically dominated CCSU numerically and politically; in 2004 they comprised a third of the student body. But Dalits had enrolled in the university in increasing numbers since the mid-1990s, and by 2004 there were as many Dalits as Jats in CCSU. The remainder of the student population was comprised of upper castes, Muslims and OBCs. The majority of students were from rural North-Western UP, and about a third of the student population lived on campus in one of four hostels—three male and one female. The female hostel contained young women from all caste and religious backgrounds. Among the men, Dalits were concentrated in just one of the three hostels, called the "Ambedkar Hostel."

CCSU was formally an "affiliating university" and its external funding came mainly from the state, via the University Grants Commission (UGC). CCSU greatly expanded the number of institutions to which it granted affiliation in the late 1990s and early 2000s, from less than 100 in 1995 to over 350 in 2004. The affiliated colleges were mainly private institutions located in North-

Western UP. A total of about 230,000 students studied in colleges affiliated with CCSU.

Meerut College was established in 1892 in the administrative center of the city. Until at least the 1970s, it was one of the most prestigious institutions in North-Western UP. The college contained several academics of international repute and enrolled students from as far away as Nepal. In 2004, however, few of MC's professors were research active and students in the college came mainly from North-Western UP—the majority from rural areas. I was not able to collect reliable data on Meerut College's academic staff, but most were either upper caste or Jat men.

In 2003–4 there were just over 11,000 students studying in Meerut College, of which roughly 40 percent were Jats and 25 percent Dalits. The remaining 35 percent was comprised mainly of upper castes and OBCs, although there were a small number of Muslims. Women constituted 27 percent of the student population. Thirty percent of students were enrolled in Arts degrees (BAs or MAs), 30 percent for law degrees (LLb or LLM), 20 percent in Science (BSc or MSc) and 20 percent in Commerce (BCom or MCom). Meerut College had not established self-financing courses along the lines of those that ran in CCSU.

At MC roughly a quarter of students lived on campus in one of six hostels in Meerut College—one female and five male. The women's hostel contained students of all caste and religious backgrounds and Dalits were distributed across all the male hostels; but Muslim men were exclusively housed in one hostel.

A mainly upper-caste executive committee with twenty-one members managed MC affairs. Before the mid-1980s, Meerut College funded itself through fees and private donations. But the government began to provide aid in the 1980s, and in 2004–5 the college received most of its external funding from the UGC. The government therefore had considerable control over the curriculum and other aspects of the colleges' functioning.

The remainder of the chapter is divided into four sections. In the next section, I discuss a widespread sense of ennui and disillusionment among young men in higher education in Meerut. These feelings were closely linked to educational decay and often expressed with reference to the idea of timepass. The second section develops my analysis of timepass by concentrating on the increasing numbers of male students who had tried unsuccessfully to acquire salaried employment. These men, typically from lower middle-class Jat backgrounds, often responded to their exclusion by remaining in MC and CCSU to study, and they referred to their rather purposeless "waiting." The third section examines links between young men's sense of limbo and masculine cultures in Meerut. By engaging in acts of timepass, students constructed vibrant forms of inclusive male sociality. The conclusions draw out the wider implications of my argument about timepass for the themes of the book.

Enduring Timepass

During their school careers, young men had been fairly closely monitored by parents and teachers. Teenagers were typically required to attend tutorials before and after secondary school, and teachers and parents reviewed their progress on a daily basis. By contrast, students typically found little to structure their time in MC. The British in India established a system of higher education based around yearly written examinations and which provided little scope for continuous assessment or group project work (Kumar 1988, 1994; Spivak 2004). MC teachers spent little time lecturing; they simply instructed students to memorize material in advance of key tests. Students in Meerut obtained the majority of their knowledge in the period immediately preceding examinations and in spaces off campus, for example via private tutorials held in the basements of professors' homes or from textbooks written by their teachers, which they read in tea stalls or their hostel rooms.

Pitched into a situation in which they were encouraged simply to wait for end-of-year tests, many students at MC complained of an overabundance of time. In contrast to rich Jat farmers, who tended to imagine time as a commodity that should be "invested" (Chapter Two), many young men appeared to think of time as valueless—to be "passed" or "killed." The following statement typifies the response of many young men to questions about their daily activities:

> Time has no value in India. Look about and you will see what we are doing, just timepass: maybe chatting on the roof, sitting about in our hostel room, wandering, chatting to friends, going to the tea stall, etcetera. That's it.

Not all young men studying in MC and CCSU subscribed to these views. Some referred to being too engaged in their studies to worry about timepass. Others had family commitments, health issues or paid employment outside college that required them to manage their time carefully. Still other students referred to timepass as a morally reprehensible idea. One young man told me, "It is wrong for students to engage simply in timepass: it is our responsibility to use our time carefully."

Moreover, some students said that surplus time was not the paramount problem; indeed, they claimed that time often moved too fast on campus. At CCSU and MC the timing of examinations, issuing of results and other key events connected to students' passage through their degrees were often scheduled in an unpredictable fashion. Students complained of a need to galvanize themselves into action at short notice in pursuit of a textbook, examination paper or result. A language of "cramming," "rushing," and an absence of time existed alongside ideas of timepass. It is the combination of panic and inertia—the need to "hurry up and wait"—that best describes the temporal anxieties of some young men.

But among male students in Meerut the notion of being surrounded by an expanse of featureless time—merely "chronic time" (cf. Kermode 1967)—had taken deep root. The idea that it was necessary to discover distractions was also frequently discussed. Discourses of timepass acted as a type of "structure of feeling" in Raymond Williams' (1977) sense of a social consciousness that gives a distinct form to people's actions and sense of their place in the world.

There were few opportunities for hostel students to engage in organized recreational activity on the MC campus. The college arranged only limited sporting, cultural and intellectual activities. Moreover, young men tended to regard their hostels as unattractive places to hang out: the only leisure facilities in many hostels were badminton nets. Many young men therefore spent long periods somewhat self-consciously "passing time" at tea stalls or on street corners close to MC. They chatted, played games, caught up on news or simply "waited for things to happen," a phrase I heard several times. Some young men said that they had performed similar forms of timepass before they arrived at university. Parents in mid-1990s rural Meerut district did not expect boys to participate very actively in household labor, and some tolerated timepass in public areas of their village. But most students said that they practiced timepass in Meerut with a new intensity. As one student put it, "Now we are in Meerut, timepass is everywhere."

Timepass in this sense was a privilege of gender. Young women were typically unable to participate in the types of public timepass in which young men engaged. In line with broader patriarchal ideas, professors, government officials and young men's parents imagined young men as by nature (*fitrat*) wayward and somewhat detached from daily tasks and young women as essentially diligent, obedient and conscientious. Parents, professors and urban society at large considered it inappropriate for unmarried young women to "hang out," except in certain public spaces, such as the sweet shops and confectionary stores near MC and CCSU.

In addition to employing the term timepass to refer to passing surplus time, young men used the term to express their sense of detachment from their studies. Timepass was commonly perceived to be the opposite of "serious" practice and therefore connoted a type of distancing. In the context of the poor quality of higher education, students often referred—either semi-humorously or more seriously—to their studies as forms of timepass. To be sure, there were some Meerut students, especially those recently arrived from poorer rural parts of North-Western UP, who regarded CCSU and MC as good places to study, and were impressed by the facilities and professors. Moreover, it is important not to suggest that young men were the only ones who imagined their studies as timepass; women enrolled in Meerut also engaged in this type of waiting. Since at least the 1960s, higher education has been a means through which parents have tried to enhance the attributes and skills of their daughters before marriage. One of the effects of this strategy has been to instill in young women a sense of being "in wait" (see Vatuk 1972; Roulet 1996). Among the twenty young women I interviewed in MC and CCSU, four made unsolicited remarks about their position in a type of "limbo" and two referred to their studies as timepass.

Young men's feeling of being stuck in a poor educational environment—and therefore engaged only in timepass—was nevertheless widespread. Many MC students, as well as those in traditional subjects in CCSU, bemoaned outmoded curricula and inadequate facilities. The colonial educational regime privileged subjects and styles of teaching that bore little relation to students' milieu. Syllabi in MC and CCSU were structured around the accumulation of facts and rote learning and the memorization of information for examinations. The majority of courses in MC and CCSU were arcane and irrelevant to students' futures; for example, a BA in Military History involved students memorizing maneuvers during the Napoleonic Wars, and geography at MC was taught using equipment employed by surveyors in the 1950s and without reference to the work of scholars writing since the 1960s. Most professors in MC and CCSU adopted a didactic teaching style and did not ask students to express their views.

Students also complained about a decline in the standard of higher education in Meerut in the 1980s and 1990s. In 1996, I heard teachers and students in MC and CCSU refer to problems in local higher education, linked to a shortage of funding and growth of private educational institutions. By 2004, this despondency had deepened. A further withdrawal of funds for higher education in UP combined with irregularities in educational administration meant that classes in MC were often short, infrequent and disorganized. Extracurricular activities and educational facilities were almost non-existent. For example, MC had just five functioning computers for its 16,000 students in 2005. The college's hostels, designed in the 1900s to resemble Oxford quads, were crumbling. Many hostellers lacked regular access to even basic amenities, such as drinking water, functioning washrooms and nutritious food.

Conditions in CCSU were slightly better. Several CCSU departments had used profits from private courses to improve facilities in traditional disciplines, such as Sociology and Biology. An Internet laboratory was opened in CCSU in 2003, the library was relatively well funded and teacher absenteeism was less marked. Yet the quality of education had declined in CCSU since the 1980s, and especially since the late 1990s. A common refrain among students was that, while CCSU increasingly looked like a university, as a result of administrative efforts to beautify the campus and construct new buildings, it lacked any type of educational atmosphere (*mahaul*) (cf. Jeffery et al. 2006): professors frequently neglected their formal duties and most departmental libraries were starved of textbooks.

The reputation of CCSU declined rapidly after the late 1990s, as evident in a sharp drop in the enrollment of students from outside UP and a wave of negative media reports regarding the institution. Some advertisements for private-sector jobs in Delhi in the early 2000s included a note that "Meerut students need not apply." Moreover, the processes of arranging admissions, constructing new university buildings, scheduling examinations and publishing results were riddled with malpractice, inconsistencies and confusion, opening up opportunities for bureaucrats to make personal side incomes, disrupting the everyday workings of the institution and further undermining CCSU's reputation. In 2004 alone, there were nearly a hundred newspaper articles in *Dainik Jagran* and *Amar Ujala* that documented maladministration in MC or CCSU. Students were keenly aware of this deterioration. In the type of statement I heard repeated many times, a Jat young man living in a CCSU hostel said:

> The university has a name but it has no real reputation. In the 1980s, many people used to come from Kenya and Tanzania to study at CCSU. In Meerut College there used to be a hostel reserved for foreign students. You will hardly find a single foreigner now studying in these institutions. Compared to the Delhi universities, these Meerut institutions are useless. The laboratories in CCSU are like laboratories in your country fifty or sixty years ago. We should take that equipment out of the university and throw it down a well.

It was precisely such awareness of Meerut's position low down within regional and global hierarchies of education that led many men to emphasize their detachment from local educational regimes—study was only timepass.

Students not only used timepass to reference their boredom and disengagement but also to convey feeling "left behind" in Meerut. Students contrasted their own timepass in Meerut higher education, with the buzz of metropolitan India. MC students, especially, often led me around the campus pointing to signs of educational decay, such as the uneven wall around the cricket ground, half-built because the administration pocketed the money; the decrepit gymnasium, once the best facility in North-Western UP; and the abandoned hostel near the center of campus, which was covered in undergrowth and garbage. What particularly galled many students was the contrast between such images of torpor and the signs of speed and globalization that surrounded the campus on all sides—the glossy signboards on the round-about outside campus, for example, and the Principal's flashy new Sports Utility Vehicle parked near the main road. Like the tired-looking waiting rooms that abut government offices, clinics and railway stations across north India, young men perceived the physical landscape of Meerut College to be patently removed from the spaces where things were happening.

Other studies that have referred to the idea of timepass in India have tended to emphasize leisure and pleasurable distraction (e.g. Abraham 2002; Nisbett 2007). In these accounts, based usually on research in metropolitan India, timepass connotes a welcome period of rest conducted between bouts of work. But students in Meerut commonly spoke of timepass in a forlorn manner. Timepass was what one had to do in a context in which other more meaningful and "serious" ways of engaging with the world were unavailable.

The melancholy that characterized young men's discussion of timepass also reflects public disapproval of young male idleness. The visibility of young male timepass had contributed to powerful discourses wherein educated young men were imagined as a moral threat. In many instances, my presence seemed to spur professors and bureaucrats to reflect on young men's purported languor and disinterest. Professors and university officials complained that students spent all their time "just hanging about" wholly disengaged from studying. The media played a large role in communicating such ideas; the college layabout was a stock figure of local newspapers and magazines and of the regional and national press. In 2004–5 alone, *Dainik Jagran* and *Amar Ujala* newspapers carried five articles that lamented the carnal appetites, sloth and irresponsibility of male college students in Meerut. These stories focused especially on the criminal and sexual threat allegedly posed by idle men, and the susceptibly of the male body to evil influences from outside the region: satellite television, Western sexual mores and Bollywood images of men who hang out.

Heightened concern over a dissolute culture of male timepass came to a head in Meerut in December 2005, when Meerut police beat young men and women presumed to be engaged in "lewd behavior" in a public park close to MC. The police justified the attacks on the grounds that the couples were having "illicit affairs." The police said that the attacks formed part of a larger effort—codenamed Operation Romeo—aimed at countering young male sexual harassment of young women and cleansing public space. Commenting on the incident in 2007, a policeman in Meerut told me: "Those who hit the young people were wrong, but the public are fed up with idlers, bad men and vagabonds."

The police incident is more broadly indicative of the state's approach to timepass. Rather than trying to address the needs of long-time students, for example though the provision of career advice or construction of spaces for them to socialize, the Indian state tried to discipline and punish young men. The police were part of a broader state apparatus that included the more militarized Provincial Armed Constabulary and Border Security Force as well as the Local Intelligence Unit, the purpose of which was to prevent young men from expressing discontent.

In sum, young men arriving to live and study in Meerut were pitched into a rather unfulfilling educational environment in which the need to pass time became a pressing concern. As they became more aware of the scale of educational decline, young men extended the reference of the term timepass to include not only their hanging out around the city but also their academic study. In addition, they used timepass to signal their removal from spaces of relative "modernity."

Stuck at the Crossroads: Unemployed Timepass

Students' common failure to find salaried work while studying in Meerut exacerbated their feelings of boredom, detachment and social relegation. While students at all stages of their college career were apt to talk about timepass, it was those who had tried and failed to get middle-class jobs and who remained in higher education for long periods who spoke most readily on this theme.

The example of Rajesh gives a sense of the experiences and opinions of these self-consciously unemployed students in Meerut. Rajesh came from a rich Jat family in a village about six miles from Meerut. He was in his early thirties in 2005 and lived in a MC hostel. I first met him in January 2005 on the bare patch of ground where hostel students congregated to play games, chat and hang out. Rajesh had more the appearance of a professor than a student: his hair was flecked with white and crow's feet lines surrounded the corners of his eyes. Rajesh had been living in MC for thirteen years, during which time he had obtained a BA, BEd, MA Political Science, MA History, MA Agriculture and a PhD. Rajesh said that there had been no particular overall logic to his degrees: "I just moved from one to the other, hoping to increase my chances [to obtain work]."

Rajesh had failed to find government work or secure employment in private service. He described himself as "unemployed," although he occasionally worked as a part-time lecturer at a degree college close to Meerut. Rajesh stressed the frustrations that punctuated his job search:

> There has been nothing suspect about my education. My results have been maximum first class. I got a distinction in four subjects. The trouble is that in order to get the sort of job appropriate to someone of my education I need to pay a huge bribe. . . . I would have to pay Rs. 300,000 or Rs. 600,000 [for a good job]. I have twice had an interview for the [Uttar Pradesh Provincial] Civil Services. On both occasions, people below me on the merit list got priority. The Commission Liaison Officer coordinates the interviews. This man asked me to give him Rs. 170,000 as a bribe. This was five years ago. The man was acting as a broker between me and the Chairman of the board. My brother [a distant cousin] is an MLA, so I had the contacts. But nothing happened.

Rajesh characterized his experience over the past thirteen years as one of "taking the blows" (*dhakke khannā*). He explained that students wait in college to obtain certain goods—a degree, a recommendation letter, a tip about a job—but these apparent advantages make little tangible difference.

Rajesh's desperation is indicative of wider social struggles occurring in Meerut. Young men had learned to expect a government job, and teachers, the media and development organizations in UP had promoted notions of personal development through formal education and service to the state. Students said that they had grown up reading school textbooks that proclaimed the value of dedicated work for the nation, by becoming a teacher, doctor, soldier or civil servant. The presence of a large army cantonment in Meerut made the prospect of military employment especially alluring for many students in the city. In general, dreams of entering government work predominated over ambitions to enter IT employment and similar sectors of the new economy in 2004 and 2005 in Meerut. Certainly, Jat students were adamant that, as educated people, they should not engage in manual wage labor, which they regarded as "lower caste" and "uneducated" work.

Young men studying in MC and CCSU had often spent several years applying for middle- and lower-ranking government jobs, especially posts in the military and university lecturer positions that required students taking the All-India National Eligibility Test (NET). Upper castes and richer Jats and OBCs had also often applied unsuccessfully for high-ranking government work in the Indian Administrative Services (IAS) or UP Provincial Civil Services (UP PCS). Like Rajesh, many of these students referred to themselves as "unemployed" and had a keen sense of being "over age" with respect to the institution in which they were studying. When I lived in Meerut college in 1996 I only occasionally heard students talking about being unemployed; in 2004 and 2005 this topic was common.

Students spoke of the hardships of navigating the arena of government employment competition, which they sometimes spoke of as a "field," using the English word. For lower-ranking government work, candidates often had to take a written examination and physical tests and undergo a series of interviews. For IAS and PCS positions, the recruitment process is longer and more demanding. In the case of almost all government jobs, candidates quickly become embroiled in a punishing program of memorizing general knowledge answers, preparing resumes and learning how to comport themselves in interviews. Young men were frequently anxious about whether they should be bribing government officials and whether they possessed the right connections. All the while, they tried to persuade friends, relatives and well-wishers to write letters of recommendation or give money for bribes.

Almost all men, regardless of class and caste background, were failing to find secure salaried work in Meerut. The rate of failure among Jats was much higher in Meerut in 2004 and 2005 than it was in rural Meerut district in the mid-1990s or in rural Bijnor district in the early 2000s (Jeffrey et al. 2008). The combination of a decline in the size of the state following economic reforms in the 1990s and a rapid rise in the number of qualified job aspirants in North-Western UP had led to spiraling demand for government positions. There were sometimes several thousand applicants for a single low- or middle-ranking government position in Meerut, and the competition for higher-ranking posts in the UP PCS and IAS was similarly intense. Students said that bribery and favoritism did not entirely dominate these employment markets; some young men got jobs without paying a bribe or using connections. But stories such as Rajesh's—of apparent foul play and of others cheating one out of a job—were ubiquitous. I was able to corroborate some of these accounts through interviewing brokers in government employment markets and government officials. Young men in Meerut, even those like Rajesh from relatively prosperous Jat households, were regularly losing out in competition for low- and middle-ranking government jobs to young people from better-connected, richer sections of the middle class. A young man in MC said that in the fevered market for government work, even "source" (social connections) and "force" (physical strength) are no longer enough: "Now, to get a job, you need a high level political contact or a close relative in the relevant bureaucracy." There was a consensus among students, professors and state officials that there existed a small self-perpetuating clique of families with good access to jobs in the military, education and government health care and, outside of this closed elite, a vast sea of frustrated young people and parents—a picture which accords with Parry's (1996, 1999) analyses of markets for government jobs in central India. Students said that caste-based reservations had become almost irrelevant in the search for a government job. Competition for reserved OBC positions was almost as intense as it was within the general quota, and Jats' acquisition of OBC status in 2000 therefore did little to improve their chances of obtaining government work.

With the exception of a few students from urban, upper middle-class backgrounds, young men studying in Meerut usually lacked the social contacts required to obtain well-paid private jobs in metropolitan India, such as the IT and outsourcing positions that were emerging close to Delhi. In my hostel surveys, I heard of only six students who had successfully captured private-sector jobs paying more than Rs. 10,000 a month. Four of these men came from upper middle-class urban families and had close kin in Delhi. Many other students had tried and failed to acquire well-paid private sector positions. These men, including many rich Jats, not only lacked connections within relevant industries but also the friends and well-wishers who could accommodate them while they searched for jobs in Delhi, NOIDA or Ghaziabad. They also referred to lacking the embodied traits that are a prerequisite for employment in multinational firms. A rich Jat young man studying in CCSU told me: "We lack the demeanor for the new jobs, and our accents give us away." Students sometimes said that the competition for jobs in the new economy was a "field" geographically centered outside Meerut district and in which the rules of the game did not operate to the advantage of provincial lower middle classes.

The failure to acquire secure salaried work not only jeopardized young men's social and economic standing but also threatened their ability to marry and thereby fulfill locally valued norms of adult masculinity. The parents of young men unsuccessful in government employment examinations found it difficult to arrange the marriages of their sons. The parents of prospective brides typically wanted to marry their daughter to a young man with a stable job. Ninety-four percent of those living in four hostels in MC and two hostels CCSU which I surveyed were unmarried and most of these men said that they were unlikely to marry in the next five years.

Some students left higher education after completing their first degree and returned to work on their family farms. These young men tended to adopt a rather lackadaisical approach to agricultural labor, checking their farms on a haphazard basis, driving a tractor, but remaining largely removed from the daily business of cultivating the soil. These men said that it was demeaning for educated people to conduct farming work. The sons of rich Jat farmers were especially likely to respond to educated unemployment by entering agriculture. Dalits, Muslims and MBCs were typically unable to pursue this strategy, and they usually entered artisanal work or manual laboring employment.

Other students in Meerut drew upon social contacts with fellow caste members living in urban North-Western UP to obtain temporary private employment in the informal economy within Meerut or the Delhi region. Such employment included positions as teachers in private coaching institutes, marketing agents for telecommunications and pharmaceutical companies, managers of Internet and international phone dialing services and facilitators in pyramid sales operations. Such positions were especially popular among Jat young men from prosperous rural backgrounds. These service-type occupations were usually part-time, insecure and offered little in the way of long-term prospects or skills. Many of the men in such employment earned between Rs. 1,500 and Rs. 3,000 a month, only slightly more than agricultural laborers in their home villages. At the same time, however, parents of richer students, including Jats from prosperous rural backgrounds, could absorb the opportunity costs associated with having a son in poorly paid employment. Furthermore, parents and young men valued private service for its aura of modernity; many of the enterprises had names that suggested their affiliation with modern, urban India, such as "Highlife Internet Café" and "Advanced Coaching Institute." Corporations or private entrepreneurs recruiting young men were quick to provide them with the trappings of urban service work, such as imitation leather briefcases, an office and an impressive sounding moniker. The sociologist Dipankar Gupta (2000) is critical of these aspects of contemporary Indian urbanism; he sees in such names and paraphernalia a "mistaken modernity." But for many young men with whom I worked, modern-style Internet cafes, coaching institutes and job titles offered a sense of cultural security and belonging in the city. Such stylistic strategies also allowed young men to construct themselves as people fulfilling the "modern" cultural ambitions of their rurally based parents. Rich, middle- and upper-caste young men, including the sons of prosperous farmers, tended to be much better equipped to enter this face-saving work in the private informal economy than were Dalits, MBCs and Muslims, who usually lacked the requisite social connections, cultural capital and parental financial support.

But perhaps the most common response of young men to their inability to obtain government employment was simply to stay put, keep on collecting degrees and hope that their luck would change. Students depended on their parents, and sometimes also their siblings, to continue in college or university. Parents were aware that, while their sons were in college, they could advertise them as "students" on the brink of salaried work (*naukrī milnewālā ādmī*), and this improved their chances of marrying their sons into good families. The mean age of male students in two hostels in MC in 1996 was 22.6. Nine years later this figure had risen to 24.4. Ultimately, however, these long-time students were forced to leave higher education, often in their late twenties or early thirties, when they would usually either return to farming in their home village, enter the private informal economy, or, in the case of poorer students, become manual laborers. Wealthier students were usually able to remain in formal education for longer than poorer students. The majority of long-time students I met in Meerut were Jats from prosperous farming backgrounds, who lacked the social connections to acquire good "fallback work" in Meerut or Delhi, but possessed enough money to support a long job search while nominally studying in Meerut. But even MBCs, Muslims and Dalits tried to remain in higher education and thereby postpone as long as possible the point at which they fully acknowledged their failure to find secure salaried work.

The tendency for young people and their parents to reinvest in formal education in the context of economic uncertainty has been widely noted in the global south (e.g. Dore 1976; Levinson 1999; Hansen 2005). What was perhaps remarkable about Meerut in 2004 and 2005 was the growing importance of varied educational consultants in encouraging a search for credentials (cf. Lynch 1990). There were two especially important sets of players in emerging markets for educational qualifications and job-oriented skills. First, there was an assortment of upper middle-class men (and more rarely women)—many of them professors, administrators or lawyers—who traded on their inside knowledge of government employment markets. These consultants offered coaching in their large middle-class mansions in the richest parts of Meerut. They provided guidance on various dimensions of obtaining government work, especially instruction on civil service interviews and advice on how to pass NET examinations. A second set of players consisted of rich businessmen and very rich farmers, including many Jats, who had profited handsomely from agriculture or industry and saw in education an opportunity to diversify their portfolio. These men were often able to purchase land on the edge of Meerut and establish private educational colleges. Colleges offering courses oriented to specific careers, such as hotel management, dentistry and engineering, were strung out along the Meerut bypass and other peri-urban roads. What united employment consultants and educational entrepreneurs was an effort to persuade students that it is possible to acquire a perfect bundle of qualifications and skills, a "magic formula" that would unlock opportunities for secure salaried work. Switching metaphors, many of these educational and employment gurus also told students that the field of competition for government employment was a "game," and that, if they could just learn the rules and the correct improvisational strategies, they would succeed in their quest. I met many employment consultants and educational entrepreneurs in Meerut in the mid-1990s. But by the mid-2000s they had become even more prevalent. They often had strong ties with caste associations (*mahāsabhās*), Lions Clubs and Rotary International, and educational consultants used the cultural capital that accrued from such membership to bolster their reputation as gurus.

Large numbers of young men in Meerut studied for several degrees in succession while also scouring the educational informal economy for other sources of distinction. Many began by studying for a BA or BSc at Meerut College and then enrolling in CCSU for Master's-level qualifications. Others, like Rajesh, accumulated bachelors and postgraduate qualifications in one of the government-funded colleges affiliated with CCSU, such as Meerut College. Of the 245 young men in my survey of MC and CCSU hostels, 64 percent had already obtained at least one degree and 43 percent had obtained two or more. The slow accretion of degrees, skills and knowledge acted to a certain extent as a prophylactic against the hardships of perceived unemployment; students felt that they were proceeding through small steps towards a definite goal.

But most long-time students recognized that there was no simple recipe for success, in spite of what they had read in the flyers mailed to them in the college or on the signboards for private classes that surround Meerut's colleges. Indeed, I heard several students refer to the idea of a tipping point beyond which educational credentials actually diminish one's employability: they referred to being "over-educated." The idea that studying is only a means of timepass was especially common among these men. Many long-time students told me that, while they had deliberated over the choice of their first degree, it hardly mattered what they studied after that. "We are just studying *vaise* [haphazardly or without purpose]," several students said.

Of course, young men often knew that they were likely to face a protracted, possibly fruitless search for work when they arrived in Meerut; those in their late teens studying in secondary school were not blind to what awaited them. But students tended to believe that patience and hard work might put them among the lucky minority who did obtain a secure government job. Moreover, their parents, whose knowledge of government job markets was mainly acquired in the 1970s and 1980s, and educational consultants, who had an economic interest in heightening youth expectations, encouraged young men to hope. When young men failed to acquire secure jobs—and were confronted, too, by evidence of the declining value of their education—they felt indignant and dispirited.

Students at MC and CCSU were especially angry about the scale of educated unemployment and the failure of the state to address this problem in a convincing manner. An MC student told me:

> The biggest problem facing students is unemployment (*berozgārī*). When I think about my life, I think that first of all I should get salaried employment, I should get a base. Once I have done that, I can start to think about other things. Ninety percent of students think in this manner. But there is no way forward.

Underlying this frustration was a sense of entitlement to salaried work on the grounds of being "educated." Young men repeatedly drew attention to their qualifications, knowledge and capacity to display an educated demeanor, for example to move, eat, talk and think with equanimity, patience and in a civilized manner. Students posited a fundamental difference between the idealized "well-mannered educated young man," who pays respect to older people and thinks carefully before speaking, and the allegedly disrespectful, loud and boorish behavior of "illiterates" (*unparh log, jahīl log*) of their own age living in their home villages or in Meerut (cf. Jeffrey et al. 2008).

Thus, many long-time students in Meerut were contending with multiple, linked forms of temporal anxiety: concern over a lack of fulfilling distractions, provincial educational decay and perceived unemployment. What did they feel about this situation of apparent limbo? A few long-time students remained cheerfully optimistic. Two young men at MC believed fervently that the processes of economic development occurring in NOIDA and Ghaziabad would soon spread to Meerut and that they were focused on preparing for the moment at which IT industries began advertising locally. Five young men I met in MC and CCSU, all of whom were preparing for government (mainly IAS or PSC) examinations, told me that, while they occasionally felt "low," they remained sure that the right job would materialize in the end. Tarul, a thirty-five year old man studying at MC, was typical in this respect. Tarul had been at MC for 13 years and collected degrees in Physics, Chemistry, Political Science and Sociology. He was formally registered as a Research Scholar in Physics, which assuaged his parents and allowed him to retain his college room, "but in practice I do absolutely no work in Physics." Tarul explained that he was entirely focused on trying to obtain a job through the UP PSC—he had five years left before he reached the maximum age for candidates. Tarul had failed multiple times, but continued to prepare for the exams in his room, apparently undeterred. Tarul often broke off our conversations to discuss his general knowledge and understanding of how to behave in interviews for government jobs. He said that he was only dimly aware of day-to-day happenings on the college campus and oriented his thoughts and actions instead towards specific points in the future: the exam, the interview and, hopefully, entry into government service. Tarul, like the rich Jat farmers discussed in Chapter Two, sometimes spoke of a need to "wait" for the right opportunities to come along, and he also referred to the moral value of patience and determination.

At the other end of the spectrum were young men who had seemingly lost all sense of a viable future in the face of repeated disappointment in the job market and a more general sense of limbo in Meerut. One Jat young man in MC said that he was contemplating suicide as a means to escape feelings of disappointment. Four other young men whom I interviewed, three of them Jats and one Yadav, were dependent on drugs and alcohol. Jats' history of working in the army meant that this community had longer experience of contact with liquor than had Dalits and Muslims, and alcoholism was becoming common among Jats. In addition, Jat young men had had greater exposure to drug cultures emerging in Delhi, either because they had visited the capital more often than had Dalits and Muslims or because the schools and colleges they had attended had more of a metropolitan feel. I heard of eight young men in the four hostels I regularly visited across MC and CCSU who were habituated to cannabis or opium, six of them Jats. Three young men, two Jats and one Dalit, killed themselves in the 1990s and early 2000s in colleges affiliated with CCSU.

Yet most long-time students were neither brightly optimistic nor wholly despondent. Instead, like Rajesh, they were ambivalent about their future and present position in society. They were dispirited about their situation and cynical about any attempt to plan for the future. But they also retained a sense that, if they could just hold out long enough, a job might just materialize in the end. This openness to possibility can be glossed as a form of waiting that is neither straightforwardly purposeful nor purposeless but shares elements of both forms.

As one would expect, long-time students had a keener sense of being "left behind" than had students earlier in their college careers. In spite of the irregularity of much higher educational functioning, the monthly or yearly college events—the term tests, annual examinations and arrival of new students in the hostels—did impose a type of rhythm on students' lives, which, when placed alongside their sense of unstructured time, served as a nagging reminder of their disappearing dreams. Indeed, long-time students often used the term "timepass" in a more directly relational way than younger students on campus. The periodic arrival on campus of the few former peers who had obtained prestigious employment sharpened unemployed students' sense of having somehow "failed." Many of my informants said that they had developed an "inferiority complex" (*hīn bhavnā*), in which they contrasted their own "timepass" with the "serious" work of those who had managed to get jobs, marry and make money. In other situations, young men contrasted their own "timepass" with the "serious" work required by their parents to keep them in higher education.

The social importance of ideas of being left behind—or stuck in-between—became especially clear to me in October 2004, when I was chatting with a group of students over a breakfast of hot milk at the busy junction outside the Meerut law court. I was recounting an interview I had given with a journalist about unemployment in the UK. One of the students present responded by telling a story, one I heard repeated many times. The story centers on two characters: one, Rampal, a man in his late thirties, who was studying in the local degree college (Meerut College), the other, Jaibir, a former classmate of Rampal, who had obtained a position in the IAS. Both men were lower middle-class Jats. As the story goes, Jaibir comes back to

Meerut every so often to see his family. The first time he returns he has just finished civil service training and has recently acquired a position as a SDM. He sees Rampal outside the Meerut College gate and asks him what he is up to. Rampal replies "Well, I'm studying and doing a bit of student politics." Five years later, Jaibir has become a DM in south India. Jaibir returns to Meerut, sees Rampal again outside the college gate and asks him how things are going. Rampal replies, "Well, I'm studying and doing a bit of student politics." Another five years pass, and by this time Jaibir has secured the lofty position of Commissioner and traveled abroad. Again, Jaibir comes back to Meerut, sees Rampal beside the college gate and asks him how he is getting on. Rampal replies: "Well, I'm studying and doing a bit of student politics."

Timepass as Affirmative Culture

In what sense might Rampal actually embody a particular form of power? Is there any context in which Rampal might be considered Jaibir's superior? Commenting on the story, many students said that Jaibir is the obvious hero of the tale; "Jaibir is Jaibir, Rampal is Rampal, one is successful, one is a flop," was the type of response I heard several times. When students told this story, the audience would often move their thumbs from side to side when Rampal's name was mentioned, a gesture that suggested foolishness and non-achievement. But other students offered alternative readings: "Jaibir is more successful, but Rampal is more experienced," one student suggested. Another said "Jaibir has become a snob . . . Rampal is a type of hero." Another student focused on Rampal's location at the MC gate: "I think if Rampal had been standing in that spot for ten or twenty years, he would have seen some very interesting things!"

These comments hint at the possibility that timepass is not only an expression of social suffering, but also something else—perhaps a cultural and political practice, a mode of self-fashioning and self-expression somewhat akin to the "styles" studied by Birmingham School scholars in 1970s UK (see Corrigan 1979). Other work on cultures of young male idleness points to the socially productive nature of hanging out (e.g. Cowan 1991; Chakrabarty 1999; Weiss 2002; Nisbett 2007). Brad Weiss (2002) has described the importance of particular sites of apparent male apathy—especially barbershops—in the efforts of unemployed young men to remake urban public space in Tanzania. In India, Chakrabarty (1999) identifies varied culturally important spots (*addās*) in urban West Bengal, often street corners or tea stalls, in which apparently idle young men have crafted nodes of masculine conviviality. At the *addās*, they "chat with intimate friends" and engage in "self presentation" (see also Heuzé 1996; Favero 2005). Mazumdar (2007: 99) has argued that the *taporī* (loafer) of Indian cinema is often depicted as a type of hero, a person challenging received social categories through the display of an uncompromising street masculinity: "a form of empowerment which expresses the fact of 'powerlessness.'"

The work of Weiss, Chakrabarty and Mazumdar resonates with my findings in Meerut, where timepass occurred within and across various city *addās*, involved young men in developing distinctive masculinities and frequently proceeded through the performance of a type of defiant public admission of failure. In a manner somewhat akin to the young men casually smashing milk bottles on the wet pavements of Sunderland in 1970s Britain, described beautifully by Paul Corrigan (1979), young men in Meerut—male students in general as well as long-time students such as Rajesh—seemed to proclaim more or less explicitly "we've nothing much to do, but we're here and you must notice us." Moreover, they found ways to acquire knowledge and skills while hanging out at university.

Young men tended to gravitate towards *addās* that suggested movement, travel and escape from Meerut and which offered the opportunity to catch up on news and display their unemployment. Outside MC most mornings and early evenings, educated unemployed Jats and jobless Dalit and Muslim young men often stood around together at the main street intersection near the Meerut courts. In CCSU, they congregated around a string of tea stalls on the major round that runs along the edge of the university. The tea stalls outside CCSU and MC, as in the many other areas of provincial north India, typically consisted of rickety wooden tables and hard plastic chairs or straight-backed wooden benches. The floor was usually of compacted dirt covered with cigarette butts and discarded chewing tobacco wrappers. In summer, the tea stalls were fiercely hot and in winter they were grimly exposed to the chill

winds that blow through the city. The roadside tea stall had an air of stark-
ness that contributed to their function as sites of tough male sociability. In
the somewhat inhospitable space of the tea stall or standing about at street
intersections, young men intermingled, traded stories, exchanged gossip and
argued about sport, films and news events. They smoked, drank tea, fooled
about, enacted mock fights, got into real fights and lounged around with their
arms draped around each other's shoulders. I very rarely saw young women
spending long periods at any of these tea stalls or street corners.

Chakrabarty (1999) defines the *addā* as a meeting place, but *addā* can also
mean workplace, site, stand, station (for vehicles) or perch (for birds). The
spaces of male social exchange I came to know provided *addās* in a double
sense: a perch from which they could view the flow of goods, images and
people in and out of Meerut and a meeting place for unemployed young men
keen to expand networks of male conviviality.

As Chakrabarty (1999) suggests, the urban *addā* was an important space
of social mixing, in which men from unlike backgrounds exchanged jokes
and developed friendships. It is worthwhile recalling that the male hostels in
CCSU and MC were differentiated to some degree by caste and religion. Yet
in the small shops, tea stalls and street intersections outside CCSU and MC,
Jats, Dalits, Muslims and other castes often mixed fairly freely. I was repeatedly struck by small gestures of friendship between diverse young men: such
ordinary actions as paying for another's tea or passing a cigarette from mouth
to mouth provided a window into a cultural substratum of male solidarity.
Other scholars have noted how street settings may kindle a group egalitarian
spirit among young men (e.g. Vale de Almeida 1996; Weiss 2002; Mains 2007).
What makes the forms of solidarity emerging in Meerut tea stalls stand out
is their tendency to cut across caste and religious boundaries. The sharing of
salty snacks and tea and the passing of cigarettes from one mouth to another
among Dalits, higher castes and Muslims signals a suspension of caste ideas
of pollution through the sharing of food or contact with another's saliva (cf.
Nisbett 2007: 941). The secular orientation of Jats and histories of brotherhood associated with the BKU movement might prime us to expect such
casual exchange. But I was surprised by these examples of young male camaraderie in the context of my previous research on middle-caste discrimination

against Dalits in rural Meerut district (Chapter Two; see also Jeffrey 2000; 2001) and the work of Brass (1997) and others on students' involvement in communal violence in Meerut in the 1980s.

Humor, horseplay and banter featured prominently in young men's time-pass activities at various points around the city, as it did in the male street cultures studied by Corrigan (1979) in the UK in the 1970s. Many of the jokes displayed a wry, self-deprecatory wit laid on partly for my own benefit and in which the hardships of being young and unemployed in provincial north India were offered up for ironic reflection. In several instances, students referred to themselves semi-humorously as *bekār*, a word which might be translated as "not at work" but also suggests worthlessness and uselessness. At other moments they referred to themselves as people "doing nothing" or "doing something or other" and derived much merriment from my fumbling efforts to get them to expand on what this "nothing" or "something" might mean. The idea of wandering also provided a basis for humor. Students often drew out the long "ooh" sound of the Hindi word for wandering—*ghūmna*—while weaving their hand through the air to suggest their capricious drift through the city. The notion of timepass itself was also a focus for humor. Jokes often arose out of how young men deployed the antonyms "timepass" and "seri-ous" in everyday conversation. During a discussion outside MC, a Jat student provoked much laughter when he distinguished between his "serious" and "timepass" girlfriends (see also Abraham 2002). On other occasions, young men generated mirth by engaging in "reverse speak" (*ulte bolte*): describing activities that were evidently "serious," such as going to hospital or interview-ing for a job, as simply timepass, and vice versa. The rather illicit nature of young men's idleness made discussions of timepass especially funny and a particularly good basis for forging cross-caste and cross-class alliances. Stu-dents' stories of timepass operated as a type of "intimate culture" in Michael Herzfeld's (2005) sense of a feature of social life regarded as somewhat embarrassing when exposed to outsiders but viewed by insiders as a basis for shoring up community spirit and building trust.

In his work on intimate culture, Herzfeld records several instances in which he miscalculated the mood of his respondents; the investigation of intimate cultures by outsiders is characterized by risk (see also Gutmann

1996). On one occasion I asked a set of Jat young men where they had been. One replied in a rather disinterested tone that they had been chatting outside the library. "Timepass?" I asked casually. The young man smarted, "No! I was talking about some important business—a job opportunity that has come up. Who said that I was doing timepass?" Timepass offered insiders a sense of solidarity, meaning and humor, but many of the young men with whom I worked did not take kindly to my second-guessing the game of cultural intimacy. Moreover, for all my hanging out with young men, there were still many situations in which my status as a foreigner with secure employment came to the fore. I often felt uncomfortable being able to "dip in and out" of a situation of social and economic hardship, and many of my respondents sensed this unease: "What do you care? You will be out of here soon!" were words I heard on several occasions.

At other moments students stressed their superiority to me; they said that they had mastered the delicate art of hanging out, something which I—as a cosseted foreigner—would never be able to appreciate. Indeed, students sometimes presented timepass as a valuable skill connected to being able to act judiciously within different fields of social endeavor. As people spending long periods occupying and observing nodes within the city, many young men said that they had developed certain types of knowledge (*gyān*). In particular, they frequently argued that they are distinctively equipped to straddle and combine a provincial space, which they equated with their rural homes and small town North-Western UP, and the modern world, which they associated not primarily with the West but with ideas, images, symbols and information that came from metropolitan India. Many unemployed students demonstrated a form of what Gidwani and Sivaramakrishnan (2003) have called "subaltern cosmopolitanism" wherein they imagined themselves as poised between two spheres—rural UP and metropolitan India—and uniquely able to bestride these different arenas. Just as rich Jat farmers in mid-1990s Meerut made much of their ability to navigate webs of social relationships that traversed the rural and urban, a younger generation in 2000s Meerut—not just Jats but also some higher castes, Muslims and Dalits—imagined themselves to be juggling cultural forms and practices that bisect and dissolve boundaries between the "provincial" and "metropolitan." In this optic, being at the crossroads offered students an opportunity to rethink their status as people "in-between" or "in the middle"—socially, spatially and temporally—and present it in a positive light.

Students also sometimes argued that the cultivation of the skill of "hanging out" in Meerut had become such a ubiquitous feature of their everyday life as to constitute a "job" (*kām*)—and it is useful to remember that *addā* can also mean "workplace." In developing this notion they referred to the multiple benefits (*fāydā*) that can flow from spending long periods on street corners or in tea stalls. For example, young men said that as people engaged in timepass they have come to learn about and appreciate the varied ways in which people dress, speak and move around in Meerut. Young men also said that by hanging out they obtain information that may be of use in the future, for example regarding new job openings or local political shenanigans, and thereby obtain political leverage in relation to others. In 2004, I interviewed four young men whom I had known in 1996 and who had obtained government jobs, and all four remembered a period of urban timepass as a time-space in which they cultivated useful social contacts and acquired information pertinent to their search for employment.

Ideas of caste and class shaped how young men elaborated on timepass in local *addās*. On the one hand, students from all caste and class backgrounds, even the Dalit poor, were keen to distinguish their style of hanging about from that of working-class young men in Meerut. The students with whom I worked did not imagine themselves as *taporī*, such as those depicted in Indian cinema of the time. Rather, they tried to distance themselves from what they regarded as the rather uncouth, "semi-educated" or "uneducated" practices of the *taporī*. The very word "timepass," because it is derived from "pastime," suggested some familiarity with English, and, by extension, connoted separation from working-class life. Students often counterposed an image of civilized, well-mannered and accomplished "educated men" passing time about the city against a vision of embarrassing and ill-kempt uneducated men, standing about uselessly or engaged in what some termed "timewaste." These discourses of male idleness bear comparison to the distinction made by Walter Benjamin (1983) between the Parisian *flâneur*, an upper middle-class wanderer judiciously and impassively sampling the city's delights, and the *badaud* (gawper), a working-class rubberneck, who becomes emotionally and violently involved in the events he witnesses (see also Buck-Morss 1986). In a somewhat similar manner, the educated unemployed young men depicted themselves as relatively intelligent observers who remained unflustered and self-consciously disengaged while passing time and contrasted this self-image with a picture of slack-jawed, easily riled, uneducated men—the lowest common denominator of urban street culture. Such narratives helped young men to deflect public criticism of their idleness onto a set of young men—the urban "illiterates"—who students felt were the ones who were really wasting time. But the rehearsal of such ideas occasionally unsettled the sense of male solidarity established within *addās* across the city. Middle- and upper-caste students sometimes used the terms "uneducated," "Chamar" and "Muslim" interchangeably when discussing the timewaste of the urban poor. Such "slips of the tongue" sometimes passed unremarked among mixed groups of young men hanging out at the tea stall, so ingrained had derogatory references to low castes and Muslims become. At other moments, Dalits and Muslims silently removed themselves from the conversation or muttered objections to the dominant narratives. In still other cases, Dalits and Muslims struck out against upper- or middle-caste comments and fights erupted.

At the same time as separating their practices from those of the urban poor, students also drew attention to the difference between their timepass and the leisure practices of upper middle-class students and older upper middle classes in the city, such as the private entrepreneurs from whom they took tutorials. Young men spoke disparagingly about "silver spoon" or "high class" students: those from upper middle class, urban backgrounds, who had not been pushed into timepass but had the money required to engage in ostentatious leisure practices, such as eating at the new metropolitan-style restaurants around the city. Among Jats and OBCs, these discourses sometimes had a caste element. Jats occasionally slipped between lambasting "high classes" and casting aspersions on "Brahmin people" or "Baniya people" in a manner that exposed further fractures in the communities of solidarity established at the *addās*. Young men's disdain for upper middle-class student cultures emerged especially clearly during a discussion of a locally available snack called Time-pass, which was launched in 2001 by Brittannia Industries, a large Indian corporation. Advertisements for the Timepass snack featured well-dressed university students popping chips into their mouths at various urban *addās*. Brittannia was clearly targeting a youth market. But most of the young men with whom I worked lacked the money to buy Timepass, and they perceived the snack to be a symbol of the wasteful leisure of their upper-class, usually upper-caste, peers.

Gender also influenced the performance of timepass. A type of hypermasculine bravado characterized much of young men's ostentatious hanging out (cf. Rogers 2008). Some young men made repeated references to sexual liaisons that were performed as a means of timepass, and others referred to the importance of "eve-teasing," a euphemism for sexual harassment, or watching young women in order to while away the hours in urban areas (cf. Osella and Osella 2002). A few Jats argued that teasing Dalit young women was an especially good means of passing time. These and other young men also tended to imagine campus space as one populated by young women, objectified as "goods" (*māl*) or "features," in the sense of "landscape features." Male students commonly said that, as educated people, they are able to cruise the campus in search of these goods or features, stopping to appreciate beautiful young women or trade "frank talk" with the few young women who spent time at urban *addās*. These self-constructions also resonated with Benjamin's description of the Parisian *flâneur*; young men projected an image of themselves as leisured observers of multiple "scenes" laid out for their amusement and titillation across campus and urban space (cf. Abraham 2002; Osella and Osella 2002; Rogers 2008). Through cultivating personas as sexually promiscuous timepass men or detached male observers, the unemployed reproduced prevalent gendered assumptions about the respective roles of young men and young women in Meerut.

Socially constructed meanings about gender and sexual difference were also embedded in the way in which young men discussed different *addās* around Meerut. Male students alluded to a gender division of leisure between, on the one hand, the starkly arranged tea stalls in which they most commonly hung out and the confectionary stores or sweet shops frequented by young women. The substances consumed in these different places were ascribed particular gendered meanings. Young men sometimes imagined tea, hot buffalo milk, deep-fried vegetables (*pakorās*) and three-cornered salty snacks (*samosās*) as male refreshments and Nescafe coffee, brand-name confectionary and soft drinks as female delectations. In her work on everyday sociality in provincial Greece, Cowan (1991: 201) argues that sugary images evoke the domesticated woman: "delicious to men; yet good, safe and unthreatening." Thus, "ingesting and enjoying sweets, a woman shows herself properly socialized as well as sociable." Similar ideas appeared to inform the gendered discourses of young men in Meerut, where sweets and female leisure were often discussed together. A number of my Jat informants referred disparagingly to Meerut's "ice-cream students"—a phrase that conjured images of wealthy female students and therefore simultaneously condensed Jat young men's suspicion of the urban rich, upper castes and young women.

Young male students' masculine show reinforced gender inequalities in access to public space. Young women felt that the ostentatious idleness of young men was undermining their studies and limiting their ability to move about the city and campus. Young women at MC and CCSU recounted numerous instances in which men had intimidated them at or around urban *addās*, either by making explicit sexual overtures or through more subtle but equally disturbing practices. In spite of increased police presence in and around CCSU and MC in the 2000s, and the introduction of security guards at the CCSU gate in 2002, young women studying at these institutions feared intimidation. Between September 2000 and March 2005, local newspapers reported six separate incidents of young women being physically assaulted by male students; and, by 2007, a female friend studying at MC said that sections of the campus and surrounding city space were effectively "out of bounds" for young women—"timepass is ruining the environment [*mahaul*] of the college," one young woman said.

At the same time, gender relations were shifting in the face of urban change. Between 1996 when I lived briefly in Meerut College and my return to Meerut in 2004, several coffee shops were established in the city, often within shopping malls or close to new private educational colleges. These coffee shops presented a marked visual contrast to the tea stall: they were well-lit, comfortably furnished and occasionally served expensive espresso drinks. A few of my young male respondents in 2004 and 2005, especially upper castes and also some rich Jats, visited these coffee shops to meet young women. Like the cyber cafes studied by Nisbett (2007) in Bangalore, the coffee shops offered a relatively private space in which young men and young women could flirt and develop relationships. Coffee shops blurred the divide between the masculine space of the tea stall and relatively feminine sweet shop. The new coffee shops had what Cowan (1991), writing about parallel developments in Greece, refers to as an "irritant effect" on entrenched gender norms: needling parents and other Meerut citizens who were already anxious about the hyper-masculine threat presented by idle young men.

The emergence of coffee shops as spaces for young people to meet casts a new light on the 2006 arrests in a Meerut park. The police heavy-handedness in dealing with young couples suspected of "illicit affairs" was connected to public concern over the visibility of gender mixing in new nooks within the city. But such social mixing was still limited when I conducted field research in 2004 and 2005. The dominant picture was of a gender division of leisure in the city between tea stalls, street corners, bus stops and similar sites that were almost exclusively male and sweet shops and confectionary stores, occasionally frequented by young women.

To summarize, timepass was Janus-faced; on the one hand it served as a means for young men to express their sense of loss in the face of the disappointments of higher education and protracted exclusion from salaried work. On the other hand, timepass offered young men a feeling of fun, social worth and lower middle-class masculine distinction. Moreover, hanging out may have been important in their efforts to obtain information and contacts relevant to their job search. Unemployed young men's waiting constituted a form of productive idleness and alertness to possibility, even as it tended to reproduce gendered forms of power.

Conclusions

A remarkable feature of students' lives in Meerut was their sense of unstructured time. As school students their activities were fairly closely monitored. By contrast, at university they often had little to do but wait for examinations and pass time. Young men also felt disengaged from college in the

context of a decline in the quality of higher education, a point they sometimes made by referring to their studies as "timepass." In addition, young men
used the idea that they were only doing timepass to mark their subordination
relative to youth who had moved out of Meerut and who were therefore presumed to be living more "serious" lives.

Different notions of timepass—as a means to counter boredom, sign
of disengagement and marker of being "left behind"—were especially pronounced among a set of self-consciously "unemployed" students. These men,
who were mainly from wealthy rural Jat backgrounds, had repeatedly failed to
find secure employment. They frequently responded by remaining in higher
education and hoping that their lives would change.

I have also described how young men built a youth culture around the idea
of "timepass"—a culture which they performed by mooching around at tea
stalls and street corners in Meerut. Timepass, far from being a passive activity,
emerges as a means by which young men mark their social suffering and begin
to negotiate unemployment. This argument resonates with research with
apparently idle men in other contexts, for example in Britain (Corrigan 1979;
Jackson 1998) the US (Whyte 1993) and the Mediterranean (Cowan 1991; Vale
de Almeida 1996). More than existing research, I want to stress the humor and
irony that characterized timepass cultures and the capacity of unemployed
young men to engage in cultural practices that bridged social divides.

The next chapter reflects on how the experience of limbo among young
men not only generated irreverent youth cultures but also somewhat creative
and mischievous forms of collective youth politics. Compelled to wait, Jats,
Muslims and Dalits sometimes joined together to organize protests on campus
and in the city. Moreover, a set of community activists had emerged in MC
and CCSU—including Jats, Dalits, Muslims and upper castes—who served
as lightning rods for student protests and facilitators in students' everyday
engagements with the state.

4   Collective Student Protest

This chapter examines the forms of collective student mobilization that emerged out of young men's experience of limbo. Other research with young men "hanging out" in different parts of the world commonly depicts unemployed youth following one of two courses: either engaging in reactionary politics (e.g. Hansen 1996) or channeling their energies into more progressive forms of democratic action (e.g. Bundy 1987; Krishna 2002). In Meerut young men were engaging in both forms of politics simultaneously. A widespread sense of limbo had led many young men to imagine themselves as "social reformers." These men played important social and political roles in Meerut and surrounding rural areas, as I demonstrate in this chapter. But unemployment had also led to the emergence of a small set of "fixers" who engaged in narrowly class-based, self-interested practices, and whose strategies I discuss in Chapter Five.

Higher education is often an important site for youth activism, in India as elsewhere. Universities commonly bring young people from different backgrounds into close proximity, offer opportunities to learn about others and encourage young people to develop a more political understanding of their lives. University may also be a time when young people have relative freedom to engage in social critique. This notion of the university as a political space became especially prominent in the 1960s and 1970s, when students took to the streets in the US and Western Europe in "new left" and "anti-war" protests (e.g. Bottomore 1970; Ross 2002) and when student involvement in nationalist and democratic movements in Africa and Asia also came to light (Jayaram 1979; Altbach 1984; Hazary 1987).

In India, the evidence of universities' role in political transformation is more fragmentary (Rudolph and Rudolph 1987). In the colonial era, Indian universities played a prominent role in the nationalist struggle (see Hazary 1987: 66 ff). In the postcolonial period, student protests occasionally fed into broader political agitations, most noticeably in 1974 in Bihar when students participated in a social movement led by the politician and social reformer Jai Parakash (JP) Narain. The "JP movement" involved students in State-wide strikes and demonstrations regarding price rises, corruption and electoral reform. These protests enrolled students across caste, religious and party political divides and contributed to Indira Gandhi's decision to call a National Emergency in 1975–77 (see Masani 1979). Yet for most of postcolonial period in India, student politics has remained rather limited in scope and conservative in character. Thus, for example, in the 1960s and 1970s, it was issues of students' progress through the university and a perceived decline in educational facilities that provoked the majority of student demonstrations (e.g. Rudolph and Rudolph 1987). In the 1980s and 1990s, student demonstrations continued to be largely conservative in tone and focused on educational issues. For example, the Mandal controversy resulted in furious demonstrations on campuses during the late 1980s and early 1990s, typically staged by higher castes angered at reservations for OBCs in education and government employment (e.g. Balagopal 1991). Universities were also important sites in which usually upper and middle castes expressed Hindu nationalist ideas and expanded grassroots Hindu political organizations. Hindu students were central players in religious riots and pogroms in the 1980s, 1990s and early 2000s (Béteille 1992; Heuzé 1992; Brass 1997; Engineer 2002).

I argue in this chapter that Meerut students' resentment regarding higher educational mismanagement and their position in limbo was generating lively forms of collective mobilization in 2004 and 2005. A set of middle-caste (often Jat) social reformers worked alongside young men from other castes to petition and critique the local state. Moreover, these political entrepreneurs frequently persuaded students from different backgrounds to come together in sizeable demonstrations. The prevalence of student mobilization across caste and class lines reflected students' common experience of educational decay and the existence of certain shared assumptions among students about how to mobilize vis-à-vis the state. At the same time, collective student demonstrations were often ineffective, occurred sporadically and tended to reproduce dominant gender norms.

The next section of the chapter identifies four sets of important political animators who came from different backgrounds but were often able to work together. I then examine how political animators were able to generate collective student action in Meerut with particular reference to the main issues raised during protests in 2004 and 2005. The penultimate section considers the degree to which student activism was achieving its goals. The conclusions link the discussion to the principal themes of the book.

Political Animators

Student mobilization in Meerut in 2004 and 2005 occurred not through the actions of formal student parties but in a rather haphazard fashion in response to the appeals of a range of charismatic political animators. This aspect of the organization of student activism reflects the distinctive history of Meerut student politics. Prior to 1947, MC drew its students mainly from upper-caste urban families (Nevill 1922: 56). This socially homogeneous, all-male body of students was involved in India's nationalist struggle. Meerut students joined in Gandhi's *swadeshi* (self-provisioning) drive, and, in 1919 and 1920, they were at the forefront of the Non-Cooperation Movement in North-Western UP. In 1929 students established an ostensibly communist organization—the Naujahan Bharat Sabha (NBS)—which pledged its commitment to "demolishing British imperialism by all means, fair or foul, and preparing the masses for revolution" (quoted in Mittal 1978: 45).

After 1947, the MC campus became an arena for party political competition. In the 1950s, the Congress Party cultivated support in MC and its student wing, the All-India International Student Federation, was prominent in Meerut at that time. From this period until his death in 1987, Chaudhry Charan Singh, a graduate of MC, used the college as a political recruiting ground. Four student leaders in MC in the 1950s and 1960s went on to become

State- or national-level politicians, three in the parties led by Singh. Student leaders in 1960s and 1970s Meerut were primarily concerned with creating a personalized support base and links to politicians who could assist them in their careers. As a result, student politics in Meerut between 1960 and 1980, as in other parts of India (e.g. Hazary 1987: 15ff), was mainly oriented around university issues, especially the welfare of students, administration of higher education and distribution of patronage associated with the privatization of education (see Gould 1972).

Such political activity disrupted campuses; Charan Singh banned student union elections in MC in the late 1970s in response to growing fears about the effects of student politicians on urban life. The policing of student life in Meerut intensified after the religious communal riots in the city in 1982 and 1987, in which some Hindu students from MC and CCSU were involved (see Brass 1997). The absence of student union elections in the most politically important college in the district (MC) and tight restrictions on students' involvement in mobilization meant that political parties were much less active in Meerut student politics in the 1980s and 1990s than they were in other historically significant sites of student political activism in UP, such as Allahabad University (see DiBona 1969) and Lucknow University (Syed 1997).

The late 1990s and early 2000s witnessed a revival in student politics in Meerut. The foundation of a student union at CCSU in 1991 encouraged students interested in developing political careers. But the real reawakening of student interest in politics related to the rapid commercialization of higher education and enormous expansion in the numbers and diversity of young people studying in Meerut institutions from the late 1990s onwards. The sheer number of students—nearly a quarter of a million in institutions affiliated with CCSU in 2005—combined with educational decay and rising unemployment, created fertile ground for collective assertion around issues such as corruption, joblessness and the privatization of higher education. At the same time, however, student political organizations were notable by their absence in CCSU and MC; only the Akhil Bharatiya Vidhyarthi Party (ABVP), the youth wing of the BJP, arranged regular meetings, had well-known office bearers and possessed a large number of members—roughly two hundred in 2004 and 2005. Two other student wings of political parties had some bearing on student activism: the Chatra Lok Dal (CLD), student wing of the Rashtriya Lok Dal; and the Samajwadi Chatra Sabha (SCS), the wing of the Samajwadi Party. These organizations occasionally sponsored candidates in the CCSU student elections, convened student meetings in advance of the visits of notable party politicians and lent assistance in CCSU student elections. But the CLD and SCS did not intervene in everyday campus politics, and even the most politically active of my informants were largely unaware of these organizations. The Bahujan Samaj Students Forum of the BSP, National Students Union of India (NSUI) of the Congress, the Students' Federation of India (SFI) of the Communist Party of India-Marxist, and All India Students Association (AISA) of the CPI-ML (Liberation) had even less institutional presence in Meerut. Students in CCSU and MC only encountered these organizations when visiting State-level youth leaders came to discuss politics with students—something that only tended to happen in advance of CCSU student union elections. Political parties were reluctant to invest scarce resources in creating an institutional base in Meerut in the absence of student elections in MC. The lack of party political activity also reflects young men's disinterest in national- and State-level representative politics. With the exception of a few Dalit student politicos, who strongly supported the BSP, most students regarded politicians as universally corrupt. They also said that political parties were disinterested in the plight of students and youth.

Collective student action in Meerut in 2004 and 2005 occurred through the efforts of a range of political animators to mobilize other students. Men dominated these everyday processes of student assertion on and around campus, in large part because of the masculine culture of student activism and the difficulties young women faced in occupying Meerut public space. Young women were not entirely excluded from leading protests. There were four young women, two Brahmins and two Jats, who sometimes became involved in public efforts to promote student protest: two worked mainly behind the scenes, instructing politically conscious young men among their peers on issues that required students' attention, and two engaged in more public protests with a view to securing a position on the CCSU student union in the future. Yet men almost always played lead roles during agitations.

Four "analytic sets" of young male political animators were especially notable in Meerut. These sets were not neatly self-contained; some young men moved between one set and another. Nor did all politically active young men belong to these four groups. It is nevertheless broadly possible to discern different categories of political animator and to identify the distinctive ways in which each set worked to achieve political goals.

First, a collection of self-styled middle-caste (mainly Jat) "social reformers" (*samājik shudhāran*) were often at the forefront of protests. One of the effects of a widespread awareness of unemployment among students in CCSU and MC in the early 2000s was to encourage the emergence of strong-willed young men from middle-caste backgrounds who believed passionately in "social service" (*samāj sewā*). These social reformers commonly looked back to youth politics in Meerut in the colonial period for their inspiration, and they imagined that through their efforts they might create a "new age" of radical student protest in the city.

Although comprising only about three percent of middle-caste men studying at CCSU or MC, there were between twenty and thirty self-identified social reformers working as political entrepreneurs on and around these campuses in 2004–5, and I was able to interview nine of these men. These nine middle-caste social reformers all defined themselves as unemployed and said that their negative experiences of competing for government employment had been important in their decision to engage in social reform. Some referred explicitly to their experience of boredom and emptiness on campus, which partly motivated them to become political entrepreneurs. Yet middle-caste social reformers did not imagine their political practices as "timepass." For these social reformers, politicking was "serious" work that required application and strenuous effort.

Consideration of the experiences of a Jat young man named Balraj provides insights into the activities of the nine middle-caste social reformers with whom I worked. I first met Balraj at the hustings for the student union election. Balraj was smartly dressed in white slacks and a blue shirt. He was delighted to hear that I was interested in youth politics in Meerut. Our first meeting was almost entirely given over to Balraj asking me questions about the UK: the nature of the party political system, whether the hospitals and schools were privatized, the social organization of higher education and whether students engaged in paid work outside their classes.

During our second interview, at a tea stall near CCSU, I learned more about Balraj's life. He was in his late twenties in 2004 and came from a village about 25 miles southwest of Meerut in neighboring Ghaziabad district. Balraj's father owned 8 hectares of agricultural land and a small sugar cane crushing business. He had wanted his sons to enter non-farm work. Balraj attended private nursery, primary and secondary schools close to his rural home then enrolled in a private college in Delhi for a Pharmacy Diploma, Meerut College for a Physics BSc and then CCSU for a degree in Mass Communications. Balraj had applied unsuccessfully for government work. He said that he had spent much of his twenties "unemployed."

Balraj referred to himself as a social reformer to distinguish his actions from *rājnitī* ("politics"), which he defined as the self-interested competition for government posts, and *netāgirī* ("leadership"), which denoted cultivating useful political contacts and building a student following. Balraj got his first taste of student activism at a rural degree college where he led demonstrations against an increase in hostel fees. By 2004, Balraj's aims had expanded considerably to embrace a suite of short-term goals: to rid higher education of corruption, widen access to the university and prevent officials from harassing students. During his studies at a rural degree college he also developed a lifetime political ambition: "to change India through sustained youth struggle against inequality and oppression."

Balraj remained committed to these immediate and lifetime goals at CCSU. He was often to be found at the head of demonstrations in CCSU related to students' welfare, and students often contacted him when they felt they had grievance against the university. Balraj said:

> Our role is to spread awareness about corruption. Let me give you an example. We found out that a submersible pump installed in the hostel three years ago cost Rs. 17,200 to put in. But the amount shown on the audit was Rs. 42,500. Students now have the right to see the audits. They should recover the money from the contractor. The problem, though, is that the student body does not have any knowledge about the administration. I protested about this matter. Nothing happened as a result, but I showed the officials that students are not blind to what is happening and that we have some power in our hands.

Balraj was a skilled orator, and he enjoyed giving short speeches in his hostel aimed at galvanizing support. When I asked Balraj about the issues he brings up in his speeches he said:

> [I tell them that] politicians and officials in this city are sucking (*chūsna*) young people dry. The senior officials at the university are sometimes the worst. They have to pay huge bribes to get their jobs and then they devise exploitative strategies to recover what they have spent. They usually give out some more money to bad elements, who then go and do bad work. This bad work yields a high return and the senior officials can then spend this money on maintaining their positions and buying off their critics. The senior officials—like all politicians—feed other people, give them alcohol, weapons and praise.

In 2004–5, Balraj was involved in demonstrations aimed at preventing students who had enrolled half-way through a year having to pay a full year of fees. He also led a campaign to ensure that students registered for private professional courses at CCSU had voting rights in the student union elections. In addition, Balraj made a sustained effort to persuade a police official who had injured a student to be brought to justice. Balraj said that these were his main campaigns; there were a host of smaller, everyday political drives in which he had also taken a lead.

For Balraj, the importance of his everyday protests resided, in part, in the opportunities they offered for deriving wider socio-economic and political lessons. Balraj was preoccupied with the challenge of developing what C. Wright Mills (1959) called a "sociological imagination" among students: the capacity to link personal struggle to broader processes of social transformation. Balraj criticized student leaders in Meerut in the 1960s and 1970s for putting their own political advancement before the needs of poor students and other oppressed communities and for failing to think about how their own insecurities might be connected to the concerns of other students in other places. Balraj said that students in Meerut needed to recover the spirit of anti-colonial student protests, a spirit that involved understanding the connections between political movements in multiple contexts.

Balraj repeatedly used events that emerged in the life of the university as a starting point for generating reflective discussion among students and young people more broadly. For example, he made monthly trips to his village and surrounding rural areas to hold workshops among rural youth on land reform, unemployment, youth rights and environmental issues. Balraj said that during these trips he tries to address caste, class and age-based inequalities and instill in young people a thirst for change. Balraj made similar efforts within CCSU and affiliated institutions. His enterprise was impressive. In the first three months of 2005 alone, Balraj followed up on a CCSU student campaign about rising fees by putting information on the notice board outside the library about educational privatization. After an incident in which a young woman was physically intimidated on campus, Balraj convened a public debate on gender rights. In the wake of a fresh scandal relating to the Vice Chancellor's alleged misuse of CCSU funds, Balraj staged a series of impromptu discussions around the campus about corruption. Balraj did not work alone; there were at least ten middle-caste social reformers living in CCSU hostels and another ten or fifteen in MC hostels who engaged in these types of social reform work.

Balraj imagined himself as a "radical." He and two other social reformers established a cell of the Naujawan Bharat Sabha (NBS) in 2004 to coordinate their work. Balraj had read about the history of NBS struggles in Meerut district and wanted to reference the efforts of previous generations of students when conducting protests. Balraj and his friends collected literature on the NBS, kept in contact with NBS cells in three other colleges and pasted photographs of the NBS hero, Bhagat Singh, in his room. Bhagat Singh (1907–34), often referred to as "Shaheed (martyr) Bhagat Singh" was a freedom fighter influenced by communism and anarchism who became involved as a teenager in a number of revolutionary anti-British organizations. He was hanged for shooting a police officer in response to the killing of a veteran freedom fighter (see Nair 2009). Balraj and his compatriots did much to promote the image of Bhagat Singh in CCSU (see Pinney 2002). But the NBS in CCSU in 2004 had no formal office, committee members or membership, and most hostel students regarded the institution as moribund.

Balraj's story offers insights into the background and strategies of the eight other middle-caste social reformers whom I met in 2004 and 2005, five of whom were Jat, two Gujar and one Yadav. Seven of the social reformers came from farming families located within fifty miles of Meerut. These young men heralded from households possessing between 4 and 10 hectares of land, and they had acquired their schooling in rural areas. All of the middle-caste social reformers had tried unsuccessfully to obtain salaried employment. They did not regard themselves as politicians or leaders (*netās*); indeed three social reformers said explicitly that their practices were "anti-political," using the English phrase. Middle-caste social reformers were energetically involved in political mobilization at the local level in Meerut, and they believed that local actions could ignite more ambitious, expansive and ideologically informed political demonstrations. Yet there were limits to their influence; middle-caste social reformers had done little to build an institutional base for their action.

There are certain parallels between the community-minded activism of middle-caste social reformers and the political efforts of Jat leaders in the early years of the BKU movement to build inclusive political constituencies. During the late 1980s, several rich Jat farmers in Muzaffarnagar district, North-Western UP, tried to build a broad rural alliance—comprised of laborers, poorer farmers and richer farmers—against the state and urban upper middle classes. But there was nevertheless a marked contrast between the strategies of Jat rich farmers in rural Meerut district in the mid-1990s and those of middle-caste social reformers' in Meerut in 2004 and 2005. As I argued in Chapter Two, most Jat farmers in the mid-1990s practiced narrowly self-interested forms of politicking rather than broad-based forms of mobilization.

Middle caste social reformers worked with another group of middle-caste young men who—either seriously or with a measure of self-effacing humor—called themselves *netās* ("leaders" or "politicians"). These men constituted a second key set of political animators on Meerut campuses. Unlike the middle-caste social reformers, this set of men either possessed a position on the CCSU student union or, more commonly, planned to contest student union elections in the future. The example of Surendra, a Jat aged 22 in 2004 and based in MC, brings out some of the chief activities of these student leaders in the arena of collective student politics. Surendra was from a wealthy Jat family living about 40 km from Meerut and had a room in HG Hostel, MC. He was keen on obtaining a government job and had already failed three times in this quest when I first met him in 2004. I did not hear him refer to himself as "unemployed," but he was intensely concerned about his employment future and he lamented young men's difficulties in finding work.

Surendra said that boredom was a constant problem in MC. He had responded to ennui through developing a reputation as a leader in HG hostel. HG hostel students with grievances against the MC administration typically went straight to Surendra's small room on the second floor of the hostel or to the local tea stall where Surendra hung out and described their complaint. After listening to a student's appeals for assistance, Surendra often called together those present in the hostel or tea stall and made contact with friends via his cell phone. He then discussed possible courses of action with his confidants and, in many cases, proceeded to organize a demonstration.

Surendra was relatively young to be a prominent student political figure, but he was charismatic and had what he termed a "political eye." He said that a political eye was not about having close contacts in formal political organizations; he had not developed good links with a politician or political party in 2005. Nor did Surendra seem especially concerned with political ideologies, for example of the left or right. Instead, Surendra explained that a political eye amounted to a "feel" for the "game" (*khel*) of politics in MC (cf. Bourdieu 1984). He elaborated on this notion with reference to strongly gendered ideas that pitted the image of the experienced male student equipped with knowledge and improvisational skill against that of the disoriented Freshman or young woman.

Surendra said that his desire to assist students was something that emerged "from his heart" (*dil se*). But he was also aware that there might be an opportunity to capitalize on his growing popularity in the future, and Surendra and his peers frequently spoke of the process of building a good reputation as a field of activity analogous to the field of competing for government employment. Surendra said: "There are two roads I could follow: either I go into government service or I enter student union politics at CCSU. To keep the politics route open I need to develop a political reputation (*nām*) among students."

In each student hostel, there tended to be two or three young men like Surendra, usually Jats but also sometimes Gujars or Yadavs, who had become the "go to figures" for their fellow hostellers and who aspired one day to become CCSU student union leaders—thus probably thirty young men across MC and CCSU as a whole. These men were often the "easiest" to interview in that they were typically bursting with ideas and keen to involve me in their schemes. Like Surendra, aspiring middle-caste leaders had not typically developed close links with a political party but concentrated instead on organizing and participating in student protests on campus.

Aspiring student leaders typically worked closely with social reformers such as Balraj. Leaders' charisma and political acuity enabled them to raise support among other hostellers at short notice. Moreover, leaders such as Surendra often had a keener sense than did middle-caste social reformers of performative dimensions of student protest, for example what to wear during a demonstration or how to comport oneself when confronting university officials.

A third important set of political animators on campus was comprised of Dalit and Muslim politically minded young men, many of whom also referred to themselves as "social reformers," or, more rarely, "leaders." The backgrounds and activities of Dalit and Muslim leaders were diverse, but the example of a Muslim young man named Iqbal is instructive. Over tea in a small textile shop in a Muslim neighborhood of Meerut, Iqbal enthusiastically documented his background and activities. He was the son of an uneducated Muslim tailor in Meerut and had eight siblings. In the face of competing demands on their meager resources, Iqbal's parents tried to persuade him to abandon school. But he was determined to continue his studies, and Iqbal worked for long hours in a shop to finance his education. He then began selling computer software products on a freelance basis. In his early twenties, Iqbal was studying for a MA in CCSU in 2004 and described himself as underemployed.

Until his late teens, Iqbal imagined joining the UP PCS. He changed his mind when he saw a visiting politician abusing the District Magistrate on a visit to Meerut. Iqbal: "The corrupt politician was able to scold and humiliate the highly educated civil servant. I realized that to acquire power in India it is necessary to become a politician." Iqbal had not joined a political party. Instead, he said that building good networks was the cornerstone of his political activity, and he hoped to run for a position in the District government within five years. He spent time and money developing good relationships within the police, local intelligence unit, newspaper offices and university administration. I often wondered at the extraordinary energy Iqbal invested in the construction of social links. I remember this in a series of images: Iqbal screaming to a halt on his motorcycle to shake hands with a policeman, frantically checking his watch to ensure that his speech would coincide with an official's arrival and carefully signing multiple copies of a petition to the District Magistrate. When I commented on his restless energy, Iqbal grinned and told me that his life is "*purā rājnitī*" he then repeated the phrase in English "total politics."

Iqbal denied that his politics was oriented to helping Muslims in particular. But he frequently complained that statues of Muslim freedom fighters should be erected in colleges. He also criticized the BJP for anti-Islamic policies and expressed his concern over Muslims' lack of confidence in the face of institutionalized communalism.

In addition to creating good networks, Iqbal spent much time engaged in social service in Meerut. In 2004–5 he arranged for schoolchildren injured by a bus driver to receive compensation, secured the release of students arrested by the police, improved facilities in college classrooms and questioned senior officials over illegal admissions to higher education. Iqbal said that a combination of network building and efforts to assist with students' problems would guarantee his political success. He claimed that he had a political identity that allowed him to "get work done" quickly and effectively in a wide variety of offices around the city. A muscular masculinity also ran through Iqbal's politicking and that of some other Dalit and Muslim politicos whom I met. Iqbal asked me once whether I had successfully obtained data from a college office. I said that I was having some difficulties. He spat on the ground and said: "Ack! Do you want me to come to this office? You need to pick up the clerk and give him a good slap."

This sketch of Iqbal's actions and preoccupations casts light upon key features of the strategies of Dalit and Muslim political entrepreneurs more generally. There were between six and ten Muslim politicos and ten and fifteen Dalit "reformers" or "leaders" in MC and CCSU combined, and I interviewed fourteen of these men. Like Iqbal, the Dalit and Muslim reformers or leaders were usually from poor backgrounds. Their power rested in large part on their vigor, determination and capacity to enroll other sympathetic officials in their schemes. Dalit and Muslim reformers, even more than their middle-caste counterparts, insisted that their local political activity was "serious"—committed, absorbing, "total," to recall Iqbal's words—rather than "timepass." Dalit and Muslim reformers and leaders were points of contact for Muslims and low castes living in CCSU and MC hostels and for Muslim and Dalit kin. Even middle and higher castes often saw men like Iqbal as alternative political mentors and lobbyists, for example when members of their own caste had refused help.

A fourth set of political animators that emerged from my research was a group of seven male students, four Brahmins and three Yadavs, who provided much of the intellectual ballast and some financial support for student protest on campus and who came from upper middle class, urban backgrounds. These men shared middle-caste social reformers' interest in linking local student issues to broader national and global dynamics. Three of these seven men had rooms in CCSU or MC hostels and the other four lived with their parents.

The example of a Brahmin young man, Om Prakash, offers insights into the activities of this set of young men. Om Prakash was in his late twenties in 2004 and always smartly dressed. I first heard from him via cell phone. He said that he had heard about my research and wanted to talk. Om Prakash often convened small discussion groups involving me and his close friends in his urban middle-class home near CCSU. He labeled himself as "underemployed" and hoped that through diligent study and learning English he would one day work for an international news organization.

Like other Brahmin and OBC young men in this set, one of Om Prakash's main roles was to offer middle-caste social reformers guidance and friendship. Om Prakash read newspapers and watched local television reports avidly. He was often quick to phone a middle-caste reformer friend to comment on an issue or express indignation at a recent turn of events. Om Prakash also offered middle-caste social reformers logistical support, for example by providing transport on motorcycles around the city or arranging hospitality in his urban home. In addition, he was an excellent source of ideas for how to frame social protest. Quick to learn of a breaking story and good at coming up with sound bites, Om Prakash was often able to spur other students to action.

Thus four sets of politically motivated young men studying in CCSU and MC in 2004 and 2005 were significant in generating collective student protest: middle-caste social reformers (such as Balraj), middle castes who aspired to become leaders or who held positions on the CCSU student union (Surendra), Dalit and Muslim politicos (Iqbal) and Brahmin and OBC young men relatively removed from student politics but important as sources of information and advice (Om Prakash).

It is important to note that individual young men sometimes moved from one "set" to another. For example, urban intellectuals, such as Om Prakash, occasionally became aspiring student leaders, like Surendra. In other cases, aspiring student leaders abandoned their attempts to acquire student union positions and adopted the role of social reformers. The boundaries between different sets of actors were also rather fuzzy. For example, in the early 2000s, there were several Dalit and Muslim social reformers who harbored ambitions to acquire positions on the student union, and some had been successful at capturing such posts.

There were certain characteristics that all political animators shared. They had weak links to political parties, did not participate actively in youth party organizations and usually displayed a detached attitude towards State and national elections and the machinations of local politicians. The gendered character of male agitators' practices was clearly evident. Young men belonging to all four sets of political animators constructed images of themselves as guardians of students' rights (*haq*) and protectors of young women's security. These gendered discourses, and the sometimes blunt masculine manner in which politicos went about their business, discouraged young women from becoming involved in collective student demonstrations and further marginalized the few female students who did sometimes work to encourage student protest.

At the same time, however, the four sets of political animators comported themselves differently with respect to the idea of student "politics" (*rājnīti*) and "leadership" (*netāgirī*). Middle caste social reformers and OBC and Brahmin young men, like the few female agitators I met on campus, regarded *rājnīti* and *netāgirī* as immoral and dirty. In contrast, aspiring middle-caste leaders and some Dalit and Muslim politicos sometimes embraced their roles as adroit political entrepreneurs and future politicians.

Collective Student Action?

It is important not to exaggerate the "collective" nature of student pro-tests, in part because political animators often had different ideas about which issues should form a basis for concerted student action. The four young women who occasionally worked as agitators tended to focus on issues that directly affected female students. They argued that there were too few politi-cal animators representing the interests of young women and that they should therefore prioritize issues such as sexual harassment of young women on campus and women's lack of access to university facilities. There were also disagreements within and among the four sets of young male politicos. In some instances, aspiring politicians took up a concern that was of little inter-est to other sets of political animators. This was especially the case where the issue had a strong populist dimension, for example where students' capac-ity to pass examinations was threatened. In other instances, OBC and Brah-min students, Dalit and Muslim reformers and middle-caste social reformers orchestrated protests that did not appeal to middle-caste *netās*. This occurred especially where the topic had some broad social justice dimension and was framed in intellectual terms, for example when the commercialization of higher education was at issue.

Reflecting divides among political animators, not all students participated in protests on campus. Most obviously, young women, especially Dalits and Muslims, tended to avoid demonstrations—whatever the topic—that entailed physical confrontation or long periods protesting in public. Moreover, collec-tive student protest mainly involved hostel students; those living off campus rarely joined agitations. In addition, senior students were sometimes pitted against those newer to the university or MC. In 2004 the Chief Minister of UP issued a directive that would have prevented students over the age of 26 contesting student union elections, a measure that senior students successfully opposed but which some junior students regarded as just in the light of older students' dominance of campus politics. There were other divisions: protests over fees tended not to interest the richer students enrolled in MC and CCSU; students who were academically able were not very interested in the rights of failing students; and social science, law and humanities students tended to be more active in political demonstrations than those studying for science and engineering degrees, probably because arts and humanities students were the most adversely affected by unemployment.

It was also clear that the issues that provoked interest in MC were not necessarily ones that caught students' imaginations in CCSU, and vice versa. In MC protests focused most often on the poor standard of educational facilities and the college administration's embezzlement of funds ear-marked for educational development. In CCSU, where the educational facilities were better but courses were more expensive, demonstrations more commonly concerned the rising costs of education. In addition, since CCSU students tended to be older than MC students and were pursuing at least their second degrees, students in CCSU hostels were commonly more sensitive than were MC students to issues that affected their ability to pass their degrees quickly and obtain work.

For all these fissures, however, political animators often worked in tandem and students did sometimes come together across caste, class, religious and to a lesser extent gender boundaries to protest against university bureaucrats and state officials. Political animators had pragmatic reasons for collaborating. Middle caste reformers and leaders possessed a political know-how and influence within some local bureaucracies that other animators lacked. Muslim and Dalit reformers were useful to other animators because of their power to mobilize low-caste and Muslim students. Upper middle-class students from urban backgrounds were relatively adept at pitching issues to the student community.

Of course, the manner in which different animators worked together should not be romanticized, but I was often impressed at how the four sets of men acted in concert; like different parts in a machine, one set frequently moved into action when another set had performed their function. This became especially evident at the beginning of student agitations and at the *addās*—tea stalls and street corners, for example—that featured prominently in the discussion of young male cultures in Chapter Three. *Addās* were located between major political arenas in Meerut; the tea stalls frequented by MC students, for example, were close to the District Magistrate's residence, the Senior Superintendent of Police's office, the district court and Meerut

College. After some event—for example a disciplinary incident or police harassment of students—a diverse collection of political animators standing on street corners gathered news. It was often the upper middle-class politicos from urban backgrounds who assumed responsibility for converting the incident into a "triggering event" that would galvanize student support (Tambiah 1997: 234). Long before police officials or journalists arrived on the scene, these men would be spinning the story of crisis to suit their political ends. As conversations turned from what had happened to what should be done, young men would often disappear into the bowels of a tea stall to plan their strategy. At this point, middle-caste social reformers and *netās* often took the lead, drawing on their relative political acuity to craft specific tactics. At the same time, Dalit and Muslim reformers might contact members of their communities at other *addās* and in hostels around the city.

When political animators managed to rally students behind a cause, the cross-caste, cross-class nature of student mobilization became more evident. In roughly half of the cases of student unrest that I observed, students began their political campaigns by visiting a university administrator or government official to plead their cause. Students usually went directly to the highest authorities in the district rather than lobbying lower- or middle-ranking officials for help. Agitating students were often to be found in the offices of the VC of CCSU, Principal of MC, DM, SSP or SDM. Students sometimes explicitly discussed the importance of ensuring that the delegation be comprised of students from different caste, class and religious backgrounds so that the group of students appeared representative of a wider student body. At the same time, they often wanted several aspiring student leaders in the group, since these men had the all-important "political eye" and possessed the nerve to manage negotiations. Delegations typically numbered eight to twelve students, but sometimes included up to forty. Young women were rarely present—they usually regarded it inappropriate to be part of a large male gang.

When students were unable to achieve their task through visiting university or government officials, they typically engaged in public demonstrations of strength—and here young women were more likely to be involved. Students frequently laid siege to the principal or VC's office to prevent people from either leaving or entering the building (*gherāo*) or barred professors' access to sections of the university to stop classes taking place (*band*). Other common protests took the form of roadblocks (*rāstā roko*), processions (*jalūs*), hunger strikes (*bhūk hartāl*) or sit ins (*dharna*). Sometimes protesters simply shut down CCSU or MC altogether. These varied protests usually involved men and women and included upper castes, middle castes, Dalits and Muslims. Indeed, political animators sometimes went to considerable effort to broadcast the cosmopolitan nature of the agitation, for example by arranging for local journalists to take photographs of an obviously diverse collection of agitators.

Why did students from widely different backgrounds sometimes come together to protest against the state and university bureaucracy in Meerut? The prevalence of collective student mobilization partly reflected the ability of political animators to uncover "issues" (they occasionally used the English word) that could provide a nucleus for protest. Political animators were quick to identify events in the lives of students that could serve as a type of window on underlying student anxieties regarding time, education and jobs.

The student agitations orchestrated by political animators commonly addressed one of four interlinked topics. First, students protested about the costs of higher education. In 2004 students were especially concerned with the expense associated with obtaining admission to higher education institutions affiliated with CCSU. Admission to private institutions with CCSU affiliation was organized such that 50 percent of places in courses were reserved for students with high merit in admissions examinations and the remaining 50 percent, termed the "management quota," could be disbursed at the whim of a college's private managers. In practice, even those high on the merit list had to pay large bribes to enter professional courses in private institutions, and the amounts that students had to pay for management quota seats had become astronomical: Rs. 200,000 for a position in a college offering BEd or engineering degrees, Rs. 1,000,000 for a place at a dental institute and Rs. 2,500,000 for a seat at a private medical college, according to several student estimates. Students argued that private educational entrepreneurs and their cronies were ruining students' futures and preventing ordinary students from obtaining a good education.

Irregularities surrounding university examinations was a second major issue animating student agitations. A particular focus of anger among middle-caste social reformers was a proposal made by CCSU in 2001 to end the practice of awarding grace marks to students who failed their exams. During the 1990s, CCSU and affiliated government-aided colleges frequently allowed students who obtained a grade within 10 percent of a pass to be given be given extra "top-up" marks to prevent them having to retake a year of study. In 2001, the CCSU decided to abolish this provision, arguing that the practice cheapened the value of a CCSU degree, and students reacted furiously.

In 2004 and 2005, concerns over students' movement through university fed into a campaign to defend young people's right to cheat in examinations. Late in 2004 it emerged that nearly a hundred students had copied en masse while retaking an examination they had earlier failed. When political animators heard that the students concerned had been apprehended by university officials, they set to work chivying other students into action on behalf of those who had cheated. Animators argued that it was unfair to single out those who had copied because cheating was institutionalized within CCSU and affiliated colleges; questions are regularly leaked and there are books for sale in the bazaar that print model answers to questions that later appear in examinations. Some students said that the university system is in itself a form of "cheating" since graduates lack access to jobs and Meerut degrees are increasingly meaningless. The irony here—that defending students' right to cheat might have been contributing to the direful reputation of Meerut degrees among Delhi employers—was keenly felt by some of my informants.

Third, student political animators frequently launched protests regarding university corruption. Akhil Gupta (1995) has argued on the basis of field research in the 1980s in Bulandshahr district, North-Western UP, that ordinary people in north India tend to regard misappropriation of government funds by state officials as unacceptable, immoral and "corrupt" (*bhrushtāchārī*). Gupta (1995) shows that local people's critiques of "corruption" are a central means through which north Indians articulate political goals, express their sense of marginalization and define what they regard as acceptable state practice. My work in Meerut supports Gupta's conclusions in many respects: students were eagerly involved in perpetuating a public culture of anti-corruption protest, where corruption was principally defined, as it is in much of the social science literature, as the abuse of public office for private gain.

The issue of corruption became especially prominent in 2002 when the VC of CCSU was removed from office after being found guilty of embezzling university funds. It emerged powerfully again in 2004, when the new VC of CCSU was accused of similar chicanery, and he was also subsequently removed from his post. While students tended to regard all instances of university officials earning private money from their positions as corrupt and wrong (*gullit*), they reserved their greatest ire for instances in which administrators' corruption interfered with students' progress through higher education or compromised their ability to acquire jobs. For example, concerns over corruption erupted violently in August 2006 in CCSU when it emerged that the University Registrar had economized on the cost of administering degree examinations by subcontracting the grading of postgraduate dissertations to students at other educational institutions. This practice was occurring at other UP universities, where undergraduate students were charged with assessing the work of postgraduates. But at CCSU the scandal took an especially extreme form; it was widely alleged that school students as young as eight years old had been grading Master's dissertations, a practice which, when uncovered, brought students into the streets to burn their degrees.

At a more everyday level, students were incensed about the litany of ways in which university administrators, criminals and low-level clerks colluded to extract resources from ordinary students. They complained about the frequency with which the university administration appropriates money officially ear-marked to improve educational facilities. Students also referred to the need to bribe a network of low-level university officials in order to obtain the results of an exam, a degree certificate or other official documents.

Fourth, political animators launched protests on the issue of the harassment of students. For example, they occasionally accused local shopkeepers of verbally or physically abusing those enrolled at CCSU or MC. In 2004 there was an intense street battle between students and traders in one of Meerut's main bazaars that occurred after a shopkeeper insulted a senior Meerut student. Students also complained about exploitative professors and university administrators. Students engaged in four days of protest when it emerged that a professor had sexually assaulted a student in a college close to Meerut in 2004, an incident which they felt exemplified the much wider physical and psychological abuse of students within higher education. Students' complaints about harassment also focused on the police. The first recorded police raid of a MC hostel in search of firearms or criminals occurred in 1929 (Mittal 1978). By the 2000s, such raids had become a regular feature of university life, and hostel students, in particular, deeply resented this invasion of their privacy. They were unhappy about the failure of the police to inform the university administration about raids, and they were equally unsettled by what they perceived to be the heavy-handed treatment doled out by the police. There were sixteen reports of police injuring students between 2000 and 2005 in *Dainik Jagran* and *Amar Ujala* newspapers. Simmering resentment about police cruelty boiled over in December 2002 when the police killed a student allegedly involved in criminal activity, and again in July 2004, when students felt that the police were dragging their heels in investigating the murder of a MC student on campus.

In sum, students' shared experience of educational decay and unemployment provided political animators with a fund of populist issues—rising costs, corruption, blocked progress and harassment—that could spur students from different backgrounds into action. The four issues that typically triggered student protests were closely connected. For example, the issue of the cost of education was linked to students' fears over their progress through university and rising corruption. Similarly, students were often angry about harassment on the part of administrators or teachers because they felt that these officials and professors were also corrupt. The skill of many political animators resided in part in their capacity to connect a specific event to all four issues at once. Thus, for example, student agitators could spin the expulsion of a student on spurious grounds to show how the incident exemplified administrators' harassment ("they picked on the student"), the rising cost of education ("look at how much the student spent on his studies!"), corruption ("was the principal being paid to expel the student by some third party?") and students' blocked progress through universities ("the authorities are preventing us from getting our degrees!"). Political animators were equally adept at linking each of these issues to the question of youth or student "rights" (*haq*)—a theme that appealed to young people regardless of class, caste, religion or gender.

Ideas of time and temporality repeatedly surfaced during agitations on the issues of rising costs, blocked progress, corruption and harassment. For example, it was stories of students having to wait for degree certificates that served as the most charged indicators of students suffering in the context of corruption. Similarly, in MC students frequently voiced their anger about educational decay by describing instances in which their teacher had failed to appear for lessons; the experience of waiting for a professor indexed their wider sense of purposeless waiting.

If the prevalence of collective agitations reflected shared student anxieties about time and mobility, it was also based upon certain assumptions commonly held among students about how protests should occur. Across class, caste, religious and gender boundaries, students in CCSU and MC tended to agree on two points regarding student mobilization. First, they frequently maintained that student mobilization should involve a measure of fun (*mazā*), even if the goals were "serious." An irreverence and sense of mischief often characterized the agitations in which students engaged. This came across when I was observing students involved in sit-ins (*dharnā*). As Cohn (1961: 615–16) observed, sitting and fasting at the door of an adversary to force the settlement of a dispute is a long-standing political tactic in India. If the person died while fasting, the curse of the death fell on the person against whom the *dharnā* was directed. In Meerut, students simultaneously drew on this idea of *dharnā*, while also ironically subverting it. For example, in CCSU in March 2005, students organized a "relay hunger strike" outside the main administrative block of the university, which involved students taking turns to fast for an hour each. At the end of each hour, supporters rushed to the hastily constructed stage on which the hunger striker was sitting and crammed food into the mouth of the protester, who feigned hunger and faintness for comic effect.

The importance of humor and irony in students' protests emerged in some unlikely circumstances. For example, on one occasion I saw a snack vendor congratulating students on a roadblock that they had built. The barrier had resulted in the vendor receiving extra business, and much laughter was extracted from the man's pledge to help them in future demonstrations. In another instance, students went to complain to the owner of a plant nursery, who had laid out potted plants on an area of ground that belonged to

Meerut College. The confrontation seemed destined to turn ugly, until a photographer from a local newspaper arrived. Some students and workers at the nursery proceeded to stage a mock fight, which the photographer happily snapped.

Such playfulness was closely related to the humor often found on Meerut street corners and described in Chapter Three. Young men were used to standing around at tea stalls and on street corners, laughing, teasing each other and engaging in horse play. The relationship between everyday joking and student protests was two-way: street corner irreverence informed political protests and humorous stories from political campaigns were often recounted and embellished at popular hangouts around Meerut.

A second point upon which students from different caste, class, religious and gender backgrounds tended to agree was that mobilization should, if at all possible, proceed in a civilized manner and with due regard to the law. This emphasis on civility is somewhat counterintuitive. In an influential recent book, Partha Chatterjee claims that those occupying the realm of "political society" in India tend to ignore protocols about ethics and civility: "political society will bring into the hallways and corridors of power some of the squalor, ugliness and violence of popular life" (2004: 74). By contrast, an ethic of respect for the university and for state power ran through student collective action in Meerut.

Students' civility and concern for the law emerged during their efforts to bargain with state officials. Political animators commonly stressed that it was important to dress well in front of officials and maintain an attitude of humility. They also claimed that the top officials in the district are people with a sense of fairness, who could be won round by making convincing arguments in a civilized manner. Students often told the DM or SSP about the misdemeanors of low-ranking state officials, policemen or university teachers in the expectation that the high-ranking officer would intervene on students' behalf. This appeal above the heads of lower officers is part of a wider genre of north Indian politics (see Corbridge 2005 et al.) and had a strong performative element: students pretended that they believed in the integrity of the DM or SSP in an effort to ingratiate themselves with the higher official even where they knew that the officer was in cahoots with subordinates. Yet students' courteous demeanor also reflected their belief in the authority and essential fairness of the state.

Students' concern with civility and the law emerged still more strongly in the letters they wrote to officials. Letter writing had become an important component of the political strategies of students in Meerut. Dalit and Muslim reformers and leaders were especially adept at composing letters to government officials, which were almost always written in a polite, high-flown Hindi. The letters frequently alluded to the condition of "students" or "youth" and typically contained multiple references to legal concepts: both specific laws and more general ideas such as "rights" and "duties." Students said that they had learned how to write these letters in school—composing a letter of complaint to a government official is a popular assignment for schoolchildren learning Hindi and English in UP. The following letter composed by a friend of Iqbals' for Meerut's District Magistrate is broadly typical of those I read:

10th February 2005

Sir,

Time and time again, it has been evident that there are multiple irregularities (*aniyamitatāyen*) in the nature of admission to Bachelors of Education degrees at CCSU. Time and time again, various enquiries have been made. But there has been no public report. As a result, up until now, nothing has been fully satisfactory (*santoshjanak*). The affiliated colleges are receiving recognition from the university, at the same time, the university is not giving admission to those who have acquired entry through the proper mechanism; also, fees are being collected from students who have been admitted while there is nothing in the way of facilities within the institutions. The university administration has granted admission into its affiliated private colleges in the wrong way. . . . This must be evidence of collusion (*milībhagat*) between the university and the owners of the private institutions. Although fee collection is the responsibility of the university, the owners of the private institutions in league with the university are collecting greater fees. Finally, it is the demand of all students that whether the private management, university or workers are at fault, strict action be taken against them. Otherwise, the students will be forced to launch a movement.

Yours,
United Students
Chaudhry Charan Singh University
Meerut

The commitment of students across caste, class, religious and gender lines to the principles outlined in such letters served to hold together diverse constituencies of student protesters.

Students' concern with due protocols emerged in other contexts. For example, in March 2005, while I was interviewing a student involved in a small demonstration outside the main administrative building in MC, a senior figure at the college emerged on the steps of the building with a piece of paper. The official told the young men involved in the demonstration that he had an important notice, and the students lined up in front of the building alongside staff and professors. The official proceeded to announce the death of a former member of the university who had a distinguished record of military service. The students listened attentively to the notice, participated in a minute's pin-drop silence and then quickly decided to abandon the demonstration in the context of the news.

There were obviously limits to students' ethic of respect and adherence to the law. For example, I did not observe students issuing formal apologies to university and government officials after the cessation of a protest, as did DiBona (1969) in work on student politics in Lucknow in the 1960s. Indeed, student deference in Meerut was sometimes combined with defiance. Students occasionally tried to suggest through their tone, posture and gestures that the failure of an official to cooperate might have dire and violent consequences. Moreover, students sometimes engaged in collective forms of violence. For example, early in 2005 a group of students from MC beat up a local shopkeeper who had allegedly humiliated a student. More dramatically, in October 2004 a group of students tried to punch senior CCSU officials. I was not present at this confrontation, but a headline in the next morning's paper stated that the students had "converted the VC's office into a makeshift boxing arena" (*Amar Ujala*, 4 October 2004).

Contradictory attitudes to violence and legality also surfaced in my discussions with different sets of political animators. For middle-caste social reformers and upper middle-class urban intellectuals, violence and illegality were to be avoided and critiqued. By contrast, aspiring middle-caste student leaders and Dalit and Muslim politicos tended to regard violence and illegality as political tools.

Notwithstanding this ambivalence, there was a gap between the manner of students' everyday engagement with the state in Meerut in 2004 and 2005 and Chatterjee's (2004: 74) argument that political society is generally violent and uncouth. Student mobilization in Meerut was often characterized instead by a type of calculated restraint (cf. Bailey 1996).

Meerut students' emphasis on civility and good order partly reflects their education. Respect for state authority is a theme that recurs in many school textbooks in North-Western UP. Students' concern with civilized mobilization also relates to their sense of themselves as "educated people" (*parhe likhe log*). Political animators and students who participated in protests were often keen to distinguish their relatively "educated" politicking from the indiscriminate violence (*goondāgardī*) purportedly characteristic of uneducated urban young men. In addition, students had pragmatic reasons for remaining on the right side of the law. Even relatively wealthy Jat students with good links in the local police force were worried about harassment and arrest at the hands of law enforcement agencies, such as the Provincial Armed Constabulary and Border Security Force; violence and illegality were risky.

The collective character of much student mobilization can therefore be explained with reference to two main factors. First, broad-based protest reflected the skill of political animators in identifying and publicizing issues of common concern. Second, collective student action was underpinned by the existence of shared assumptions about how political protests should be carried out—with a certain measure of irreverence and in a reasonably civilized, legal and restrained manner.

Were Student Protests Effective?

Collective student mobilization was at least partially successful. For example, sustained protests regarding the costs of higher education in 2002 led the CCSU administration to backtrack on a proposal to raise tuition fees. Similarly, student demonstrations regarding the corruption of high-level university officials were important in the UP Government's eventual decision to remove two VCs from their positions at CCSU in 2002 and 2006. In addition, protests regarding harassment regularly led to small victories for MC and CCSU students: professors had to apologize to students they had beaten, for example, or students successfully compelled shopkeepers to back down in a dispute. In addition, even short-lived student protests often left certain traces on the UP educational landscape that could provide part of the inspiration for future struggles, such as graffiti complaining about university bureaucrats' negligence, photographs of agitation that were subsequently circulated by newspapers and local television stations or stories of student heroism that became enshrined in the memories of particular *addā* communities or hostel populations. Moreover, middle-caste social reformers were occasionally able to stage-manage wider demonstrations regarding the privatization (*nijīkaran*) of education, social inequality and the politics of environmental change within and outside Meerut district and India. For example, broad protests regarding privatization occurred in February 2005, when the Supreme Court in India issued an order requiring six private educational institutions affiliated with CCSU that had not received recognition from the central-level University Grants Commission (UGC) to suspend operations. These six institutions had received recognition from the State government in the newly established state of Chattisgarh. The Chattisgarh Universities Act of 2002 allowed educational entrepreneurs to establish universities without obtaining formal recognition from the UGC. Businesspeople were only required to apply to the Chattisgarh State Government, which did not conduct inspections prior to approval. Entrepreneurs had exploited this opportunity by opening a range of so-called "universities" with woefully poor facilities, and often without any educational facilities. In a notorious incident, seven universities were opened in a single hotel in Chattisgarh. Since universities could establish branch campuses in other states, the Chattisgarh University Act had had a significant effect on higher education in many parts of India, including North-Western UP. In February 2005, a large number of MC and CCSU students joined with those studying at the six threatened institutions to demand that the educational entrepreneurs who had opened the "fake (*naqlī*) universities" return the money that students had paid in fees, which they did, in part.

In spite of a few successes, however, middle-caste social reformers and their associates were unable to generate sustained, widespread collective student protests in Meerut on the type of national and international questions—concerning poverty, illiteracy, capitalist change and political freedom, for example—that animated student protest in the colonial period in Meerut. Students in the 2000s were largely concerned with a narrower student or youth agenda and, within this, on issues that directly affected their studies in Meerut and future employment prospects. Political animators and students participating in demonstrations often claimed that this was no simple omission on their part. Some said that it is better to concentrate on protesting about local matters, where there was a possibility of success, rather than spending long periods trying to connect their grievances to those of students in distant locations. Other students explained their lack of attention to national and international issues by drawing attention to a regional split in north Indian student politics, between "Delhi student politics," in which students more routinely displayed the type of sociological imagination that Balraj desired, and "provincial student politics" wherein students' immediate concerns were paramount. Krishnan (2007) offers a picture of politics in Jawaharlal Nehru University in Delhi in 2005 and 2006 that lends some credence to this notion. Still other students said that the lack of attention to the connections between "Meerut issues" and wider social and political change reflects weaknesses in the UP education system. Middle-caste social reformers and Brahmin and OBC urbanites complained vociferously about the low value attached to critical inquiry and the social sciences within Meerut higher education, and they discussed the failure of professors to politicize the student body with respect to questions of curricula change. It is also possible that the focus of collective protests on student and youth issues reflects the importance to many animators of trying to build links across caste, class and religious lines: more narrowly ideological mobilization might have divided the student population.

Students showed little interest in joining a small band of middle-caste reformers in organizing trips to rural areas to discuss social and economic issues with the poor. There was also a strong sense in which student protests were detached from the political campaigns of other sections of college society. Whereas students often involved the lowest-ranked government workers in universities and colleges in their collective protests in the first half of the twentieth century, such broad collective action was rare in the 2000s. Students were usually at loggerheads with cleaners, clerks and other poorly paid staff. Similarly, the political activity of students and that of bureaucrats and professors typically moved along different tracks. Government officials, university bureaucrats and professors usually perceived student demonstrations to be bothersome and counterproductive. The short-term political aims of principals and professors were often diametrically opposed to collective student demands. Professors tried to protect their income from private tutorials and avoid being compelled to spend long periods on campus, and principals wanted to defend their access to bribe money and kickbacks. One of the central goals of a union of college principals in North-Western UP in 2001 was to discourage students from organizing politically to express demands. In 2005 the police and college principals in Meerut called the parents of leading political animators to campus to complain about the actions of their sons. They also "rusticated" one aspiring student leader, a richly suggestive word connoting expulsion into rural isolation as well as being barred from the university.

It is also telling that Balraj and his allies were unable to institutionalize their protests. This partly reflects the unwillingness of political parties to invest resources in gathering up the strands of collective youth frustration into a durable organizational form. During the 1990s and early 2000s, political parties tried to mobilize Meerut students, and the BJP was particularly keen to support young people through the ABVP. In 2005 the Lok Dal leader and son of Chaudhry Charan Singh, Ajit Singh, made two high-profile visits to Meerut during which he unsuccessfully attempted to obtain student support for the creation of a separate state of "Western UP" (Paschim Pradesh). Yet political parties remained largely unwilling to invest resources in student politics in Meerut in the 1990s and early 2000s. Students occasionally tried to establish their own collective organizations, such as the NBS, but there were little signs of any interest in these organizations. Similarly, a "united students' group" at CCSU was set up in the early 2000s, but survived mainly as a letterhead in 2005. Collective student protest in Meerut remained piecemeal, sporadic and largely organized around individual incidents occurring on or close to campus.

Conclusions

A collective feeling of timepass and associated resentment over educational decay, corruption and privatization had resulted in the emergence of different sets of young male political animators among unemployed students in Meerut. These varied agent provocateurs coordinated with each other to mobilize students, who were able to make small but significant gains through their petitioning and demonstrations. These protests cut across caste, class, religious and to a lesser degree gender divisions; Muslims, Dalits, Jats, Brahmins and others sometimes worked side-by-side to raise their voices against the university administration and the state. This collective action reflected students' somewhat similar structural position within society—as people preoccupied by the problems of boredom, joblessness and educational decline—and a type of political commonsense among students wherein it was imagined that protests should be both fun and civilized.

The types of demonstrations in which students engaged and the topics of their protests are broadly similar to those of students in Meerut and other parts of India in the 1960s and 1970s. Like male students in an earlier period, politically active young men in Meerut were preoccupied with issues that related to their progress through the university and access to employment. But the rapid privatization of education and the scale and extent of malpractice within CCSU and MC in the mid-2000s perhaps lent a distinctive intensity to Meerut student activism. It also encouraged alliances across social boundaries within the student community that might not have been forged had students' anxieties been less pronounced.

This chapter has provided a critical perspective on Partha Chatterjee's idea that politics in India commonly occur either within a bourgeois civil society—rational, legal and civilized—or within subaltern political society: mischievous, illegal and unruly. Students' collective action in Meeerut straddled this divide, combining elements of both the "civil" and "political," but characterized most notably by a type of old-fashioned civility and respect for the law.

This chapter has diverged, too, from the focus of Bourdieu on the class-interested, self-maximizing strategies of middle-class sections of society. In

Meerut, the sons of many rich Jat farmers responded to unemployment and associated feelings of being only in "timepass" by trying to imagine a less competitive way of relating to local political fields and other players in those fields. Rather than trying to outmaneuver poorer groups, for example by charging money to help students acquire degree certificates, some Jat social reformers assisted those subordinated within local arenas of competition. But before dispensing with Bourdieu as a guide to the everyday politicking of a Jat middle class, it is useful to remember that social reformers were few in number. And many of those who professed to be assisting other students, such as the aspiring student leaders discussed in this chapter, soon became more interested in capitalizing on their political know-how to make money. The next chapter examines these more self-interested political entrepreneurs.

5   Fixing Futures: Improvised Politics

A section of the Jat students with whom I worked combined collective protests against corruption with efforts to collude with government and university officials. This chapter considers how young men manage and make
sense of such apparent "hypocrisy" with primary reference to research that I
conducted with Jat student leaders in Meerut in 2004–5, men who also sometimes called themselves "fixers" (*kām karānewale*). I argue that Jat fixers were
keenly aware of how to work various fields of social relations to their personal advantage and rationalize their corrupt practices to others. More than
this, Jat fixers had developed a powerful discourse in which they imagined
their double-dealing as a form of creative improvisation (*jugāṛ*).

Many scholars have shown that unemployed youth profit from political
brokerage (e.g. De Vries 2002; Hoffman 2004; Li 2007). Within India, the rise
of a set of educated unemployed young men who make money as intermediaries between the government and ordinary people is a theme of Hansen's
(1996) account of urban life in Mumbai and Heuzé's (1992) work in small town
central India. My main contribution to this broader scholarship is to identify
the capacity of self-styled unemployed men in Meerut to critique malpractice
while also engaging in activities that reproduced malfeasance and to highlight
the salience of a vision of youthful improvisation.

The following section of this chapter uses the story of Girish to outline
the political strategies of Jat student leaders. I then consider the nature and
limits of Dalit resistance to Jat duplicity. The next three sections discuss how
Jats justified their involvement in "corruption," the importance of notions of

shrewd improvisation (*jugār*) for micro-political practice, and some of the links between the material discussed in this chapter and the wider themes of the book.

Girish

Twenty-seven in 2004, Girish came from a prosperous rural Jat family owning 5 hectares of agricultural land. Girish's father, Ompal, had been *pradhān* of the local village *panchāyat* and he had good social connections with politicians and government bureaucrats in Meerut. Ompal had sent Girish to an English-medium school on the outskirts of Meerut with a view to his son obtaining a government job. Girish studied History at Meerut College and in 2002 he enrolled in a Master's degree in Political Science at CCSU.

Girish tried and failed to obtain a job in the UP State Government several times between 2000 and 2002, and he viewed politics as an alternative career. Between 2002 and 2004, Girish attempted to establish a good name among his CCSU peers. He led voluble demonstrations against malpractice within the university, acted as lobbyist for other students in their negotiations with the local state and assisted his peers in their quest to obtain admission and degree certificates from university officials.

During my first interview with Girish, soon after his victory in the student union elections in Fall 2004, he spoke in rich tones of the importance of his "social service" (*samāj sevā*) among students:

> I am a type of social reformer. I feel that my vocation is to help other students. Whoever comes to my hostel room, I am ready to help them. If they have a complaint against the VC, I will be with the student in the VC's office. If we need to organize a protest about some wrongdoings in the [university] administration, I will be first to lead a delegation to the office of a failing official. I am ready to go to jail for students.

In referring to going to jail for students, Girish harked back to discourses of sacrifice among students during the nationalist movement (see Mittal 1978) and especially to the image of Bhagat Singh. He also drew on idioms of student hardship and stoicism that emerge out of recent Bollywood movies depicting campus activism.

In 2004 Girish decided to compete for a CCSU student union position. In the autumn of that year he was thoroughly absorbed in what he termed the "game" (*khel*) of developing a good name. He spent Rs. 200,000 producing color posters and hired twenty new jeeps to ferry his supporters around Meerut. Girish also paid for a local tea stall to distribute free tea and *samosās* to students two days before the elections. On top of this, Girish attended meetings of other Jats on campus at which he persuaded his fellow caste members to rally behind him.

When I met Girish in February 2005, four months after the student union elections, he stressed his continued commitment to helping other students. Girish took my presence in his student union office as an opportunity to rehearse his achievements in assisting his peers. Flanked by a friend from a local television channel who was taking notes on our conversation and another journalist who was photographing us, Girish gave me what seemed like a well-worked speech:

> Globalization has created a class of capitalists (*pūnjīpatī*). These capitalists just work for their own benefit. They do nothing for anyone else. The capitalists are controlling education as if it is a market commodity (*bikne kī vastu*). The capitalists just want education to be profitable (*amdān*). They just want marketing, marketism. In this environment, no one takes any notice of students' welfare (*chhātron kī hit*). We are part of the age of youth (*yuwā*). I am also a political science research scholar so I am aware of these things. During the age of youth, before people get married, people are active politically. If I don't think politically now, when will I think politically?

In spite of such rhetoric, Girish became steadily more interested in accumulating money from his post. By the summer of 2005, he had bought a car, allegedly out of money he had earned through acting as a broker between private educational entrepreneurs and the CCSU bureaucracy. When I visited Meerut in March 2007, Girish continued to refer to himself as "unemployed" but he was earning Rs. 8,000 a month—a reasonable salary compared with many of his peers—working as a political fixer for a Jat businessman who had established several private colleges close to Meerut.

The example of Girish signals much broader forms of political double-dealing among the nine Jats whom I interviewed who held powerful positions in the CCSU student union between 1991 and 2004. On the one hand, these men ignited the dry tinder of collective student angst in fierce campaigns against university professors and administrators. On the other hand, most of them were colluding with university officials to make private incomes.

Like Girish, many Jat young men who had failed to acquire salaried employment tried to obtain a position in the CCSU student union, which was the preeminent source of money, prestige and political influence within higher education in Meerut district. Of the thirty men who held one of the top two positions in the CCSU student union between 1991 and 2004, sixteen were Jat, six Gujar, four upper caste, three Yadav and one Dalit. No women, Dalits or Muslims obtained the post of Student Union President in CCSU between 1991 and 2004. The young men who acquired student union posts were usually in their late twenties or early thirties and unmarried. Many of them defined themselves as unemployed, and they typically came from relatively wealthy rural families.

Girish's story highlights four important aspects of the political strategies of Jat student leaders or fixers in CCSU. First, Jat student leaders spent considerable effort developing a good reputation among students in preparation for student union elections. They launched high profile demonstrations against university and government officials, and these agitations were reported in favorable terms by friends within local newspapers and television stations. Student leaders usually kept a dossier of articles and photographs recording their protest activity, which they sometimes displayed at the public debates that preceded student union elections. In their descriptions of their goals, the candidates in the 2004 student union election in CCSU frequently mentioned their commitment to improving facilities for students, preventing fee rises, tackling the commercialization of education and ending teachers' harassment of students—precisely the issues that featured in broader, collective student agitations.

Student leaders were especially keen to present an image of moral probity during their campaigns. In public settings before elections, Jat fixers emphasized their vegetarianism, aversion to alcohol and respect for young women. Student leaders were aware of young women's concern about male timepass and cultivated an image of chivalry. This was evident in the demeanor of young men as they walked around the campus in the weeks before elections; they always greeted young women by pressing their hands together, instructed supporters to remain a respectful distance from young women during meetings and self-consciously referred to female students as "sisters" to suggest that the young women were sexually inaccessible. After the elections, the leaders often abandoned this brotherly approach. The night after student union election results were announced in 2004, the successful students and their supporters gathered outside one of the female hostels in CCSU and joined together in sexually explicit chants—"letting off steam" as one of the students put it.

Student leaders relied on caste solidarities to win power. Arild Ruud (2008) has written of the importance of control over hostel rooms in the reproduction of student leaders' dominance in a university in Dhaka, Bangladesh. In a similar vein, Jats adopted a conscious strategy of manipulating the allocation of rooms in college hostels in order to expand their influence within their caste, and more rarely among other students. Many Jat fixers colluded with hostel wardens and higher university officials to register multiple hostel rooms in their name and then sub-let the rooms to caste peers entering the university.

In the immediate run-up to elections, Jat student leaders often enlisted the help of one or more so-called "campaign managers"—other Jats, often arts and humanities students who seemed to be especially adversely affected by unemployment and were therefore most likely to be among CCSU's long-time students. These men specialized in mobilizing members of their caste and seeking strategic alliances with upper-caste, OBC and Dalit candidates. The campaign managers arranged parties at which students celebrated a common identity, for example through eating meat, drinking whisky and swapping tales of rural life. Jat campaign managers were also sometimes responsible for inviting notable political figures to campus in order to cement feelings of Jat or middle-caste solidarity among students. In 2006 the BKU leader Mahendra Singh Tikait visited CCSU to pledge his support to a Jat student leader. In 2007 Ajit Singh came to campus for the same purpose. Politicians perceived campus visits as an opportunity to widen their support base and recruit charismatic students as local party spokespeople or rabble rousers.

Jat student leaders also typically spent between Rs. 150,000 and Rs. 300,000 prior to elections on producing posters, hiring vehicles and organizing feasts for students—Rs. 300,000 was roughly equivalent to the annual income of a 5-hectare farmer in rural Meerut district at the time. In 1996, the poster campaigns associated with the CCSU student union election were modest; by 2004, candidates produced over 50,000 posters each, which were then festooned across campus. This inflation in the cost of elections was also reflected in students' decisions around transport. In 1996, candidates for the CCSU student union elections typically borrowed jeeps from rural relatives for their campaigns. In 2004, students also hired many vehicles in order to spread their message in advance of elections and to transport students to campus to vote on election day. It was uncommon for students to offer feasts in the mid- and late 1990s, yet in 2004 most candidates had an arrangement with one of the tea stalls or small restaurants outside the campus to provide tea and snacks to CCSU students. This campaign tactic heightened the role played by *addās* as places of student timepass and political mobilization.

Jat student fixers sometimes received financial help and assistance with campaign strategies from the youth wings of political parties in urban areas. In particular, student leaders tried to obtain the endorsement of the ABVP, which would deliver organizational assistance and might also bring with it student votes. Jat students seeking ABVP backing typically viewed this quest in entirely pragmatic terms and rarely demonstrated an enthusiasm for Hindu nationalist ideas.

Students also sometimes received logistical advice from student leaders visiting Meerut from other parts of north India. During the run-up to the 2004 student union contest, a student fixer said that a visiting SFI representative from Delhi had given him the idea of organizing feasts at a local hotel and another leader had received material for a campaign brochure from a visiting NSUI student leader from Lucknow. Jat fixers also contacted ex-student leaders in Meerut for assistance in their campaigns. In 2004 and 2005, Jats who had held a CCSU student union position during the previous five years had usually made large sums of money. They typically remained in Meerut and often possessed contacts within political parties. By convincing recent student leaders to help them, candidates for CCSU student union posts could obtain what they termed, in English, an "approach" to an MLA or MP and sometimes financial and logistical support with their campaigns. A Jat student leader explained:

> One of your first steps in preparing for a CCSU election is to contact an ex-student leader and ask them for help. The ex-student leaders will ask you some questions about your commitment. They will check that you are serious and that you have to right character and fighting power. Once they approve of you, they will open their address book and your power will increase.

But advice from youth wings of political parties or ex-student leaders in Meerut was less important than the rural support upon which Jats could draw. Jat fixers obtain much of their political inspiration from having observed the strategies of senior kin in rural areas. Jat student leaders were adept at redeploying tactics derived from rural politics to acquire student union posts. The organization of feasts for supporters before elections and efforts to intimidate voters on polling day, for example, were both tactics used by dominant castes in rural North-Western UP. Village politics and CCSU politics were intertwined in other ways. Students often requested funds from rich families in their village, invited senior kin onto campus to give speeches on their behalf and sometimes enrolled members of their village in CCSU to help with their campaigns. A friend of Girish's who won a student union election in 2003 registered several siblings in the university to act as political representatives in different hostels. Small wonder, then, that celebrations following a Jat's victory were often as lively in a leader's home village as among his supporters on the CCSU campus.

A second key theme illustrated by the example of Girish is the importance of student politics as business. Reddy and Haragopal (1985: 1149) argue that the expansion of the state in south India in the post-independence period led to the emergence of a set of fixers (*pyravīkār*) who traded on their capacity to travel between government offices and knowledge of the niceties of the administrative system. Reddy and Haragopal's analysis suggests that lower middle classes are especially likely to engage in brokerage work, since they possess the time and money required to barter with government functionaries but not the funds and contacts to acquire secure well-paid work. Consistent with this argument, a section of the middle-caste student body—especially

Jats like Girish from relatively prosperous rural backgrounds—was energetically crafting careers as fixers. In the mid-1990s, it was possible to earn only small sums from a student union post: Rs. 20,000 according to some estimates. But the privatization of education in the late 1990s and early 2000s and rapid expansion of the size of the student body greatly increased possibilities for enterprising Jats to use their social, cultural and political capital to acquire money. There was a general consensus among older students, that, from the late 1990s onwards, student leaders had usually abandoned their pretence to be assisting "the ordinary student" after winning the student union elections and devoted time instead to building social networks that would provide rapid economic profits. As an aspiring Jat student politician explained, looking ahead to his own possible future:

> To win an election you need to be able to show that you are fighting for students' rights. After the election you enter a totally different phase. You establish a commercial relationship with the university administration. You agree not to protest about particular issues, and in return the university administration grants you certain favors.

Not all Jat *netās* sought rental incomes from their union posts; some continued to concentrate their efforts on critiquing corruption and educational decline. Many aspiring student leaders—men like Surendra (Chapter Four)—said, "I will be different from the others." Nevertheless, after winning the student union elections, Jat student leaders usually focused on making money from their positions. Even those who competed for student union positions but failed to secure victory could often profit financially from their accumulated influence. One keen observer of student politics in Meerut said that "all you need is 20 or 30 students behind you and you can capitalize on your position."

According to the most reliable estimates, student leaders occupying the top positions on the CCSU student union in 2004 and 2005 could earn between Rs. 800,000 and Rs. 1,000,000 in a year. Student leaders worked alongside university officials in extracting money from students seeking admission to CCSU and affiliated institutions. Jat fixers would often take small sums—sometimes called a "convenience fee"—from students in return for accomplishing an administrative task related to the process of admissions. A Jat student leader explained that:

> Rural students wanting to register for admission have little idea how things work. They have two choices. They can wait a few days to do all their paperwork or they can see a student leader, pay a few hundred rupees and accomplish the task right away [*ek dum*, literally "in one breath"]. Staying in the city for one night or two nights is more expensive than paying the small amount. Also, the student [seeking admission] will have to pay bribes anyway to gain admission, so why not pay a student leader a little to help?

As aspiring student leaders seeking to build a following, Jats often embellished tales of the delays and difficulties students' faced in acquiring resources from the university in order to spur young people to protest. Once safely ensconced in student union office they engaged in similar forms of exaggeration in order to make money as fixers (cf. Parry 1999).

Jat fixers' intermediary activities threatened the ability of officials to make money from the admission process, and we might therefore expect CCSU and MC bureaucrats to resist pressure from student leaders to obtain a slice of the pie. But administrators lived in fear of being targeted by students in protests against corruption. Administrators also benefited from student leaders' contacts in the student community.

Jat student leaders also worked as facilitators for private educational entrepreneurs in their negotiations with CCSU and the state administration. The period between January 2004 and April 2005 witnessed a remarkable growth in private educational institutions across North-Western UP. There was an especially marked growth in the number of colleges offering BEd degrees. In 2004, the Chief Minister of UP, Mulayam Singh Yadav, announced 46,000 new positions in primary schools for people with BEd degrees (*The Hindu*, 4 June 2004). Many parents saw in this initiative a possibility for their sons, and sometimes also daughters, to obtain a government job. Educational entrepreneurs were quick to pick up on this burgeoning demand, and over 20 colleges offering BEd degrees opened in Meerut in 2004 alone. In order to establish a private higher education institution in Meerut it is necessary to obtain a No Objection Certificate (NOC) from the Governor in Lucknow and affiliation from CCSU. Colleges offering BEd degrees also required accreditation from the National Council for Teacher Education (NCTE). Student leaders lobbied CCSU university officials to grant affiliation to private colleges and also contacted politician friends for assistance in obtaining NOCs and NCTE accreditation. By interviewing different players related to a particular event, I was able to cross-check several stories in which student leaders acted as go-betweens in negotiations, forged documents on behalf of businessman and prevented unrest among students in poorly staffed and ill-equipped private colleges.

There were a few journalists in Meerut, including some young men who had formerly worked as social reformers in Meerut higher education, who were active in exposing educational malpractice, and seven stories of corruption in the process of affiliation and acquisition of NOCs appeared in *Amar Ujala* and *Dainik Jagran* in 2004. But Jat fixers said that in Meerut in 2004–5 the majority of instances of misconduct in the affiliation and recognition process were undetected.

In return for assisting educational entrepreneurs, student leaders received seats in the private college concerned, which they could auction to students and their parents. Since parents and students were willing to pay Rs. 100,000 for places in many private colleges in 2004 and 2005 (and sometimes more for colleges offering BEd degrees), student leaders could make substantial sums by selling one or two college positions. Student leaders pointed out that this opportunity to make money from politics only emerged in the early 2000s, although before that time leaders sometimes earned smaller amounts by auctioning places at engineering colleges to students.

Student union leaders were sometimes able to influence appointments to teaching and administrative positions within CCSU or affiliated colleges, and they could earn money through taking a job themselves, allocating a post to a close relative or gathering bribes from others in return for recommending them for the position. Student politicians also had some say over the disbursement of contracts and tenders for the construction of government and private educational institutions. Fixers often received bribes from business interests to channel contracts their way and after leaving university some leaders became contractors themselves. Jat fixers also sometimes blackmailed contractors by threatening to launch student demonstrations about the poor quality of their buildings.

The commercialization of education in Meerut district and the continuing forms of state regulation that shaped private markets for qualifications had therefore offered enterprising young men possibilities to make large private incomes. Student leaders redistributed a portion of their earnings to those who had financed their student union campaigns. They also invested money in fighting future student elections and a few students paid university professors to provide extra-university tutorials and assistance writing Master's or PhD dissertations.

The capacity of a few Jat student leaders to insert themselves in advantageous positions within densely tangled networks of state officials, business-people and criminals parallels the similar enterprise of Jat rich farmers in mid-1990s Meerut. But the broad similarity between rich farmers' practices and those of Jat fixers should not obscure differences in their respective politicking. Rich farmers' tended to approach the business of building and capitalizing on social links with a heavy dose of caution. The metaphor of "cultivating fields" that I employed in Chapter Two works well because it connotes judiciously tending relationships. Rich Jat farmers emphasized a need to think carefully before investing in a link and expending political capital. By contrast, Jat fixers needed to make money quickly; they knew that they could typically only trade on their student union post for a year and needed to recoup the expense of acquiring a student union post. Two fixers told me that, when they returned to their rural homes, they sometimes encouraged senior kin to be more mercurial in their relations with local state officials. A Jat student leader said: "We tell our seniors: 'You have been sending those officials mangoes and butter for years, you should make some money from your link!' We give our fathers a course in brokerage."

After leaving their student union post, Jat leaders sometimes used their contacts to acquire temporary work as political fixers for educational entrepreneurs or State- or district-level politicians, in the manner of Girish. These positions were insecure and offered only moderate salaries, indeed many young men playing these fixing roles continued to consider themselves unemployed. In other instances, Jat student leaders had been able to obtain permanent employment as university professors or advocates, jobs they could combine with political activity. Of twenty Jats who had developed reputations for political leadership in CCSU between 1991 and 2005 and whose whereabouts I could trace, ten had become political fixers, three had secured teaching positions in government colleges, two had entered law, two were building contractors, two had returned to agriculture and one was in jail. Between 1991 and 2005, no Jat leaders entered district representative government, let alone State-level or central politics. Jats argued that the chances of becoming a state- or central-level politician were remote relative to earning opportunities within the informal economy. Jat fixers were uninterested in BKU politics and the relatively piecemeal opportunities for rent-seeking associated with *panchāyat* politics.

Many Jat student leaders referred to their new-found social mobility in the wake of student union electoral victory in class terms. These men said that that their elevation to a post in the union precipitated their entry into a "middle class," using the English term, evident in the possession of a car, cell phone, and relatively expensive clothes. Purchasing a car was an especially important rite of passage, and students often measured the political skill of a CCSU President by his mode of transport. In the late 1990s, CCSU Presidents bought Marutis, a small Indian car; by the early 2000s they were driving high-powered Indian-made jeeps such as Tata Sumos; and by 2005, student leaders were seeking to order cars constructed in the US and Germany. At the same time, these students were not simply imitating a "new middle class" (Fernandes 2004). They continued to set great store by their rural roots and frequently projected an image of rustic simplicity. Moreover, student leaders continued to cast aspersions on the urban rich: the "ice-cream eating students" living in the wealthiest parts of Meerut (see Chapter Three).

Even while making money from their student union posts, student leaders continued to engage in collective action targeted against university and government officials. Hansen (1996, 1998) and Corbridge et al. (2005) have persuasively argued that ordinary people in India operate with a split notion of the state, what Hansen (1998) calls a "dual consciousness" (see also Shah 2006). On the one hand, they view the state as a craven, partial and disorganized set of institutions. On the other hand, they believe in the state as a sublime institution and source of authority, rationality and power. Student leaders dramatized such a dual consciousness through their daily activity: vociferously critiquing state corruption with their right hand, while slyly doing deals with state officials with their left. The amount of time fixers spent in protesting against corruption relative to the time engaged in colluding with officials varied from leader to leader. Some fixers concentrated their energies on collective protest and only occasionally took a bribe or kickback. Others half-heartedly participated in demonstrations and devoted their energies to personal gain.

In addition to offering cash and middle-class status, a position on the CCSU student union provided Jat student leaders with a sense of spatial and temporal security and belonging. Fixers no longer talked about themselves being engaged in long-term timepass. They stressed instead their thorough absorption in the hustle of politics. One student leader commented: "From where would I get time for timepass? Timepass is for the other students."

For Jat young men, escaping feelings of limbo in Meerut meant engaging in a new way with the state. At a mundane level, these young men no longer had to wait for an audience with state officials. As we walked into the DM's office on one occasion, I touched a leader's arm: "Surely we should wait on this side of the curtain?" I asked (the side on which members of the public wait for an audience with the DM, often for several hours). "Tschk" the leader replied, "it's not like that." He grinned, flicked back the curtain screening the DM's inner sanctum and sat down in one of the chairs nearest the officer's desk. Tellingly, when I asked a student leader who had just won a position on the CCSU student union how he felt about his victory, he replied, "The biggest difference is that whenever I go to a government office, people always leave me a chair." Student leaders' sense of having immediate and rapid access to the most important government and university officials came across strongly whenever they offered to assist me with my research. Student leaders would tell me: "I can get you a meeting with the VC by this evening, if you wish" or, "Do you want me to call the DM? I can have him on the line in a second." No longer preoccupied by the state's partiality and injustice—indeed having become, in a key sense, "one of them"—Jat fixers could give expression to their sense of the state as a sublime set of institutional powers. On innumerable occasions, fixers offered animated descriptions of the workings of the DM's office, the various ranks within the police force and the cost of government jeeps.

The feeling of having escaped a preoccupation with boredom, educational decline and unemployment extended beyond student leaders' dealings with the state. Jat fixers often seemed to delight in being able to obtain goods and services from shops and businesspeople surrounding the MC and CCSU campuses free of charge. I once caused considerable embarrassment when, early in my research in 2004, I refused to accept a shopkeeper's offer of a free notebook. The shopkeeper associated me in his mind with one of the leading student politicians in MC, with whom I had visited the shop just an hour before. The leader later upbraided me: "What do you think others will say if they see you paying for something like that when you are with me? Are you trying to bring me down?"

Jats' intimate connections to local businesspeople and state officials provided a sense of routine that was markedly different from the forms of waiting that young men often discussed in college hostels and at tea stalls around the city. In a typical day, a Jat student leader might visit the VC's office to discuss admissions, travel to a building site near CCSU to chat with a contractor and spend the afternoon at the home of a senior police official catching up on local gossip. Riding in a car or atop a foreign-brand motorcycle, Jat student leaders tacked between the homes and offices of some of the most influential people in Meerut. After a few weeks, the daily visits often slipped into a common pattern. Jat fixers began to follow well-known routes through the city, they began to feel that they had a "circle." Indeed, the whole business of politics often came to resemble a comfortably predictable job (*naukī*) or "game" (*khel*) and escape from the punishments of passing time.

Dalit Resistance

Most students were reluctant to contest the power of Jat student leaders. Middle-caste social reformers such as Balraj (Chapter Four) said that they deplored the activities of student fixers but did not hold these men accountable for their actions. A friend of Balraj's said that student union leaders "are part of a system." Surendra and other aspiring student leaders spoke in similar terms.

OBC and Brahmin young men were often sharply critical of Jat student leaders like Girish, but they did not tend to act on their feelings. Nor did Muslims such as Iqbal, who tended to regard Jat student leaders as beyond their reach: "It would be useless trying to contest their power" a Muslim friend of Iqbal's said.

The only set of students who steadfastly attempted to undermine the dominance of Jat politicians were Dalits among the Muslim and Dalit reformers and leaders I discussed in Chapter Four. One of the most striking developments of the late 1990s and early 2000s in higher education in Meerut district was the emergence of a small set of confident, energetic and hard-working Dalit social reformers who acted as critics of dominant caste power on campuses. In 1996 there were only two Dalits enrolled in CCSU active in student politics. By 2004, there were at least ten Dalit politicos in CCSU, all men and from the Chamar caste. The emergence of the Dalit political entrepreneur reflects the rise in the number of Dalits enrolled in CCSU, a fourfold increase between 1995 and 2005. In contrast, there were still no Dalit reformers in Meerut College; Dalits said that the "atmosphere" (*mahaul*) of MC was not conducive to low-caste political assertion.

I interviewed seven Dalits involved in politics in 2004–5. These self-styled social reformers were aged in their late twenties or early thirties. Three were studying for Master's degrees and four for PhDs. Five came from poor rural backgrounds and two from more prosperous urban families.

A sense of the goals, activities and achievements of these men can be obtained by considering Suresh, among the most energetic of the Dalit reformers whom I interviewed. Suresh was in his late twenties, unmarried and studying for a Master's in Engineering at CCSU in 2004. His parents worked as agricultural laborers in a village seven kilometers from CCSU, and his father also ran a small business stitching footballs. Suresh was one of eight siblings, and his family faced a series of financial crises during his childhood. Suresh attended a poorly run primary school and government high school in the village. After passing his Twelfth Class (senior high school) examinations in 1994, the economic hardships suffered by his family forced him to return to his village to assist his parents making footballs. In the late 1990s, Suresh obtained diplomas in computing and technical work from a private college in Meerut. By 2000, he had saved enough money to enroll in higher education; he obtained a degree in Physics, Hindi and Maths from a government degree college in Meerut in 2003 and entered CCSU in the same year. Suresh had tried to obtain government employment but he referred to himself as unemployed.

Like the other Dalit and Muslim reformers I discussed in Chapter Four, Suresh organized protests on the issues of the rising costs of education, corruption, officials' harassment and young people's stalled progress within higher education. Beyond this, however, Suresh had a keen sense of how caste discrimination exacerbates Dalits' exposure to social problems. Suresh frequently spoke in strong terms of the continuing force of caste oppression within CCSU. He told me:

> In the past, Dalits were treated as untouchables. They could not sit with upper castes. They were not allowed to eat with upper castes. This is slowly changing. Dalits are not below anyone here in terms of their cleanliness, living conditions and clothing. We are also educated. But if Dalits have problems here, the administration does not help them as much. The administration is negligent. They tell us [imitating a senior official by sneering and adopting a haughty tone], "Yes, we will do your work, but come later today or come tomorrow."

Many other Dalits made similar complaints. Dalit reformers frequently said that there is a glass ceiling for Dalits in CCSU and that Heads of Department at the university systematically discriminate against Dalits in the allocation of PhD positions. There was a consensus among Dalit politicos and Dalits who did not participate in politics that caste oppression had diminished within the university and affiliated colleges but that Dalits remained subject to multiple, often subtle, forms of discrimination.

Suresh and other Dalits argued that Jat leaders' practices encouraged educational privatization and corruption and thus contributed to the perpetuation of class and caste injustice. Suresh tried to expose Jats who were working closely with university administrators, contractors or government officials to arrange backdoor admissions, embezzle funds or take kickbacks. Suresh was especially concerned by instances in which corruption had a strong caste component, as for example when a Brahmin young man in a college affiliated with CCSU had bribed an official to let him occupy a government post reserved for a Scheduled Caste.

Suresh had little interest in seeking election to the CCSU student union.

He claimed that Jats' numerical dominance within the university made it impossible to acquire an influential position. Suresh was also uninterested in the BSP, though he had been to two BSP rallies in Meerut and had a link to a BSP politician. The other six Dalit reformers whom I interviewed also had links to the BSP, but, like Suresh, they were not active members of BSP political organizations, did not campaign on the BSP's behalf and did not contest CCSU student union elections.

Instead of working for the BSP or its student wing, Suresh and his colleagues attempted to address political goals through varied forms of social networking, sometimes collaborating with middle-caste social reformers, Muslim politicos or OBC and Brahmin students, but most commonly operating alone. Some of this networking occurred in CCSU. Suresh was often to be found helping Dalit students obtain examination results from an office, meeting the VC to complain about a negligent professor or seeking a scholarship for a Dalit student from the CCSU Registrar. Travelling usually by bus because he lacked private transport, Suresh also regularly visited private colleges affiliated with CCSU to investigate incidents that involved Dalit students and meet government officials to complain about the actions of student leaders.

Suresh emphasized his ability to negotiate with government and university officials face-to-face, but letter-writing was his speciality. Suresh told me that writing letters reduced the number of times that he had to visit offices and engage in the sometimes awkward self-presentation that personal contact entails. Suresh also said that writing allowed him to choose his words in his own time, develop the right tone and test his arguments with friends. On the day that I interviewed Suresh about his letter-writing, he had written to the DM regarding corruption in the process of admission to private educational institutions, the VC complaining about the non-payment of Dalit scholarships at CCSU and the Dean of Student Welfare regarding a bullying incident. Suresh's letters often referred to the plight of students as a whole, but he was especially interested in seeking assistance for Dalits.

In Chapter Two I discussed the patience of Dalit political entrepreneurs in rural Meerut district in the mid-1990s, and other studies of everyday brokerage in India have emphasized the importance of persistence for subaltern political entrepreneurs (Reddy and Haragopal 1985; Appadurai 2002). Suresh and his

Dalit friends were extraordinarily stoical. On one occasion, Suresh showed me thirty copies of a letter of complaint he planned to deliver by hand to government officials across Meerut. Another Dalit reformer described having waited for over six hours to see a District Magistrate regarding scholarships for Scheduled Castes. Such commitment was hardly the sole preserve of Dalits; Jat student leaders like Girish displayed considerable perseverance in certain settings. But patience, and especially the ability to absorb setbacks graciously, was a theme that emerged particularly strongly in my work with Dalit reformers. The following story told by one Dalit reformer gives a sense of their determination:

> There is an institute in Modinagar [a town south of Meerut] called Golden Future Institute. It offers BEd admission. Ten or twelve Dalit students got admission there. But they were not able to get scholarships and the management would not return their fees as they should. The manager of the institute, Balwant Singh, said that he would not return the fees. The students came to me because they had read about my work in the newspapers. I wrote an appeal to Balwant Singh. He did not respond for two months. Then, after a further letter, Balwant started to exert pressure on me to abandon the case. I then visited the Registrar at CCSU, who promised to investigate the matter "within ten days." Ten days passed and nothing happened. I went back to the Registrar and he told me to go and see the VC. I went to the VC and he sent me to the affiliations department in the university. After a few days, the affiliations department official told me that the person I really needed to see was the Registrar. I went back to the Registrar and he told me, "just wait for another ten days." I then visited the District Magistrate in Ghaziabad district. I paid him a lot of respect. He said he would investigate the matter and Balwant eventually had to pay the money.

A strong theme emerging from my interviews with Dalit reformers in 2007 was of their being able to compensate at some level for their lack of money, connections and a feel for the game by outlasting their opponents. The common idea among students that they "have time" to do politics was especially prevalent among Dalits.

Dalit reformers' social networking sometimes bore fruit. Between September 2004 and April 2005, they arranged for Dalit schoolchildren injured by a bus driver to receive compensation, secured the release of students arrested by the police, improved facilities in college classrooms and instigated a formal inquiry into illegal admissions to higher education. Less tangibly, the emergence of hard-working Dalit social reformers was important in persuading other Dalits within and outside CCSU to persist with education and to register for university courses. Dalit young men and women studying in CCSU said that the presence of active Dalit politicos on campus improved their access to education. They often said that it is "easier for Dalits in CCSU than in MC." The four Dalits—two men and two women—whom I interviewed at MC concurred. These students said that they knew of the activities of CCSU Dalit reformers and admired these men. In 2004 and 2005, Dalit reformers also had some success in changing the iconography of CCSU to reflect Dalit pride. A hostel was named after Bhim Rao Ambedkar, an Ambedkar garden was created on campus and Ambedkar's birthday was exuberantly celebrated during annual events inside CCSU.

Yet Dalit reformers' attempts to widen low-caste access to resources and critique higher caste power were limited. Upper- and middle-caste Hindus, particularly the Jats, continued to dominate formal student associations, as they did in most other higher educational institutions in Meerut. The prevailing political mood among Dalit students in CCSU, Meerut College and the other colleges I visited in Meerut was one of world-weariness.

Dalit social reformers lacked a coordinated approach to changing campus politics. Only a handful of Dalit students had shown any interest in establishing a separate student union for SCs and STs, few Dalits participated in rallies calling for increased Dalit unity on campus in the later part of 2004, and a campaign to improve Dalits' access to Master's-level research supervision was abandoned before it had started. One reformer argued that establishing Dalit institutions is dangerous in the context of continued Jat dominance in CCSU. "It gives our opponents targets," he said. Another claimed that it was very difficult to develop institutional memory in a university context. Nor did Dalits, for all their efforts to record their struggles, engage in the strategy of "setting precedents" that Appadurai (2002) describes as a key tool of the urban poor in Mumbai. Dalit reformers claimed that such an approach would be ineffective because the fields of competition in which they operated were too uncertain and unstable. "What works one year may not work the next," a friend of Suresh's claimed.

Dalit reformers' efforts to undermine Jat power also largely failed because some politically active Dalits prioritized making money over advancing a common Dalit cause. In 2004, there were three Dalit young men, two of whom I interviewed, who defined themselves as *netās* (leaders). Dalit *netās* either obtained positions on the CCSU student union or hoped to do so in the immediate future. The two Dalit *netās* whom I got to know said that the frustrations of engaging in "social service" had persuaded them to enter CCSU student union politics. One of these men told me: "I had developed a good reputation among Dalits and some other poor students, and I thought, 'Why should I not go the political route?'" The three men who had made this decision came from relatively prosperous Dalit backgrounds; two were from urban areas and one from a landholding rural family. The political trajectories of these men paralleled those of Jat fixers. Like powerful Jat politicos, Dalit *netās* typically spent at least a year building up a support base among other students before launching bids for a position on the CCSU student union. After acquiring a post on the CCSU student union, the Dalit *netās* made money from their posts. Both Dalit *netās* I met were able to purchase expensive cars shortly after securing CCSU student union positions.

The failure of Dalits to challenge Jat advantage within political spheres also reflects the small number of Dalit reformers on campus. There were simply too few Dalit social reformers to dent Jat power. In some high profile cases involving transparent state or university malfeasance, Dalit reformers were able to achieve surprising outcomes. But in smaller and everyday interactions with the state, Suresh and his peers had to ration their time and energy according to personal considerations. For all his persistence, Suresh could only assist a few Dalit students in their negotiations with government and university bureaucrats.

Dalit reformers' failure to undermine caste and class dominance more convincingly is also attributable to the counterresistance of Jats (see also Jeffrey 2008). The manner in which Jats shored up their control over access to rental incomes and broader political dominance of higher educational institutions in Meerut paralleled the reactionary strategies of rich Jat farmers in rural Meerut district in the 1990s. Jats had greater financial resources at their disposal and were therefore able to outspend and out-bribe Dalits. They also had relatively well-developed social networks. For example, Jats were often able to call on influential senior kin or Jat "muscle" in rural areas to assist with political business in town, and they also had better links within the Meerut police force, which usually sided with Jats in struggles on campus. Moreover, Jats had a type of feel for what they termed the "game of politics" in Meerut. When we were discussing this idea at a tea stall in April 2005, a leading Jat politician put it concisely: "Being a Jat in Meerut is like having an invisible licence."

The limitations of Dalits' resistance and Jats' effective counterresistance had important implications for the future of Dalit student politics in Meerut. In the absence of durable opportunities to counter Jat power in CCSU, aspiring Dalit politicians were increasingly choosing not to contest CCSU student union elections or critique the practices of dominant student leaders within social networks in Meerut. Several Dalits, including Suresh, had begun to re-orient their political energies away from campus politics and towards obtaining positions either on village *panchāyats* or in block- or district-level government representative bodies. As early as 2001, Suresh campaigned successfully to become part of a Block Development Committee (BDC), an elected sub-district council responsible for administering development resources to his village and surrounding settlements. In 2005, Suresh was looking forward to contesting the position of Vice Chair of the BDC for a second time. Suresh failed again to obtain the BDC position, but when I met him briefly in 2007 he said that he was much more interested in village and block-level politics than in CCSU politics, even while he continued to pursue particular campaigns on campus. In 2004 and 2005 there were two other Dalit reformers who were interested in *panchāyat* politics, and by 2007 I heard that one of these men had obtained a post as a *pradhān*. One Dalit told me in 2007: "our pathway in the university is blocked, so we will seek political power through the proper channels."

Rationalizing Corruption

Dalit reformers were also responding to their failure to challenge Jats effectively at the level of social networking by engaging in a politics of words: a subtle array of symbolic practices directed towards questioning the moral and political authority of Jat leaders, what Scott (1985) might term "weapons of the weak." Dalit reformers frequently counterposed a vision of Dalit plain-living and honesty with Jat student leaders' purported ostentation and duplicity. In this narrative Dalits were always depicted as "straight" (*sīdha*), while Jats were imagined as crafty (*chalāk*). Dalits frequently likened Jat political strategies to the intricate lattices of battered syrup—*jalebīs*—that are sold on UP streets; they said that Jats were engaged in a "*jalebī* politics." Dalits tried to project a sense of their own relative straightforwardness through wearing simple clothes, avoiding decoration in their hostel rooms and cultivating a civilized air around campus. Central to these low-caste discourses was the notion that Dalits were more assiduous in their studies than Jats and did not have to rely on favoritism to pass examinations. These cultural projects were strongly gendered. Dalit reformers emphasized their capacity as successful men to avoid the temptations associated with a "corrupt" lifestyle, such as promiscuity and drinking. They also celebrated their superiority to Jats in small male groups that excluded women and reinforced male control over campus public space.

Jat social reformers tended to shy away from supporting Dalits' negative characterizations of Jat fixers, a reluctance that reflected caste solidarities. But Brahmin and OBC urbanites as well as Muslim reformers frequently supported Dalits in criticizing Jat student fixers for their alleged "selfishness" and "betrayal" of a broader student interest. A young Brahmin man who worked closely with Jat reformers said: "Those Jat leaders are working for their selfish motives. They lack humanitarian qualities. It is a game of telling one lie ten times and it will become a truth." Ex-student leaders who were active in the 1970s and 1980s were equally strident in their criticisms. In a statement that mixed hostility towards "corrupt" student leaders' practices with a more general discourse about "today's youth," one Jat ex-student leader, Kuldeep, said:

> Those boys [Jat student leaders] are looking for easy earning, easy going. They want to acquire a salaried job without working. Now young people are only interested in a car, cell phone and getting food easily. The student leaders who are successful think "I've got a name."

Kuldeep accompanied these words with a gesture: he pouted and plucked his shirt collars twice with his index fingers and thumbs. The gesture suggested arrogance and a sense of having "made it."

The apparent success of Jat fixers in defending their power in the face of Dalit resistance therefore posed a moral problem for these men: how could they on the one hand claim to be in the vanguard of anti-corruption protests and, on the other, be engaged in activity that others defined as "corrupt"? Jat fixers had to rationalize their "corrupt" practice to a greater extent than did rich Jat farmers in the mid-1990s in rural western UP, and they had developed a more sophisticated toolbox of justificatory strategies.

One way in which Jat fixers countered accusations of betraying a broader student cause was by making denials. I frequently watched some of the most notoriously avaricious student leaders issuing bold challenges to their audiences at large public gatherings: "You tell me one instance in which I have been corrupt!" When students started listing examples, the student leader would dismiss their arguments as self-interested and false or accuse his opponent of failing to appreciate "true corruption" (*sahī bhrashtāchār*). These performances borrowed from the political styles of national-level politicians faced with accusations of malpractice and from images of bold student politicians that emerge from Indian films, such as *Shiva* (1989) and *Yuva* (2004). Jats' exaggerated indifference to censure may also have been influenced by their familiarity with the image of the "innocent until proven guilty" defendant in legal cases dramatized on cable television.

In other circumstances, Jat leaders grudgingly acknowledged that they colluded with government and university officials but argued that their practices paled into insignificance when viewed alongside the actions of public servants and professors. For example, when I asked a Jat fixer during a public discussion how he responded to accusations that he is "corrupt" he said:

> You want to know about corruption? I will tell you about corruption! In MC according to the official rules, there should be ninety classes for each course before the examination. But in many cases there are just ten classes before the examinations. That is it. Ten classes when there should be ninety! [pause] *This* is the biggest corruption.

Another student leader heavily involved in practices that others defined as corrupt made a similar argument:

> Yes, I will tell you about true corruption. My grades are lower than yours. I then put forward false certificates to say that I am very good in sports. This then increases my grades. I will then obtain admission to the university of my choice. Or I just give money to increase my grades. There is no right to information. We have a prospectus. We should be told how many seats there are in different faculties. If there are 80 seats, they will admit 100 or only admit 60 and charge the other 40 a huge sum. This has been going for 6 or 8 years now, since the privatization of education took hold.

In these discussions of what constitutes "true corruption," Jat leaders sometimes made moral distinctions between the giving and receiving of bribes. Jat leaders said that they had been forced to give bribes to government and university officials in order to achieve desired tasks but that it was wrong for anyone to request a bribe.

In other cases, Jat fixers elaborated on the differences between their actions and those of venal officials by contrasting their own "corruption" (*bhrashtāchār*), understood as routine efforts to work the system, with the "fraud" (using the English word) of university bureaucrats. Student leaders said that paying a 50 rupee bribe to get a degree certificate was everyday corruption, part of how things operate in Meerut. What they objected to was situations in which officials took a bribe and still failed to act or where officials engaged in some outrageous new practice that was not part of local systems of corruption. For example, student leaders said that they regularly colluded with the CCSU Registrar to raise students' grades in examinations and assist students in obtaining their results before the official date—"okay corruption" as one leader quipped. But student politicians were incensed when allegations emerged in the summer of 2006 that the CCSU Registrar had been lining his pockets by arranging for Master's dissertations to be graded by school students, an act that student leaders characterized as "basic fraud."

In other instances Jats argued that as student politicians they have no option but to engage in the practices that others describe as "corrupt." Jats claimed that they are "trapped" or "bound in" (*band hona*) within a complex

set of obligations, practices and rules that make it impossible to achieve any-
thing without bribing, flattering and intimidating others. In a typical statement, one Jat student leader said: "If a person wants to be recognized, if
they want an identity, they have to work out a way of riding at the top of the
system." He picked up on this theme later in the same conversation:

> An honest person cannot succeed in politics in UP. Politics here is about competi-
> tion. If I am on foot and competing against a person on a motorcycle, I will lose.
> If I am honest, people will bear down on me on all sides trying to pressurize me
> into taking money . . . No, to succeed in politics you need public support. This
> only comes through offering and taking bribes and through showing force.

In making such arguments, Jat young men often built upon long-standing
gendered stereotypes of their caste as comprised of blunt, pragmatic, hard-
working men (see Stokes 1986). But their discourses also reflected the influence of Bollywood films which have frequently depicted innocent college students becoming embroiled in deception and treachery (see Mazumdar 2007).
Reflecting the pervasiveness of this broader film culture of youth innocence,
Dalit leaders who made money from their political influence also referred to
being bound by the rules of corruption. One Dalit leader stated that:

> The problem is that top officials demand corruption. The problem happens from
> top to bottom not from bottom to top. Most leaders are corrupt. If you became a
> *netā* and obtained just a single car, people would think you were a fool.

Jat fixers also argued that, since everyone is involved in "the game," there
is no point outside the system from which others can critique their practices.
Several Jat leaders recounted instances in which their critics, including Dalit
reformers, had offered bribes. In a large group discussion, a student leader
who had narrowly failed to win a student union post maintained that:

> Here we have a system in which nothing is done without force. That is the system
> we have to live with. If a normal student goes to an office in this university to get
> work done—to get their results or change course—nothing will happen. If we
> [student leaders] go to get something done, it will happen immediately.

Jat fixers also rationalized their involvement in malpractice by referring to
political ambitions that operate on different temporal scales. They said that

in the short term, while they possess influence within student politics and the university, they should try to make money, but that in the long term they were keen to live "clean" (*sāf*) lives. Jat leaders sometimes expanded on this theme by arguing that their own enterprise might allow them to protect their future children from opportunistic politicking.

One way in which Dalits tried to fight back against Jats in the face of their efforts to deny, obfuscate or rationalize their collusion with government officials was to accuse Jats of casteism (*jatīwād*), especially of distributing largesse to members of their own caste. Drawing on broader narratives of Indian modernity, most students in CCSU and MC regarded casteism as an evil (*zulm*) and referred to a pressing need to root out the vestiges of casteist thinking within the university. Opposition to casteism was typically a central plank of student leaders' speeches during the student union campaign season. Jats countered accusations of casteism by referring to Dalits' prejudice towards helping members of their own caste. "Like Mayawati you are only interested in helping Dalits and have no concern with other students" was the angry jibe made by a rich Jat student during a speech by a Dalit leader at a public event on CCSU campus in 2004. At other moments, Jats acknowledged that they tend to help members of their own caste but denied such action amounted to *jatīwād*. In the type of statement I heard many times, a rich Jat student leader told me during a public discussion of caste outside the CCSU library: "It is not casteist if you help members of your own caste. It is only casteist if you actively discriminate against other castes."

Jats knew that most students would not be convinced by their efforts to deny or rationalize their involvement in activities that most other students regarded as "corrupt" or "casteist." But new students were constantly arriving at CCSU, many of whom had little idea about who could make claims to being genuinely "straight." Some Jat leaders were able to maintain a reputation for honesty for long periods while also making large personal incomes. At the very least, some student leaders were able to position themselves as loveable rogues; "Girish makes a bit of money, but he is tough and basically honest" was the judgment of a set of students from a variety of backgrounds at a mini-conference over tea that I held in CCSU.

Jugār

Many Jat leaders secretly cherished their ability to strike deals with local government officials and used references to their double-dealing as a means of cementing friendships. In small gatherings of trusted student colleagues and government officials, Jat student fixers presented their capacity to make money from their student union posts as a valuable skill and sign of their masculinity. In certain instances, my presence acted as a trigger for these conversations, but positive accounts of their capacity to bend and manipulate the state were such a marked feature of my conversations with student leaders that I believe that they represent an important aspect of an emerging culture of political entrepreneurialism.

In their analysis of "fixing" in Andhra Pradesh, Reddy and Haragopal (1985: 234) refer to the central value of flexibility for the middleman. "The institution of *pyravīkār* is highly adaptable and readily changes its strategy to suit the client, the administrator, the scheme and the time." This emphasis on shrewd improvisation, timeliness and the capacity to act "in the moment" had become a type of founding philosophy for Jat student fixers in Meerut in 2004 and 2005. Jat leaders frequently referred to their political entrepreneurship with reference to the Hindi word *jugār*. Jats sometimes used *jugār* to refer to varied forms of skillful political opportunism or mischievous ingenuity, and in McGregor's (1993) Hindi dictionary *jugār* is defined broadly as "provisioning." But discussions of *jugār* usually referred more specifically to a capacity to "fix things" through bringing together unlike practices or materials in a novel and ingenious manner. The word *jugār* approximates to the US term "jerry rigging" and also carries with it many of the associations of the northern English word "nouse." *Jugār* was most often explained with reference to visual images. Jat young men commonly argued that the idea of *jugār* is encapsulated in the image of the rural bullock cart that has been fitted with a modern engine (*jugārī gārī*). One group of Jats also explained *jugār* by referring to a young man who, on waking in the morning, slips his feet sleepily into one smart leather shoe and one plastic sandal, because these two pieces of footwear just happened to be under his bed. "The young man wears these shoes all day—that is *jugār*."

In the political sphere, fixers often used *jugār* to refer to instances in which they had improvised with available resources to achieve a particular goal. This point came across strongly in September 2004, when I accompanied a Jat leader named Balbir and his friends to the office of the SDM in Meerut. Balbir and his friends wanted to obtain the SDM's assistance in a campaign to re-establish a student union in Meerut College, which would allow influential students to obtain a larger cut of the money that accrues from back-door admissions. In the SDM's office, Balbir adopted a pleading tone: "The MC administration has been denying students the right to establish a student union. We are requesting you politely, sir, to put pressure on the principal to allow a student union in the college." The SDM interrupted impatiently: "I had the MC Principal and several professors in this office last week. They said a union would cause violence among the boys." Balbir replied: "Sir, Meerut students have contributed much to the democratic struggles of this country, and India is a famous democracy throughout the world, and . . . [Balbir appeared to look round the room for some further inspiration] that is why a foreign researcher has come to investigate these issues!" Balbir then signaled in my direction. The SDM said he would look into the matter. Two weeks later MC got its student union election. Outside the SDM's office, Balbir puffed out his chest: "That is *jugār!*"

In other situations, Jat leaders used *jugār* to refer more precisely to their ability to combine "the modern" and "the traditional" while doing political work. For example, a Jat leader cited an occasion when he had used a rope bed to break the air-conditioning system in a university official's room as an example of *jugār*. In another instance, a fixer underlined his improvisational skill by discussing how he had rigged up a speaker system in a tree during a political rally on the edge of the campus. One Jat leader explicitly linked *jugār* to visions of environmental conservation. This young man combined his efforts to extract money from private educational entrepreneurs with a program to encourage rainwater harvesting in Meerut. He said that, while others might regard these political projects as strikingly different, he considered them to be connected by their commitment to *jugār*.

In addition to the notion of the "field" employed by older Jats in rural areas to describe spheres of social networking, Jat student leaders also elaborated on their capacity to do *jugār* with reference to the multiple "games" which they play. Other scholars have noted a propensity of young men to construct illegal brokerage activities as a game (e.g. De Vries 2002; Vigh 2006). In Meerut references to varied "games of politics" (*rājnītī kā khel*) had become common in 2004 and 2005. Fixers argued that in order to be able to practice *jugār* you must isolate, study and experience a wide variety of games. Such ideas were self-perpetuating; where people imagine their practices as moves within a game they tend to act in a more game-like manner and this, in turn, reinforces a tendency for social fields to resemble complex games (cf. Knox et al. 2006 who make a parallel argument with respect to network metaphors).

The four games to which Jat fixers referred most often were obtaining a CCSU student union post, negotiating with government and university officials over backdoor admissions to higher education, making money from building construction in Meerut and intervening in markets for posts in CCSU and affiliated institutions. These games were sometimes also called fields and were analogous to the arenas of competition within which rich Jat farmers imagined that they operated in rural Meerut district in 1996–97. Jat leaders said that, like many games (such as cards and cricket), these spheres of political competition take a definite temporal form; for example, the CCSU elections occur once a year and people have "turns" at trying to win. They also said that, like any game, "you reap what you sow": skillful or committed players see their efforts rewarded in terms of money, social influence or votes. Moreover, each game was associated with particular spaces, such as the campus, building site or government office. Jats said that their gaming spaces were also complexly connected, and those fixers able to dominate a variety of games simultaneously were said to possess a "setting": a polycentric nexus of contacts which needed to be nurtured through accumulating "force," the police or caste peers willing to intimidate or beat up opponents; "source," which denoted access to a high-level political connection; and *jugār*, the capacity to deploy resources in a shrewd, enterprising and timely manner.

Jat leaders commonly stressed that *jugār* is unrehearsed. Birbal's ingenuity in the SDM's office resided in his ability to take immediate advantage of my presence to press home his case. Jats imagined *jugār* to be something that resided at a deep level within their bodies, like a spring capable of triggering certain innovations (cf. Bourdieu 2001). *Jugār* therefore suggested enterprise, élan, investment and an innate capacity to master events in the present and within a set of gaming spaces within which Jats had considerable power.

Jugār was a strongly gendered discourse. Fixers tended to link ideas of shrewd improvisation to locally hegemonic visions of successful masculinity—wealth, physical strength and sexual prowess—and, more subtly, equanimity in the face of danger and a type of sly cunning. In 2003, a young woman was elected to an influential position on the CCSU student union, and Jat leaders frequently remembered her as someone who was not only incompetent, but who also lacked knowledge of *jugār*. In other instances, fixers reinforced gendered notions of men and women's character and roles through attributing to women a capacity to practice only a particular form of feminine *jugār*. A Jat fixer said:

> Women are very skilled in certain types of *jugār*, like mending things in the home and economizing with household spending. They even do *jugār* with their husbands [everyone laughed]. But they can't do the type of *jugār* that we have been talking about: political *jugār*.

In addition, discussions of *jugār* sometimes served as a medium through which Jat leaders glorified male privilege. This became especially apparent during a conversation with a student fixer named Indu, about another leader, Kishan, who had left university and worked as a fixer in Meerut in 2005. According to Indu, Kishan had long enjoyed a good reputation with young women in Meerut on account of his alleged charm, good looks and wit. Kishan had purportedly used these attributes to recruit young women from MC and nearby colleges to perform sexual favors for government officials. Indu said that Kishan was such a master of *jugār* that people called him *jugārū* (one who does *jugār*). Kishan apparently ran an agency in an upper middle-class suburb of Meerut. People wanting to accomplish a task through a government official visited the agency and paid Indu, who then directed one of the young women to ingratiate herself with a specific officer. I did not investigate this story—it may be untrue. The key point relates to how Jats discussed Kishan's work. In a group conversation with Jat fixers and other Jats, Indu said that Kishan's actions serve as an excellent example of *jugār* because he "took advantage of the 'goods' (*māl*) that were at his disposal." It was clear that "goods" referred to young women studying in Meerut. In a tone that suggested considerable admiration, Indu then explained that Kishan "weighed up the options open to him, worked out that he has some advantage over many others in Meerut [his close contact with attractive college-age women as well as his connections within government bureaucracies], and then reassembled the 'goods' to make money."

Rich Jat farmers in Meerut district in the mid-1990s also referred to *jugār* when discussing their politicking. Like student leaders in Meerut, they used the term to describe actions which involved bending the rules in order to obtain a desired resource. Thus, for example, if a rich Jat farmer used a veiled threat to persuade a Cane Society official to hand over a sugar cane permission slip, this might be conceptualized as *jugār*. Yet Jat student fixers sometimes referred to *jugār* as a distinctive quality of the young (*jawān*). Jat fixers said that they possess a spirit of mischief and adventure that older people have lost.

They said that older people are richer and therefore lack the motivation for devising ingenious solutions to political problems. In elaborating this idea, a Jat fixer drew a contrast between his father, a rich farmer with good links in several government offices, and his cousin, another Jat leader, named Uttam Singh:

> My father certainly has power in his hands, but he does not have the energy of Uttam. I will give you an example. Last week, Uttam and four of his friends just happened to be passing a building site near the university. Uttam decided to go in to see a contractor who was overseeing the construction of a new department. Uttam and his friends sauntered onto the building site [imitating a swaggering gait]. Uttam sifted through a pile of cement and pretended to be furious. He shouted at the contractor, "This cement has the wrong consistency. You're using fake cement and endangering the lives of ordinary students!" The contractor tried to reason with him and offered to pay a bribe. Uttam said, "How dare you offer me money when you are cheating on students and risking their lives?" Then one of Uttam's friends sidled up to the contractor a little later, "Look, I think Uttam would be prepared to overlook this, but you'll have to pay up." The contractor paid the money.

The Jat fixer telling this story later commented: "I can never imagine my father being so cunning or acting so quickly."

Echoing the discourses of many rich Jat farmers in rural Meerut district in the mid-1990s, several Jat leaders said that Jat young men were distinctively equipped with the belligerence and pragmatism required to act on the spur of the moment. One Jat young man recalled the local saying that JAT stands for "Justice, Action and Truth," putting emphasis on "action." Other Jats said that their caste's history of rural toil had taught them how to economize and make strategic use of scarce resources. These ideas came together in a tale I heard repeated several times by Jat students in Meerut that concerned a Jat fixer named Rajendra. As the story goes, Rajendra, from a village in western Meerut district (an area famous for its criminality) was visiting Delhi. He had no belongings but he wanted to make money. A Delhi gangster offered Rajendra men and weapons so that he could organize a robbery. Rajendra refused the help. Instead, he took out a handkerchief and small stick he had picked up at the side of the road, approached a car at a busy traffic junction, and, hiding the stick under the handkerchief to suggest that he was carrying a gun, told the motorist, "Give me your wallet or I'll kill you." The motorist speedily handed over his money. Jats emphasized Rajendra's capacity as a Jat man and villager to instigate a crime using minimal resources—a type of "hyper-*jugār*" in which the modern (metropolitan India) and traditional (the handkerchief trick) are combined to telling effect, and in which the UP youth seemingly outplays the metropolitan gangster.

Bourdieu argues that people often regard being a player within a field as, itself, a form of cultural distinction; "There are many agents . . . for whom to exist in a given field consists *eo ipso* in differing, in being different, in asserting one's difference, oftentimes because they are endowed with properties such that should they not be there, they should have been eliminated at the entrance to the field" (Bourdieu and Wacquant 1992: 100). This statement holds true for student fixers, who seemed keen to celebrate their involvement in games of local politicking. The notion of being good at *jugār* served to remind others of one's enrollment in these different gaming spaces and consequent skill relative to ordinary students and the uneducated.

But *Jugār* was a morally uncertain concept for young men. *Jugār* carried with it associations of not doing things properly (*thīk sè*). Some dominant Jat leaders chastised their friends for celebrating *jugār* and spoke of the importance of remaining "straight" as far as possible. In addition, before experiencing a catalogue of disappointments in their search for salaried employment, many Jat fixers had spoken proudly of their desire to become part of the Indian state and, once in post, avoid or even actively oppose *jugār*. Moreover, even those Jat fixers most committed to making money from their political influence continued to spend considerable time in collective protests against the "*jugār*" of professors, university administrators and government officials— and they did not want their own future children to do *jugār*.

At first glance, the negative connotations of *jugār* would seem to make it a poor choice as a focal point for a culture of successful youth masculinity. But it was precisely the moral ambivalence of *jugār* that rendered it an effective means of developing rapport with caste peers and government officials. By admitting to doing *jugār*, Jats could bestow on their peers and co-conspirators the warm feeling of being "let in" on an intimate secret. Jokes were central to this process. On many occasions I watched Jat leaders use humorous references to *jugār* as a preface to celebrating their political acumen. For example, at a Jat chicken and whisky party involving government officials held in February 2005, a Jat fixer said that he would illustrate the nature of *jugār* by telling a story of a friend who had recently visited the government anti-corruption officer in Meerut:

> My friend approached the clerk sitting outside the anti-corruption officer's room. The clerk—he was a Jat—told my friend, "Anti-corruption sir is not here today." My friend answered, "But I can see his light on." The clerk replied, "I'm sorry sir." After a pause, the clerk said, "Sir, I may be able to let you meet anti-corruption sir, if you pay me a certain amount [pause] . . . maybe fifty rupees." My friend actually paid the money and was let inside. Once in the anti-corruption official's room, he told the official: "What is this that is happening? You are the anti-corruption official and your own clerk is sitting outside your door taking bribes! What kind of man are you to let these things happen under your nose?" The anti-corruption officer answered: "Brother, what to do? This is how it is in these times . . . even *I* had to pay the clerk fifty rupees to enter my office this morning!"

In other instances, several Jat fixers told me a joke I heard repeated on several occasions about Bill Clinton's visit to India.

> Bill Clinton came to India. He arrived at his five-star hotel in Delhi where a Jat was working. He asked the Jat, "There is a huge tangle of wires outside my window

and yet the electricity supply is good. How does the hotel manage to maintain a smooth supply?" The Jat man grinned and said "*jugār.*" The following day, Clinton was visiting a government office. The clerk at the office had a car. Clinton asked him, "How did you earn enough to buy a car?" The clerk answered: "*Jugār.*" The next day, Clinton was travelling to Chandigarh with a Jat driver. He asked, "Driver, there are bicycles, bullock carts, buses, trucks and cars all over the road, yet you manage to speed along smoothly—how do you do it?" The Jat driver replied "*Jugār.*" The next day, the Indian Prime Minister came to see Clinton off at the airport. The PM asked Clinton, "Sir, we want to expand our trade with America, is there a valuable commodity that you would like to import from India?" Clinton replied, "Yes, we need to buy some of your *jugār.*"

In some versions of this joke Clinton's interlocutors were Jats, and on some occasions Jat leaders did not refer to the caste identity of the hotel worker, clerk and driver.

Few of these jokes or stories were original; what mattered was the pleasure of listening, the skill of the teller in elaborating on familiar themes, and the stories' elevation of the figure of the Jat man as arch improviser, one working the system through a set of ingenious improvisations. Like the discourse of timepass, student leaders' stories of colluding with local state officials and engaging in *jugār* operated as an "intimate culture" (Herzfeld 2005): a feature of social life regarded as somewhat shameful if exposed to outsiders but central to the reproduction of local solidarities. The Clinton joke also hinted at the capacity for *jugār* to index other visions of belonging; the force of that joke seemed to reside in its capacity to suggest Jats' acuity and—especially where the caste identity of Clinton's interlocutor was obscured—the improvisational abilities of Indians in general.

The rapid commercialization of Meerut district and associated rise of private companies and non-state educational institutions were undoubtedly important in persuading Jat young men to celebrate *jugār*. The idea of creatively combining unlike technologies, of making bold timely decisions and of resolving difficulties through individual enterprise were common tropes of television advertisements, signboards and leaflets distributed by major firms and private universities in Meerut and other parts of north India. Moreover, the proliferation of private educational institutions, loosely regulated by the state, had expanded opportunities for graft and therefore the profits available from *jugār*. Yet Jat young men did not simply "buy in" to a regional or national ideology of political opportunism. Rather, Jat student leaders creatively reinvented a vision of entrepreneurial skill through making use of local symbolic resources and often through telling lurid stories of their involvement in under-the-table dealings.

Thus, Jat student leaders were not only dominating access to local earning opportunities within the informal economy and rationalizing their practices but also engaging in intensive cultural practices that allowed them to build relationships with Jat peers and officials, especially younger men employed in government service. *Jugār* was an ambivalent, complex and overdetermined discourse, reflecting Jats' desire to build social contacts, mark their political acuity and understand their escape from passing time.

Conclusions

Much recent research in postcolonial settings suggests that unemployed young men either coordinate democratic political action (e.g. Demerath 1999; Krishna 2002), for example by spearheading subaltern protest, or engage in forms of reactionary class-based political activity, as where they become involved in clientelism and violence (e.g. Bayart 1993; Hansen 1996); the North-Western UP example shows that unemployed young men may play both roles simultaneously. Jat political leaders were assisting students in mounting critiques of a predatory state and engaging in patron-client politics in order to enhance their own material interests. Indeed, the image of being a reform-minded representative of a general student interest was an important staging post in lower middle-class young men's efforts to develop a position within informal political networks.

This chapter supports Bourdieu's argument that young people's political practices tend to reflect their class habitus and quest for social gain, and thus that cross-class youth mobilization will be short-lived. The chapter also resonates with Harriss-White's (2003) work on the resilient hustle that characterizes much lower middle-class activity in India. For all the evidence of cooperation across caste and class lines I provided in Chapter Four, analysis of Jat student fixers points to the divided nature of youth political society. It is not just that a sphere of youth politics is split between relatively rich sections of the educated unemployed colluding with officials and disparate "others" less compromised by their associations with clientelism, but also that a small band of rich Jats had created a culture of *jugār* that was at odds with the self-constructions of many other students. When male students were not thrown together against the university in pursuit of a particular goal, they were often seeking to undermine each other through the production of gendered moral discourses.

A focus on Jat youth leaders has also revealed how class advantage is secured through the cultural production of narratives that rationalize dominant practice. Rich Jat farmers also sometimes talked about *jugār* in rural Meerut district in the mid-1990s. To a greater extent than these farmers, however, Jat politicos in Meerut in 2004 and 2005 had crafted a discourse in which the capacity to adjust one's principles to reflect local conditions, to "improvise" (*jugār*), was held up as a skill, value and marker of class and gender power. Scholars have discussed the local salience of ideas of judicious opportunism and pragmatic savoire faire in other postcolonial contexts, for example among unemployed young men in Sierra Leone, where "hustling" was a focus of youth reflection (Hoffman 2004), and in northern Cameroon, where unemployed young men used a language of "spoils" to discuss their efforts to take advantage of illegal trade networks (Roitman 2004). My material connects especially closely to Henrik Vigh's (2006) study of the Aguentas militia in Guinea-Bissau in the late 1990s. Vigh refers to the importance of a notion of shrewdness (*dubria-gem*) among young male ex-combatants, who imagined their future success to depend upon their capacity to navigate shifting terrains of political struggle in a timely and resourceful manner (see also Simone 2005). Discourses of *jugār* served multiple functions in Meerut, operating as a class-inflected intimate culture (Herzfeld 2005), basis for cultural distinction and means of celebrating a capacity to influence the state across multiple fields.

6   Conclusions

This book has examined the rise and resilience of a middle class of Jats, especially Jat young men participating in student politics. It has followed a central story: a middle class of Jat farmers emerged in North-Western UP in the four decades following Indian Independence. From the mid-1980s onwards, the liberalization of the Indian economy and the rise of Dalits threatened to undermine the accumulation strategies of rich Jats. This powerful group responded to these pressures by intensifying their quest for social and political contacts and investing in the cultural capital of their children, especially through education. Much of the book has then examined the experiences and practices of the young men who were in a sense the "product" of rich farmers' investments: the students hanging out on street corners in Meerut City in 2004 and 2005. Waiting had become a central preoccupation for these men, who had a profound sense of being "lost" in time and space.

Young men were not passive in the face of their apparent marginalization, however. Some Jat students had become social reformers and worked alongside men from other caste and class backgrounds to critique educational corruption. Other Jats used their skills and free time to become "fixers" within local networks of corruption, channeling contracts to favored businessmen and selling places in private universities, for example.

This chapter reflects on the key contributions of the book to an understanding of class, politics and waiting. In the next section I discuss how my analysis might inform broader accounts of postcolonial middle classes. I then consider the politics of middle-class reproduction through discussion of Bourdieu's notion of "field." Finally, I examine the limits of Bourdieuian theory with reference to the importance of "futureless waiting" or "limbo" as a context for politics. Distinct from many other accounts based in the global south that describe how middling sections of society become gradually subsumed within a broader "global middle class," I document a process of class reproduction strongly founded on control over local capital and the local state.

Rethinking Middle Classes

Since the early 1990s there has been increased interest in the purported rise of a "global middle class." This phrase is especially associated with the work of economist Branko Milanovic (2005) who has used income data to examine the size of the middle class globally. My account engages more closely with research in anthropology and human geography on postcolonial middle classes (e.g. Barr-Melej 2001; Fernandes 2000; Cohen 2004; Nijman 2006). These studies often focus on people's own self-definition of themselves as a "middle class" and tend to concentrate on issues of consumption, social action and politics.

A key conclusion of recent studies of the middle classes in postcolonial countries is that these classes have tended to reproduce their power through cultural and social strategies. In the context of an underdeveloped formal economy, middle-class status often depends upon being able to marshal cultural capital and social connections successfully (e.g. Berry 1985; Barr-Melej 2001; O'Dougherty 2002; Cohen 2004). For example, Barr-Melej emphasizes how lower middle classes in Chile in the early twentieth century contested the power of the bourgeoisie not primarily through improving their economic position but rather via a process of "cultural production" founded on education and social reform work. Similarly, Joshi (2001) argues that prosperous sections of urban society in colonial Lucknow, UP, established their position as a new middle class through a process of social and cultural entrepreneurship rooted in, and routed through, new forms of communication, especially newspapers.

Scholars working on postcolonial middle classes often make the further observation that the cultural capital formation and social networking of middling strata is typically oriented towards events, processes and goods occurring outside their country, and especially towards "Western" cultural forms and social networks. Among recent accounts, O'Dougherty (2002) refers to the centrality of private education and foreign consumer goods in the accumulative practices of the Brazilian middle classes in the 1980s and 1990s. Cohen (2004) argues that a Moroccan middle class explicitly turned away from strategies that emphasized national development in the 1990s towards a celebration of Western culture and efforts to acquire jobs abroad. Similar points have been made in India. For example, Leela Fernandes (2006) identifies growing enthusiasm among middle classes in the 1990s and 2000s for investing in westernized cultural markers. Indeed, Fernandes (2006) argues that the image of being part of a "new middle class"—global in outlook and style—has become hegemonic in India, acting as a cultural beacon for other middle-class strata.

My work supports the emphasis of O'Dougherty, Cohen and Fernandes on the social and cultural processes through which middling strata seek to constitute themselves as a class, but differs from their accounts in some other important respects. The emergence of a Jat "lower middle class" from the ranks of the rich peasantry in the 1960s and 1970s depended centrally on their seeking education and urban contacts. When rich Jat farmers felt that their position was threatened in the 1990s, they reacted by redoubling their efforts to acquire relatively prestigious educational qualifications and good contacts in the local administration. Moreover, when Jat students failed to find secure salaried employment, they responded, again, by seeking further educational qualifications and better social connections. Bourdieu distinguishes between institutionalized cultural capital, such as educational qualifications; objectified cultural capital, for example ownership of consumer goods; and embodied cultural capital, such as the ability to comport oneself in a distinguished manner. All three forms of cultural capital featured prominently in the efforts of Jats to improve or maintain their position in local society during the period between 1960 and 2005.

Jats' emphasis on cultural capital formation and social networking, as opposed to focusing effort in the economic sphere, reflects UP's depressed economy in the 1990s and 2000s. A lack of government support for entrepreneurship, poor infrastructure and rampant corruption discouraged rich farmers and Jat young men from channeling time, effort and money into developing small manufacturing enterprises or agriculturally related industries. Jats also lacked social contacts in the areas of manufacturing and trade, which were dominated by upper castes in North-Western UP. At the same time, the lack of a land frontier, declining government investment in agriculture and legal restrictions on landownership made it difficult for Jats to reinvest in agriculture. More importantly, Jats' history of entering white-collar employment and obtaining education encouraged rich farmers to seek education and urban influence as a strategy for mobility. In other parts of India in the 1970s and 1980s, where the economic situation was more favorable to off-farm diversification into business, rich farmers devoted much greater energy to non-agricultural enterprise (see Harriss 1982; Upadhya 1988; Rutten 1995).

Unlike postcolonial and Indian middle classes featured in many other studies, the Jats did not imagine "the West" or "metropolitan regions" as a model of successful development. I must enter a caveat here: images of "new middle class" metropolitan success and broader visions of globalization certainly influenced Jats' tactics. For example, Jat rich farmers were keen to send their children to English-medium schools that supposedly offered "Western-style" instruction. Likewise, educated unemployed young men in Meerut used English words and consumer goods associated with the West, most notably cell phones, to communicate cultural distinction. But what is perhaps surprising among rich farmers and young men in Meerut was their ambivalence towards images of a globalized upper middle class. Jats continued to value qualities such as pragmatism and masculine strength, which they equated with their own caste and their heritage as farmers in provincial India. Jat young men, in particular, distinguished their strategies from the urban leisure classes, whom they imagined as "silver spoons."

It is therefore not only "slumdwellers" who provided a negative role model for lower middle classes in Meerut, as Ashis Nandy (1998) has argued in an essay on middle classes in India; Jats also distinguished themselves from Westernized sections of the upper middle classes. Such hostility to upper echelons reflects the manner in which caste and class intersected in Meerut district. Most of the urban rich were upper-caste Brahmins and Rajputs whom Jats generally disliked and suspected. What appeared to be emerging in Meerut district was a distinctive lower middle-class culture rather than widespread efforts to imitate India's globalized metropolitan middle class.

Jats' unwillingness to embrace images of metropolitan upper middle-class mobility was also reflected in the geography of their social strategies. Much work both with middle classes and unemployed young men from middling strata stresses their propensity to migrate in search of better prospects (e.g. Simone 2005; Mains 2007) or at least their overweening desire to move abroad (Cohen 2004). Of course, some Jats did migrate outside North-Western UP to metropolitan India or abroad in the 1980s, 1990s and 2000s. For example, there was a brief trend in the 1980s among some of the richest rural families to send one son to Russia or Eastern Europe for medical training, which was cheaper in that region than it was in India (Jeffrey 1999). But Jats' primary orientation was towards strengthening their control over cultural capital and social networks within North-Western UP. Rich Jat farmers imagined their sons entering salaried work in this region. Educated Jat young men studying in Meerut typically remained in North-Western UP in the face of unemployment. Similarly, Jat student leaders focused on trying to build power in Meerut and surrounding areas rather than attempting to construct a State-wide or national profile.

This localism reflects the difficulty that Jats faced in acquiring influence and power within metropolitan India. The majority of Jats from rural Meerut district and surrounding areas lacked the English-language speaking skills and Delhi-based social contacts required to migrate successfully to the Indian capital and enter jobs in the new economy. In their forays into the world of Delhi education and employment, Jats often spoke of feeling embarrassed and out of place. In 2005 Jats in several professional bureaucracies in Delhi told me that they try to conceal their caste identity for fear of being the target for jokes.

Jats also had strong reasons for remaining in North-Western UP. In this region, belonging to the Jat caste delivered organizational benefits, most obviously the capacity to access a range of contacts quickly in spheres such as education, the police and agricultural marketing. For example, rich farmers confronted with difficulties in agriculture in the mid-1990s saw that relatives in urban areas could assist with education. They took advantage of caste ties to position their children in satellite households in urban areas. In North-Western UP Jatness also often acts as a form of cultural capital. Jats could use the complexly assembled set of tastes, habits and dispositions that are associated with caste to cement social ties. When a Jat student said that being a Jat in Meerut is like having an "invisible license" (see Chapter Five), he was expressing openly what many Jats privately believed: that their caste identity was a type of trump card in the local area.

Jats are better defined as a "rural-urban middle class" than as a globalized middle class: they knit together the rural and urban in manifold ways. The capacity of rich Jat farmers to meld the rural and urban was evident during the BKU protests of the early 1990s, when many farming families worked with rural protests to coordinate mass demonstrations in Meerut (Bentall and Corbridge 1996). My research in 1996 and 1997 in rural Meerut district suggests that rich farmers spent their days tacking back and forth between their villages and local towns, seeking out contacts, negotiating with government officials, while simultaneously trying to ensure that their farms remained profitable (see Chapter Two). The rural-urban character of lower middle-class Jat strategies was equally apparent in the sphere of Meerut student politics and cultures in 2004 and 2005. For example, students waited around at particular nodes in the city partly to keep abreast of news flowing into Meerut from the surrounding countryside (Chapter Three). Similarly, social reformers and Jat leaders shuttled between the city and rural areas in order to pursue their political goals (Chapters Four and Five).

Michael Lipton (1977) argued that the line between rural and urban was increasingly difficult to trace in South Asia. Jats were not only connecting the rural and urban, they were also blurring the distinction between the countryside and city. For example, rich Jat farmers' practice of constructing urban-style homes in their villages was contributing to a process wherein rural areas increasingly looked like suburbs of Meerut. Moreover, the frequent visits of Jat social reformers and Jat leaders to rural areas and the movement back to farming of Jat university students were important conduits along which urban goods and ideas flowed into the countryside. The increased movement of large numbers of farmers into Meerut to petition bureaucrats, check on their urban-educated children or bolster their sons' political careers was contributing to the urbanization of rural social relations and "ruralization" of some parts of Meerut.

Jats were therefore stretching "the local" practically and imaginatively through rural-urban strategies. Their accumulation practices also involved developing a new relationship to time. Most notably, rich Jat farmers learned to invest in their children as a basis for reproducing class power. They lengthened their mental horizons, since obtaining a return on educational investment required Jats to wait for children to grow up and find employment. In addition, the development of social connections in urban areas involved rich farmers in waiting for the right moment to cash in on a connection. Jats spoke of these practices as forms of "waiting," and they were quick to attach to their long-term investment strategies the moral qualities of patience, prudence and foresight.

In a rather different manner, many Jat male students in Meerut imagined themselves as people "waiting for work." By stretching out the time they spent in college, these men could continue to inhabit the relatively respectable position of "student," even as they became increasingly aware that college education was not going to deliver a graduate job. A prolonged period in college also allowed many Jats to find status-saving but usually poorly paid work in the urban informal economy. Waiting on street corners and at tea stalls also offered a more diffuse set of skills and knowledge, for example regarding how the city works socially and politically. Yet Jat students rarely regarded their "waiting" as purposeful or as an "investment." Indeed, many had come to imagine themselves occupying a semi-permanent condition of limbo: "What can we do but study and hope things will change?"

Jats' spatial and temporal strategies were strongly gendered. In putting into practice their localized social networking and efforts at cultural capital formation, rich Jat farmers and unemployed Jat young men reinforced dominant visions of masculinity (cf. Connell 2005), for example around the importance of men entering paid employment and of male farmers undertaking the social negotiations associated with building links within state bureaucracies.

In a similar vein, Jat students were involved in the production of performance hierarchies of manliness in which certain social attributes, such as the capacity to hang out in an insouciant manner and negotiate with government officials, were invested with powerful gendered meanings.

Through emphasizing such masculinities, Jat men reproduced gendered ideas and practices that had negative implications for women and many men. For example, rich Jat farmers' decision to use local marriage markets to improve the employment chances of their sons threatened the security of young brides; parents prioritized financial calculations over establishing their daughters in a secure marital home (see also Roulet 1996). Similarly, a trend among some political animators and student leaders to affirm a blunt macho masculinity served to limit young women's ability to participate in politics. Willis's (1977) emphasis on people's tendency to challenge some aspects of dominant power while reinforcing other dimensions of inequality is useful here; social reformers among the Jats and Dalits were capable of only "partial penetrations" of prevailing structures of power, often reinforcing gender inequalities as they contested hierarchies based upon age, class and caste. It is important to tread carefully here, however: gender inequalities are produced by women as well as men, and there is a pressing need for future research into how young women contest, navigate and shape the gendered practices I have described in this book (see Fernandes 2004; Lukose 2005).

The rise of a large cohort of educated unemployed young men who refuse to settle down quickly into agriculture or low-paid private service work may have other more uncertain and long-term implications for gender politics in the region. Again, I am aware of a need to proceed cautiously; it is hazardous and difficult to make predictions about the social outcomes of long-term unemployment. But Prem Chowdhry's (2009) work in Haryana has shown how protracted young male unemployment in that region has had deeply unsettling effects on gender relations, boosting membership of caste organizations that violently punish those who marry across caste lines. It is also possible that the rise of a cohort of young men who make claims to be "on the verge of a service job" but who ultimately fail to acquire salaried employment may be heightening tensions within marriages. Parents may marry their daughter into a family on the understanding that their son-in-law will acquire a salaried post and then try to annul the marriage when the young man remains unemployed. In such situations, families frequently quarrel and young brides commonly become subject to harassment (see Chowdhry 1997, 2009).

Jat accumulation strategies therefore offer a vivid reminder that class and gender violence occurs not only through employment relations or divisions of labor but also via social and cultural mechanisms (cf. Bourdieu 1984; Savage and Butler 1992). It also underlines the point made by other scholars of the middle classes (e.g. Fernandes 2004; Cohen 2004) that class and gender reproduction are never guaranteed but frequently require constant effort to manage multiple "capitals." Simply remaining lower middle class was a considerable social achievement for Jats in North-Western UP. Their success rested not on their ability to imitate the consumption practices and lifestyle of global middle classes. Rather, Jat dominance was reproduced through a set of socio-political projects oriented around control over the state in North-Western UP and locally salient forms of social and cultural capital.

Micro-Politics: Rethinking the Field

In her account of the strategies of Morocco's middling strata, Cohen (2004) emphasizes middle classes' disengagement from ideas of national progress through a program of development. Rather than imagining futures working for the Moroccan state or participating in electoral politics, these middle classes looked outside the country for opportunities for their own social betterment. Cohen links such attitudes to a decline of the state in Morocco since the 1980s both materially, through neoliberal cutbacks, and ideologically, with the waning of the hopes of modernity and progressive change.

At first blush the conditions pertaining in UP in the 1990s and 2000s are similar to those described by Cohen in Morocco: economic reforms begun in the early 1990s in India had exacerbated problems of social reproduction for UP's middle classes and there was a general cynicism about possibilities for progress. But in UP governmental agencies remain crucially important as providers of money, qualifications and social support. Rich Jat farmers' attempts to manage social threats in the 1990s focused largely on trying to capture forms of state power. They attempted to influence a range of government institutions, such as the local police, Cane Societies and village councils. Similarly, Jat social reformers and Jat leaders responded to joblessness in Meerut in 2004 and 2005 by organizing collective protests against the state or working as local fixers.

If the state continued to matter materially, it also remained ideologically significant in North-Western UP. This was especially evident among unemployed young men in 2004 and 2005. Students were quick to protest about educational corruption, police abuses and other bureaucratic misdemeanors precisely because they continued to believe in "the state" (*sarkar*) as an ideal. The collective protests of students commonly referred to the strength and importance of Indian democracy, and students eagerly discussed their rights and entitlements as students and youth. Moreover, an ethic of respect for the state and belief in the rationality of the state at some higher level ran through student protests in Meerut.

Students' belief in the redemptive capacity of the state and the state's essential fairness reflects the historical and continued material importance of the state in the lives of most ordinary citizens. Many sections of student society, especially Jats and Chamars, had long histories of contact with the state, and they had benefited, at least to some extent, from jobs in government, state education and the government's development project. Students' belief in the state probably also reflects the role of the educational system, media and government organizations in persuading many students of the importance of respecting state authority. In the 1990s and early 2000s in North-Western UP, school textbooks made great play of the authority of the state, requiring students to memorize details of state functioning and write letters to district officials, for example. Students' positive regard for the state also reflected the extent to which they linked the state and the nation in their minds; students retained a deep patriotism, evident in things as mundane as their jokes—for example about Bill Clinton visiting India (Chapter Five)—and respect for members of the military, mentioned in Chapter Four. For many students the abandonment of faith in Meerut's city bureaucracy would amount to a betrayal of a particular Indian dream of democratic order.

What is also notable about Jats' engagement with the state is the extent to which it coexisted with a widespread disillusionment with party politics and the sitting governments in Lucknow and Delhi. Rich farmers and students appeared rather disinterested in party politics. They frequently voiced their frustration at the failure of parties to address social and economic concerns. Likewise, Jats were angry at politicians for their greed, corruption and ineptitude and for presiding over the criminalization of politics. Cynicism characterized many conversations that I had with Jats about "politics" (*rajniti*) at the level of the UP State and Indian nation.

Jats denigrated formal politics in part because Dalits had begun to contest elections successfully. Drawing on research in the South Indian city of Chennai, John Harriss (2006) has described a similar tendency to denounce formal politics in the context of increasing low-caste involvement in electoral politics. But Jats' disinterest in formal politics also reflects material calculations and the specific political conjuncture in North-Western UP in the 1990s and 2000s. Rich Jat farmers and Jat student leaders regarded making money through colluding with local state officials as more profitable than seeking public office at the State or national levels. Moreover, the death of Charan Singh and the Mandalization of politics had conspired to weaken the farming lobby in North-Western UP; many Jats felt that they lacked a successful party at the State level that could durably represent their interests.

One of the unintended consequences of Jats' tendency to invest more time and effort in informal politicking than contesting local or State elections was that it gave politically mobile Dalits a certain room for maneuver. Pai (2002) argues that Dalits successfully contested several seats as *pradhān* (head) of *panchayāts* in villages close to Meerut in the late 1990s. My research helps to explain this phenomenon—many Jat young men had turned away from *panchayāt* or district politics in favor of developing links to multiple arms of the local state.

Thus, while "the state" and "development" remained crucial for the Jats, their political imagination is oriented towards, and fashioned through, the informal political spheres in which they operate. Reflecting the pervasive influence of the Government on people's everyday lives, Jats and Dalits' discussion of "the state" invariably related to such questions as what the local police inspector was doing, how to persuade the District Magistrate to grant a gun license or what pressure could be brought to bear on a college principal to allow a student to remain in education (cf. Shukla 1992).

How might this everyday politics—or "politicking"—be theorized? Since the early 1990s several scholars working in the field of postcolonial studies have attempted to explain and describe the continued relevance of "the state" in people's everyday lives, and they do so by referring to exactly the type of quotidian tactics and strategies that I am claiming are important for the Jats (e.g. Gupta 1995; Appadurai 2002; Chatterjee 2004). But, as I have argued throughout this book, these accounts often present a rather simplified opposition between a bourgeois and state elite, on the one hand, and a "public culture" (Gupta 1995), "political society" (Chatterjee 2004) or arena of "deep democracy" (Appadurai 2002), on the other. In these studies, the search for a broad democratic sphere of subaltern action is prioritized over sociological analysis of how various class fractions are constituted through their interactions with the everyday state. Moreover, writers within this postcolonial strand of scholarship are sometimes rather too eager to scale up their accounts of social life to generalize about the character of non-elite politics. For example, Chatterjee (2004) uses a selective survey of recent protest movements in India to argue that everyday politics among the poor and lower middle classes is characterized by illegality and violence. My research in Meerut suggests non-elites often make use of legal and civil tactics, as well as illegal and violent ones, in pursuing their political goals. The boundary between the "civil" and "political" is permeable (see also Corbridge et al. 2004; Ghosh 2006; Baviskar and Sundar 2008). Indeed, people in Meerut actively debated whether the terms "civil" or "political" should be attached to their collective mobilization, a possibility not discussed in Chatterjee's work. For example, many students in Meerut stressed the essentially "civilized" nature of their protests; they argued that politeness, equanimity and calculated restraint is more likely to yield results than violent and illegal action.

Reflecting my dissatisfaction with this literature on ordinary politics, I have drawn on the work of the French sociologist Pierre Bourdieu, and especially his notion of field, to conceptualize how people compete for power in North-Western UP. Bourdieu leaves the question of how to define "field" productively open but it is clear that he is interested in distinctively organized social microcosms, spheres of practice that are built up through the strategies of those participating in a particular arena and by forces external to the field.

Bourdieu argued that, because people are endowed with different economic, social and cultural resources, they will tend to fare differently within fields. Moreover, a class that wins in one field will tend to succeed in other fields, too. Bourdieu stressed that a person's success or failure across varied fields becomes embodied in their system of dispositions (habitus). The rich become better able to "cultivate fields" not only because they have higher volumes of various forms of capital but also because socially effective markers of privilege become incorporated in their everyday dispositions (habitus): things as mundane as how they dress, speak and stand. Class in this analysis cannot be read off from someone's structural position. It is rather the product of people's agency: their attempts—successful or otherwise—to navigate varied arenas. "The state" can be understood in somewhat similar terms: as a set of powers, symbols and embodied practices complexly entangled within fields. At the same time, the state figures in Bourdieu's schema as an external force shaping the overall operation of fields, as for example when a State government withdraws funds from public schooling thereby reshaping the field of education.

Bourdieu's conception of field resonates very well with how people in North-Western UP talked about politics, class and the state. Jats used the very idea of "field" (often using the English word) and related notion of "game" (*khel*) to describe everyday political life. Rich farmers referred most often to fields or gaming spaces associated with influencing the police, agricultural marketing agencies, schools and government employment markets. For unemployed young men, the spheres of higher education, government employment markets, student union politics and the police, were some of the most crucial fields with respect to realizing social ambitions. Jats argued that the state (*sarkar*) was important in these fields, for example as embodied in the personage of officials. Government officers, symbols of the state and various material practices of governance were all deeply implicated in how specific fields functioned on an everyday basis. But Jats also argued that the state in Lucknow and Delhi—*sarkar* in a different sense—could influence the rules of the game within each field.

References to "playing the game" or "playing the field" also amounted to a strategy within the field. For example, many Jat student leaders used the idea that their corrupt practices were just a game to euphemize their actions. Such discourses had a self-reinforcing effect. As students began to talk of their actions as game-like maneuvers, they also came to conceptualize the fields as games. The cumulative effect of large numbers of young men imagining their actions in this way was to make the field itself more game-like.

Another intriguing aspect of local discourses of field and game was people's references to the vertical organization of fields. It is useful to recall the comment of one student, "We have to find a way of riding at the top of the system." Similarly, when chiding me for embarrassing him, a student asked rhetorically, "Are you trying to bring me down?" Ferguson and Gupta (2002) have written about the social process through which people come to attribute to "the state" the qualities of being "up there." Verticality is built into people's sense of local politics in other ways in North-Western UP. Jats and Dalits had a keen sense of who is "up" and "down" within fields, and they frequently expressed their sense of dominance and subordination in these terms.

Jats therefore reproduced their power in North-Western UP in the 1990s and early 2000s through a dual strategy. First, they invested in local forms of cultural and social capital, a strategy that is somewhat at odds with many accounts of "global middle classes" around the world (cf. Cohen 2004; Fernandes 2006) and reflects the social networking resources and cultural capital that Jats' caste status provides in North-Western UP. Second, Jats advanced their interests through interaction with the local state as it became relevant to their lives across a number of spheres.

Waiting, Creativity and Mischief

A central problem with Bourdieu's theoretical schema, however, is that it fails to account for instances in which people do not act according to self-maximizing, class-related "logics." If aggressive individualism is the norm, why did some Jats eschew opportunities to make money from the local state and act instead as social reformers? Why, more broadly, did young men from markedly different backgrounds join together to produce cross-caste cultures of timepass and collective social protests? How, too, would one explain the mischievous character of young male cultures and politics—these seem difficult to square with the general tone of Bourdieu's work?

One response to these questions would be to point to the youth of Jat young men. Several anthropologists have argued recently that young people, precisely because they are often somewhat removed from wider society, may be capable of novel forms of action (see Bucholtz 2002 for a review). Much of this work draws on Karl Mannheim's (1972) influential writing on generations and social change. Mannheim stressed the importance of examining generations as social actors. Within any particular place, there is a novelty inherent in how specific age cohorts interact with their surroundings: "The continuous emergence of new human beings in our own society acts as compensation for the restricted and partial nature of the individual consciousness" (Mannheim 1972: 105). The notion that each generation experiences a "fresh contact" with their social circumstances has been taken by some to suggest that youth may be especially imaginative social actors within particular conjunctures. For example Jennifer Cole (2004: 576) has drawn on Mannheim's ideas to argue that young people in the region in which she worked were "uniquely poised to take advantage of new social and economic conditions" (see also Keniston 1971; Bucholtz 2002). But such assertions risk suggesting that youth possess more agency than other sections of society (see Durham 2008); Mannheim argued that any generation may be capable of engaging in innovative social behavior.

A more plausible explanation for the cultures of timepass and collective student politics that I have described is that they arise out of the particular spatio-temporal experiences of Jat young men on campus: namely, their feelings of surplus time and of being left behind. It is worthwhile recalling for a moment the nature of young men's limbo. Many young men spent the years from about five to eighteen engaged in forms of learning that required them to work hard and which were monitored by ambitious parents and other relatives. Boys often had to go to tutorials before or after school. When these young men arrived at Meerut College or a similar institution in their late teens they found that there was little to occupy their time. When, after a few years, they experienced the full force of exclusion from government employment, the sense of timelessness came to be mixed with a still more potent sense of limbo and disappointment. Many young men in Meerut College asked me, "What is there to do but sit around and wait?" While there is the obvious risk of exaggerating this culture of surplus time (and of course many young men knew that they were likely to face prolonged unemployment in Meerut), young men's sense of limbo was important in the region in 2004 and 2005.

But can a sense of limbo generate cultural and political possibilities? The idea that "waiting" may be a spur to novel action was rehearsed long ago in the writing of Siegfried Kracauer (1995 [1963]). Kracauer argued that many professionals in urban Germany in the early 1920s had a profound sense of "just waiting" but that their boredom could serve as a basis for thought, politics and action. In Kracauer's view, a sense of waiting can generate a type of "hesitant openness" and "tense preparedness for action" (see also Crapanzo 1986).

The rise of National Socialism in Germany casts a shadow over Kracauer's optimism regarding waiting. But the cultural and political possibilities of waiting are also evident in other studies (e.g. Stepputat 1992; Conlon 2007; Hart 2007). For example, Finn Stepputat has described the prevalence of feelings of timelessness in a refugee camp in Guatemala. In a manner that resonates closely with my own account of youth, Stepputat (1992: 110) likens refugees' experiences of time to C. S. Lewis's description of grief: "like waiting; just hanging about waiting for something to happen. It gives life a permanently provisional feeling . . . almost pure time, empty successiveness." Stepputat proceeds to argue that common feelings of waiting among Guatemalan refugees created a sense of shared purpose, a type of moral and political community that could form the basis for numerous projects and schemes.

Paralleling Stepputat's work in certain respects, there is now a nascent literature, much of it based in Africa, on the practices of groups of homosocial young men "hanging out" on street corners (for example, Weiss 2002; Mains 2007; Ralph 2008). These studies point to how the temporal suffering and sense of ambivalence experienced by young men can generate cultural and political experiments that, in turn, have marked social and spatial effects. For example, Michael Ralph (2008) has recently written about the emergence of a strong sense of timelessness and boredom among unemployed young men in urban Senegal. Ralph documents these men's attempts to counter ennui and recuperate masculinities through a range of somewhat surprising and disparate street practices, including competitive tea-drinking competitions, impromptu concerts and city clean-up campaigns—often events that include young men from a wide variety of social backgrounds.

As the work of Steptuttat and Ralph might lead us to expect, the experience of limbo in Meerut seemed to act as a seed-bed for the generation of somewhat novel youth cultures and political protests. Young men studying in Meerut began to imagine themselves as a lower middle-class "group" precisely through hanging out together in hostels, tea stalls and on street corners. Reflecting the links between temporal anxiety and cross-class political action, collective mobilizations of the student body often began in spaces of male waiting, such as tea stalls, and young men's protests focused on issues related to time, such as their anger at being unable to pass smoothly through university degree courses.

It is not just that limbo creates action across class lines: it also generated a particular mood among young men, a sense of mischief and irreverence that ran through much of their activity. Robust horseplay, joking and banter were sometimes most apparent, for example, where young men traded humorous insults on street corners. At other moments, students used irony, for example when organizing "relay hunger strikes" in which students took it in turns to go on hunger strike for one hour each. In still other instances, young men engaged in a type of mischievous theatricality. Recall, for example, the corrupt student politicians I described in Chapter Five who cheekily asked other students at large gatherings to "name one instance in which I have been corrupt!" When regaled by their interlocutors with examples, these student politicians simply ignored their audience. Not only was the leader's reputation left intact, but they actually enhanced their power through such deliberate irony. Of course, older Jat men also joked about their activities, but humor, sarcasm and a type of spirited gamesmanship were more pronounced among young men "in wait."

As well as arising out of an enthusiasm for joking, young male mischief-making seemed to reflect an awareness of being partially detached from surrounding institutional forms. The position of being in limbo has instilled in some young men a feeling that they had only a second-hand relationship to surrounding social and spatial structures. Ross McKibbin (1994) has written of unemployed young people in Britain in the 1920s and 1930s who imagined themselves at some remove from mainstream society and culture. These unemployed youth could not afford to watch football matches. Instead, they heard about the action afterwards by hanging around outside the stadium; life, it seemed, was lived "second-hand." In Meerut I observed a somewhat similar type of second-handedness. It came out in young men's discussions of being left behind in Meerut and thus partially removed from "where things were happening" (Chapter Three). It was also evident where young men contrasted Meerut student politics with "proper" (*thīk*) student politics occurring in Delhi (Chapter Four). A certain second-handedness also emerged in young men's discussions of *jugār* (Chapter Five): shrewd improvisation was a skill but it also carried with it the sense of not doings in the right way (*thīk se*).

In sum, the contributions of this book to wider theorizing on class, politics and waiting are threefold. First, I have stressed the value of a cross-learning approach that examines Jats' practices with respect to those of lower middle classes in other parts of India and the world. Whereas some other authors have proposed the emergence of a global middle class somewhat delinked from their nation and locality, I have identified a lower middle class in India whose power is firmly rooted in control over local networks and cultural capital, even while the local is itself being transformed.

Second, my analysis of Jat accumulation strategies exposes shortcomings in postcolonial-inspired accounts of subaltern politics—such as those offered by Chatterjee, Appadurai and Gupta—that pit the bourgeoisie against a subaltern mass. I have argued instead for examining how different strata navigate "fields" or "games" of social competition. This involves thinking about people's changing location within fields (Bourdieu 1977), how fields themselves change in response to external pressures, and the field as a discursive form (cf. Savage et al. 2005).

Third, I have pointed to waiting as context for surprising cultural and political practices. Young male limbo in Meerut in 2004 and 2005 led to novel, sometimes irreverent, types of cultural and political behavior. Bourdieu's work therefore needs to be read alongside analyses that foreground counterintuitive examples of cross-class collaboration (e.g. Chatterjee 2004) and ironic dimensions of culture and politics (Willis 1977). My appeal is therefore for an organizationally and culturally sensitive political economy approach to youth, politics and the middle classes in India, one resolutely attuned to both the durability of class dominance and counterintuitive social practice.

Whilst the book is centrally concerned with theorizing class and politics, my analysis also suggests some new direction for policy. First, education is a necessary but not a sufficient basis for social mobility in North-Western UP (see also Jeffrey et al. 2008). Education is widely regarded by development institutions, and scholars such as Sen (1999), as an unproblematic "social good" that will inevitably improve people's individual and collective prospects. But prolonged formal education, on its own, often fails to promote equitable social development. In Meerut, caste and class powerfully shaped the capacity of students to be able to benefit from formal education: rich Jats were able to capitalize on their qualifications to a greater extent than poorer members of their caste and Dalits. Moreover, even among rich Jats there was increasing ambivalence about the capacity of higher education to improve people's lives. From scholarly and policy perspectives there is an urgent need for greater research that examines the contradictory effects of prolonged formal education on different sections of the Indian population as well as how education is socially constructed by various social groups. Such research requires combining the optimism of much conventional development thinking on education with the more critical perspectives offered by scholars such as Bourdieu.

Second, I have documented the considerable role played by young male "fixers" in perpetuating everyday forms of "corruption" in north India. Powerful organizations such as the World Bank most commonly imagine corruption as a problem located firmly within the state; we are accustomed to hearing about governments that are "corrupt." What these politically motivated discourses ignore, among other things, is the importance of a set of people outside the state in perpetuating "corruption" at the local level. It is important to note in this context that Jat fixers encourage corruption not because they lack an understanding of liberal democratic norms but because they see few alternative avenues for mobility in the denuded economic environment of Uttar Pradesh in the 1990s and early 2000s. Attempts to grapple with corruption in a place like Meerut must eschew a narrow focus on governmental reform to consider how to change the array of options available to young men like Girish (Chapter Five) and the associated issues of educational decay and employment scarcity.

I have also shed light on a section of youth society that actively seeks to promote social understanding and a democratic ethos at the local level. A final contribution of this book to policy debates is to uncover the importance of energetic social reformers among educated unemployed young men. Popular stereotypes of unemployed youth as a danger or as inevitably hostile to the state and civilized society risk obscuring how some young men might be enrolled in development efforts. Young men such as Iqbal (Chapter Four) and Suresh (Chapter Five) possess considerable political acuity and are keen to become involved in organizational efforts to improve the lives of subordinated youth. The Indian government and development organizations might profitably reach out to, and learn from, this social constituency.

What binds these arguments together is appeal for fine-grained social research on how "development" unfolds in diverse sites across India and other parts of the world. This point bears repeating at a time when fewer and fewer scholars have the time, inclination and resources to conduct long-term qualitative research in India.

Bibliography and Index

Bibliography

Abraham, Leela. 2002. "Bhai-behen, True Love, Time Pass: Friendships and Sexual Partnerships among Youth in an Indian Metropolis," *Culture, Health and Sexuality* 4, 3, pp. 337–53.

Ahluwalia, Montek, S. 2001. "State Level Performance under Economic Reforms in India," Working Paper No. 96, Center for Research on Economic Development and Policy Reform, Stanford University.

Altbach, Philip. 1984. "Student Politics in the Third World," *Higher Education*, 13, 6, pp. 635–53.

Amar Ujala. 1997. 28 January, "Trouble at Simbhavli Sugar Mill."

Amar Ujala. 2004. 4 October, "Vice-Chancellor's Office Transformed into Makeshift Boxing Arena."

Anandhi, S., J. Jeyaranjan, and R. Krishnan. 2002. "Work, Caste and Competing Masculinities: Notes from a Tamil Village," *Economic and Political Weekly*, 37, 24, pp. 4403–14.

Appadurai, Arjun. 2002. "Deep Democracy: Urban Governmentality and the Horizon of Politics," *Public Culture*, 14, 1, pp. 21–47.

———. 2004. "The Capacity to Aspire: Culture and the Terms of Recognition," in *Culture and Public Action*, ed. V. Rao and M. Walton. Stanford, CA: Stanford University Press, pp. 59–84.

Argenti, Nicolas. 2005. *The Intestines of the State: Youth, Violence and Belated Histories in the Cameroonian Grassfields.* Chicago: Chicago University Press.

Aries, Philippe. 1962. *Centuries of Childhood: A Social History of Family Life.* New York: Transaction Books.

Arnot, Madeleine. 2003. "Male Working Class Identities and Social Justice: A Reconsideration of Paul Willis's Learning to Labor in Light of Recent Research," in

Learning to Labor in New Times, ed. Nadine Dolby, Greg Dimitriadis and Paul Willis. London: Routledge, pp. 15–34.

Baden Powell, B. H. 1971. *Administration of Land Revenue and Tenure in British India*. Delhi: Ess Ess Publications.

Bailey, Frederick G. 1957. *Caste and the Economic Frontier: A Village in Highland Orissa*. Manchester: Manchester University Press.

———. 1963. *Politics and Change: Orissa in 1959*. Berkeley: University of California Press.

———. 1996. *The Civility of Indifference: On Domesticating Ethnicity*. New York: Cornell University Press.

Bakhtin, M. M. 1986. *Speech Genres and Other Late Essays*. Austin: University of Texas Press.

Balagopal, K. 1991. "Post-Chundur and Other Chundurs," *Economic and Political Weekly*, 26, pp. 2399–2405.

Barr-Melej, Patrick. 2001. *Reforming Chile: Cultural Politics, Nationalism and the Rise of a Middle Class*. Chapel Hill: University of North Carolina Press.

Basu, Amrita. 1995. "When Local Riots Are Not Merely Local: Collective Violence and the State in Bijnor, India 1988–92," *Theory and Society*, 24, 1, pp. 35–78.

Baviskar, Amita. 2007. "Cows, Cars and Rickshaws: Bourgeois Environmentalists and the Battle for Delhi's Streets," Mimeo.

Baviskar, Amita, and Nandini Sundar. 2008. "Democracy versus Economic Transformation?: A Response to Partha Chatterjee's Democracy and Economic Transformation in India," *Economic and Political Weekly*, 43, 46, pp. 87–89.

Bayart, Jean-Francois. 1993. *The State in Africa: The Politics of the Belly*. London: Longman.

———. 2007. *Global Subjects: A Political Critique of Globalization*. Cambridge, UK: Polity Press.

Bénéï, Veronique. 2008. *Schooling Passions: Nation, History and Language in Contemporary India*. Stanford, CA: Stanford University Press.

Benjamin, Walter. 1983. *Charles Baudelaire: A Lyric Poet in the Era of High Capitalism*, Harry Zohn, trans.. London: Verso.

Bentall, Jim. 1995. "'Bharat versus India': Peasant Politics and Urban-Rural Relations in North-West India," PhD dissertation, University of Cambridge.

Bentall, Jim, and Stuart, E. Corbridge. 1996. "Urban-Rural Relations, Demand Politics and the 'New Agrarianism' in NW India: The Bharatiya Kisan Union," *Transactions of the Institute of British Geographers*, 2, 1, pp. 27–48.

Berry, Sara. 1985. *Fathers Work for Their Sons: Accumulation, Mobility and Class Formation in an Extended Yoruba Community*. Berkeley: University of California Press.

Béteille, André. 1992. *The Backward Classes in Contemporary India*. Delhi: Oxford University Press.

———. 2001. "Race and Caste," *The Hindu*, 10 March.

Bissell Keith. 2007. "Animating Suspension: Waiting for Mobilities," *Mobilities*, 2, pp. 277–98.

Blackman, Stuart. 2005. "Youth Subcultural Theory: A Critical Engagement with the Concept, its Origins and Politics, from the Chicago School to Postmodernism," *Journal of Youth Studies*, 8, pp. 1–20.

Bottomore, Tom. 1970. "Conservative Man," *New York Review of Books*, 15, 6, pp. 20–26.

Bourdieu, Pierre. 1977. *Outline of a Theory of Practice*. Cambridge: Cambridge University Press.

———. 1984. *Distinction: A Social Critique of the Judgement of Taste*. London: Routledge and Kegan Paul.

———. 1986. "The Forms of Capital," in *Handbook of Theory and Research in the Sociology of Education*, ed. J. G. Richardson. New York: Greenwood Press, pp. 241–58.

———. 2000. *Pascalian Meditations*. Stanford, CA: Stanford University Press.

———. 2001. *Masculine Domination*. Stanford, CA: Stanford University Press.

Bourdieu, Pierre, and Lois Wacquant. 1992. *An Invitation to Reflexive Sociology*. Chicago: University of Chicago Press.

Brass, Paul R. 1965. *Factional Politics in an Indian State: The Congress Party in Uttar Pradesh*. Berkeley: University of California Press.

———. 1997. *Theft of an Idol: Text and Context in the Representation of Collective Violence*. Princeton, NJ: Princeton University Press.

Breman, Jan. 1993. *Beyond Patronage and Exploitation*. Delhi: Oxford University Press.

———. 2000. *An Industrial Working Class: Sliding to the Bottom of the Labour Hierarchy in Ahmedabad, India*. Amsterdam: Amsterdam University Press.

Bucholtz, Mary. 2002. "Youth and Cultural Practice," *Annual Review of Anthropology*, 31, pp. 525–52.

Buck-Morss, Susan. 1986. "The Flâneur, the Sandwichman and the Whore: The Politics of Loitering," *New German Critique*, 39, pp. 99–139.

Bundy, Charles. 1987. "Street Sociology and Pavement Politics: Aspects of Youth and Student Resistance in Cape Town 1985," *Journal of Southern African Studies*, 13, pp. 303–30.

Butler, Judith. 1990. *Gender and the Subversion of Identity*. New Haven, CT: Yale University Press.

———. 1997. *The Psychic Life of Power: Theories in Subjection*. Stanford, CA: Stanford University Press.

Byres, Terence J. 1988. "Charan Singh (1902–1987): An Assessment," *Journal of Peasant Studies*, 15, 2, pp. 139–89.

CABE. 2004. http://www.education.nic.in/cabe/universalisation.pdf. Last accessed 22nd Jan. 2007.

Carter, Anthony T. 1974. *Elite Politics in India: Political Stratification and Political Alliances in Western Maharashtra.* London: Cambridge University Press.

Chakrabarty, Dipesh. 1999. "Adda, Calcutta: Dwelling in Modernity," *Public Culture*, 11, 1, pp. 109–45.

———. 2000. *Provincializing Europe: Postcolonial Thought and Historical Difference.* Princeton, NJ: Princeton University Press.

Chandrashekhar, C. P., and Jayati Ghosh. 2002. *The Market that Failed: A Decade of Neoliberal Economic Reforms in India.* Delhi: Manohar.

Chari, Sharad. 2004. *Fraternal Capital: Peasant-Workers, Self-made Men, and Globalization in Provincial India.* Stanford, CA: Stanford University Press.

Chatterjee, Partha. 1998. "Beyond the Nation or Within?" *Social Text*, 56, pp. 57–69.

———. 2004. *The Politics of the Governed: Reflections on Popular Politics in Most of the World.* Delhi: Permanent Black.

———. 2008. "Democracy and Economic Transformation in India," *Economic and Political Weekly*, 43, 16, pp. 53–62.

Chopra, Radhika, and Patricia Jeffery (eds). 2005. *Educational Regimes in Contemporary India.* Delhi: Sage.

Chowdhry, Prem. 1994. *The Veiled Women: Shifting Gender Equations in Rural Haryana 1880–1990.* Delhi: Oxford University Press.

———. 1997. "A Matter of Two Shares: A Daughter's Claim to Patrilineal Property in Rural North India," *Indian Economic and Social History Review* 34, 3, pp. 289–311.

———. 2009. "'First Our Jobs Then Our Girls': The Dominant Caste Perception on the 'Rising' Dalits," *Modern Asian Studies*, 43, 2, pp. 437–79.

Ciotti, Manuela. 2006. "'In the Past we were a bit 'Chamar': Education as a Self- and Community Engineering Process in Northern India," *The Journal of the Royal Anthropological Institute*, 12, 4, pp. 899–916.

Cloke, Paul, M. Phillips and Nigel Thrift. 1995. "The New Middle Classes and the Social Constructs of Rural Living," in *Social Change and the Middle Classes*, ed. Mike Savage and Tim Butler. London: Routledge, pp. 220–40.

Cohen, Shana. 2004. *Searching for a Different Future: The Rise of a Global Middle Class in Morocco.* Durham, NJ: Duke University Press.

Cohn, Bernard. 1961. "From Indian Status to British Contact," *The Journal of Economic History*, 21, 4, pp. 613–28.

Cole, Jennifer. 2004. "Fresh Contact in Tamatave, Madagascar: Sex, Money, and Intergenerational Transformation," *American Ethnologist*, 31, pp. 573–88.

———. 2005. "The Jaombilo of Tamative Madagascar (1992–2004): Reflections on Youth and Globalization," *Journal of Social History*, 38, 4, pp. 891–913.

Cole, Jennifer, and Deborah Durham (eds). 2008. *Figuring the Future: Children, Youth, and Globalization*. Santa Fe, NM: School of American Research Press.

Coleman, James S. 1965. *Education and Political Development*. Princeton, NJ: Princeton University Press.

Comptroller Auditor General. 2008. "Auditor Report Uttar Pradesh 2007–2008," available at http://www.cag.gov.in/html/cag_reports/up/rep_2008/contends.htm, last accessed 12 Dec. 2009.

Conlon, Deirdre. 2007. "The Nation as Embodied Practice: Women, Migration and the Social Production of Nationhood in Ireland," Ph.D. Dissertation, City University of New York.

Connell, Robert W. 2005. *Masculinities*. Berkeley: University of California Press.

Corbridge, Stuart. 2004. "Waiting in Line, or the Moral and Material Geographies of Queue-jumping," in *Geographies and Moralities*, ed. Roger Lee and David M. Smith. Oxford: Blackwell, pp. 183–98.

Corbridge, Stuart, and John Harriss. 2000. *Reinventing India: Liberalization, Hindu Nationalism and Popular Democracy*. Cambridge, UK: Polity Press.

Corbridge, Stuart, Glyn Williams, Manoj Srivastava and René Véron. 2005. *Seeing the State: Governance and Governmentality in Rural North India*. Cambridge: Cambridge University Press.

Corrigan, Paul. 1979. "Doing Nothing," in *Resistance Through Rituals: Youth Sub-cultures in Post-War Britain*, ed. Stuart Hall and Tony Jefferson. London: Routledge Kegan and Paul, pp. 103–5.

Cowan, Jane K. 1991. "Going out for a Coffee? Contesting the Grounds of Gendered Pleasures in Everyday Sociability," in *Contested Identities: Gender and Kinship in Modern Greece*, ed. Peter Loizos and Evthymios Papataxiarchis. Princeton, NJ: Princeton University Press, pp. 180–202.

Cowen, M., and R. W. Shenton. 1996. *Doctrines of Development*. London: Routledge.

Crapanzo, Vincent. 1986. *Waiting: The Whites of South Africa*. New York: Vintage.

Crooke, W. 1973. [1889] *The Races of Northern India*. Delhi: Cosmo Publications.

Darnton, Robert 1999. *The Great Cat Massacre and Other Episodes in French Cultural History*. New York: Basic Books.

Das, Veena, and Deborah Poole. 2004. *Anthropology in the Margins of the State*. Sante Fe, NM: School of American Research Press.

Datta, Nonica. 1999. *Forming an Identity: A Social History of the Jats*. Oxford: Oxford University Press.

Demerath, Peter. 1999. "The Cultural Production of Educational Utility in Pere Village, Papua New Guinea," *Comparative Education* Review, 43, 2, pp. 162–92.

————. 2003. "The Social Cost of Acting "Extra": Students' Moral Judgements of Self, Social Relations, and Academic Success in Papua New Guinea," Mimeo.

Desai, Nitin. 2007. "Growth and Employment," *Business Standard*, 15th November.

Deshpande, Satish. 2003. *Contemporary India: A Sociological View*. Delhi: Viking.

De Vries, Peter. 2002. "Vanishing Mediators: Enjoyment as a Political Factor in Western Mexico," *American Ethnologist*, 29, 4, pp. 901–27.

DiBona, Joseph. 1969. *Change and Conflict in the Indian University*. Durham, NC: Duke University Press.

Dirks, Nick B. 2003. *Castes of Mind: Colonialism and the Making of Modern India*. Delhi: Permanent Black.

Donner, Henrike. 2006. "Committed Mothers and Well-adjusted Children: Privatisation, Early-Years Education and Motherhood in Calcutta," *Modern Asian Studies*, 40, pp. 371–95.

Dore, Robert. 1976. *The Diploma Disease: Education, Qualification and Development*. Berkeley: University of California Press.

Dube, S. 1998. *In the Land of Poverty: Memoirs of an Indian Family 1947–1997*. London: Zed Books.

Duncan, Iain. 1997. "Agricultural Innovation and Political Change in North India: The Lok Dal in Uttar Pradesh," *Journal of Peasant Studies*, 24, 4, pp. 246–68.

————. 1999. "Dalits and Politics in Rural North India: The Bahujan Samaj Party in Uttar Pradesh," *Journal of Peasant Studies*, 27, 1, pp. 35–60.

Economic Times. 1998. "Rs. 24 crore cane scam unearthed," May 18.

Engineer, Ashgar Ali. 2002. "Gujarat Riots in the Light of the History of Communal Violence," *Economic and Political Weekly*, 37, 50, pp. 5047–54.

Ennew, Judith. 1994. "Time for Children or Time for Adults," in *Childhood Matters: Social Theory, Practice and Politics*, ed. Jens Qvortrop. Brookfield, VT: Averbury.

Epstein, T. Scarlett. 1973. *South India: Yesterday, Today and Tomorrow*. London: Macmillan.

Favero, Paolo. 2005. "India Dreams: Cultural Identity Among Young Middle Class Men in New Delhi," Doctoral Dissertation, Stockholm University.

Ferguson, James. 2006. *Global Shadows: Africa in the Neoliberal World Order*. Durham, NC: Duke University Press.

Ferguson, James, and Akhil Gupta. 2002. "Spatializing States: Towards an Ethnography of Neoliberal Governmentality," *American Ethnologist*, 29, 4, pp. 981–1002.

Fernandes, Leela. 2000. "Restructuring the New Middle Classes in Liberalizing India," *Comparative Studies in South Asia, Africa and the Middle East*, 20, 1–2, pp. 88–112.

———. 2004. "The Politics of Forgetting: Class Politics, State Power and the Restructuring of Urban Space in India," *Urban Studies*, 41, 12, pp. 2415–30.

———. 2006. *India's New Middle Class: Democratic Politics in an Era of Economic Reform*, Minneapolis: Minnesota University Press.

Fernandes Leela, and Patrick Heller. 2006. "Hegemonic Aspirations: New Middle Class Politics and India's Democracy in Comparative Perspective," *Critical Asian Studies*, 38, 4, pp. 495–522.

Ferro, Manuela, David Rosenblatt and Nicholas Stern. 2004. "Policies for Pro-poor Growth," in *India's Emerging Economy*, ed. Kaushik Basu. Cambridge, MA: MIT Press, pp. 153–82.

Foucault, Michel. 1988. *Politics, Philosophy, Culture: Interviews and Other Writings, 1977–1984* [Translated by Alan Sheridan and others]. London: Routledge.

Frøystad, Kathinka. 2005. *Blended Boundaries: Caste, Class and Shifting Faces of 'Hinduness' in a North Indian City*. Delhi: Oxford University Press.

Fuller, Chris, and Veronique Bénéï. 2001. *The Everyday State and Society in Modern India*. London: Hurst and Co.

Fuller, Chris, and Haripriya Naramsimhan. 2007. "Information Technology Professionals and the New-Rich Middle Class in Chennia (Madras)," *Modern Asian Studies*, 41, pp. 121–50.

Gerke, Solvay. 2000. "Global Lifestyles under Local Conditions: The New Indonesian Middle Class," in *Consumption in Asia*, ed. Beng-Huat Chua. London: Routledge, pp. 159–82.

Ghosh, Kaushik. 2006. "Between Global Flows and Local Dams: Indigenousness, Locality, and the Transnational Sphere in Jharkhand, India," *Cultural Anthropology*, 21, 4, pp. 501–29.

Giddens, Anthony. 1990. *The Consequences of Modernity*. Cambridge, UK: Polity.

Gidwani, Vinay. 2001. "The Cultural Logic of Work: Explaining Labour Deployment and Piece-rate Contracts in Matar Taluka, Gujarat—parts I and II," *Journal of Development Studies*, 38, 2, pp. 57–74.

———. 2008. *Capital Interrupted: Agrarian Development and the Politics of Work in India*. Minnesota, MN: Minnesota University Press.

Gidwani, Vinay, and K. Sivaramakrishnan. 2003. "Circular Migration and Rural Cosmopolitanism in India," *Contributions to Indian Sociology*, 37, 1–2, pp. 339–67.

Gold, Ann, and Bhoj Ram Gujar. 2002. *In the Time of Trees and Sorrows: Nature, Power, and Memory in Rajasthan*. Durham, NC: Duke University Press.

Gooptu, Nandini. 2007. "Economic Liberalization, Work, and Democracy," *Economic and Political Weekly* 42, 21, pp. 1922–33.

Gould, Harold. 1972. "Educational Structures and Political Processes in Faizabad District, Uttar Pradesh," in *Education and Politics in India*, ed. Susanne Hoeber Rudolph and Lloyd I. Rudolph. Cambridge, MA: Harvard University Press, pp. 94–120.

Gramsci, Antonio. 1971. *Selections from the Prison Notebooks* [ed. and trans. Q. Hoare and G. Nowell-Smith]. London: Lawrence and Wishart.

Gupta, Akhil. 1995. "Blurred Boundaries: The Discourse of Corruption, the Culture of Politics and the Imagined State," *American Ethnologist*, 22, 2, pp. 375–402.

———. 1997. "Agrarian Populism in the Development of a Modern Nation (India)," in *International Development and the Social Sciences: Essays on the History and Politics of Knowledge*, ed. F. Cooper and R. Packard. Berkeley: University of California Press, pp. 320–44.

———. 1998. *Postcolonial Developments: Agriculture in the Making of Modern India*. Durham, NC. London: Duke University Press.

Gupta, Dipankar. 1997. *Brotherhood and Rivalry*. Delhi: Oxford University Press.

———. 2000. *Mistaken Modernity: India Between Worlds*. Delhi: Harper Collins.

Gutmann, Mathew C. 1996. *Meanings of Macho: Being a Man in Mexico City*. Berkeley: University of California Press.

Hall, Stuart. 1985. "Signification, Representation, Ideology: Althusser and the Post-structuralist Debates," *Critical Studies in Mass Communication*, 2, pp. 91–114.

Hansen, Karen, T. 2005. "Getting Stuck in the Compound: Some Odds against Social Adulthood in Lusaka, Zambia," *Africa Today*, 51, 4, pp. 3–16.

Hansen, Thomas. B. 1996. "Recuperating Masculinity: Hindu Nationalism, Violence, and the Exorcism of the Muslim 'Other,'" *Critique of Anthropology*, 16, 22, pp. 137–72.

———. 1998. "Governance and State Mythologies in Mumbai." Paper delivered to Anthropology of the State Workshop, London School of Economics and Political Science.

———. 2001. *Wages of Violence: Naming and Identity in Postcolonial Bombay*. Princeton, NJ: Princeton University Press.

Hansen, Thomas B., and Finn Stepputat 2001, *States of Imagination: Ethnographic Explorations of the Post-Colonial State*. Durham, NC: Duke University Press.

Harper, D. 1992. "Small N's and Community Case Studies," in *What is a Case? Exploring the Foundations of Social Enquiry*, ed. Charles C. Ragin, H. S. Becker. Cambridge: Cambridge University Press, pp. 139–58.

Harriss, John. 1982. *Capitalism and Peasant Farming: Agrarian Structure and Ideology in Northern Tamil Nadu*. Bombay: Oxford University Press.

———. 2003. "The Great Tradition Globalizes: Reflections on Two Studies of 'The Industrial Leaders' of Madras," *Modern Asian Studies*, 7, 2, pp. 327–62.

———. 2006. "Middle-class Activism and the Politics of the Informal Working Class," *Critical Asian Studies*, 38, 4, pp. 445–65.

Harriss, R. L. 2003. "Popular Resistance to Globalization and Neoliberalism in Latin America," *Journal of Development Studies*, 19, pp. 365–426.

Harriss-White, Barbara. 1996a. "The Green Revolution in South India," *Politica Internazionale*, 5, pp. 81–94.

———. 1996b. *A Political Economy of Agrarian Markets in South India: Masters of the Countryside*. Delhi: Sage.

———. 2003. *India Working: Essays on Society and Economy*. Cambridge: Cambridge University Press.

———. 2005. "India's Socially Regulated Economy," Paper for the 7th International Conference on Institutional Economics, University of Hertfordshire.

Hart, Jason. 2007. "Dislocated Masculinity: Adolescence and the Palestinian Nation-in-exile," *Journal of Refugee Studies*, 21, 1, pp. 64–81.

Hasan, Zoya. 1995. "Shifting Ground: Hindutva Politics and the Farmers' Movements in Uttar Pradesh," in *New Farmers Movements in India*, ed. Tom Brass. Ilford, UK: Frank Cass, pp. 165–94.

———. 1998. *Quest for Power: Oppositional Movements and Post-Congress Politics in Uttar Pradesh*. Delhi: Oxford University Press.

Hazary, Subas C. 1987. *Student Politics in India*. Delhi: Ashish Publishing House.

Hebdige, Dick. 1979. *Subculture: The Meaning of Style*. London: Methuen.

Heller, Patrick. 2000. "Degrees of Democracy: Some Comparative Lessons from India," *World Politics*, 52, pp. 484–519.

Herzfeld, Michael. 2005. *Cultural Intimacy: Social Poetics in the Nation-State*. New York: Routledge.

Heuzé, Gerard. 1992. "Shiv Sena and 'National Hinduism'," *Economic and Political Weekly*, 27, 41, pp. 2253–61.

———. 1996. *Workers of another World: Miners, the Countryside and Coalfields in Dhanbad*. Delhi: Oxford University Press.

The Hindu. 4 June 2004, "BEd Boom."

Hoffman, Danny. 2004. "The Civilian Target in Sierra Leone and Liberia: Political Power, Military Strategy, and Humanitarian Intervention," *African Affairs*, 103, pp. 211–26.

http://rethinkingdemocracy.wordpress.com/, last accessed 10 Jan. 2010.

http://www.guardian.co.uk/profile/craig-jeffrey, last accessed 8 Jan. 2010.

Jackson, Peter. 1998. "Domesticating the Street: The Contested Spaces of the High

Street and the Mall," in *Images of the Street: Planning, Identity, Control in Public Space*, ed. Nicholas R. Fyfe. London: Routledge, pp. 176–91.

Jaffrelot, Christophe. 1996. *The Hindu Nationalist Movement and Indian Politics*. London: Hurst and Co.

———. 2003. *India's Silent Revolution: The Rise of the Low Castes in North Indian Politics*. Delhi: Permanent Black.

Jayaram, N. 1979. "Sadhus No Longer: Recent Trends in Indian Student Activism," *Higher Education*, 8, 6, pp. 683–99.

Jeffery, Roger, and Patricia Jeffery. 1994. "The Bijnor Riots, October 1990: Collapse of a Mythical Special Relationship?" *Economic and Political Weekly*, 29, 12, pp. 551–58.

———. 1997. *Population, Gender and Politics: Demographic Change in Rural North India*. Cambridge: Cambridge University Press.

Jeffery, Roger, Patricia Jeffery and Craig Jeffery. 2005. "Social Inequality and the Privatisation of Secondary Schooling in North India," in *Educational Regimes in India*, ed. Radhika Chopra and Patricia Jeffery. Delhi: Sage, pp. 41–61.

———. 2006. "*Parhāī ka māhaul*? An Educational Environment in Bijnor, UP," in *The Meaning of the Local: Politics of Place in Urban India*, ed. Geert de Neve and Henrike Donner. London: Routledge, pp. 116–40.

Jeffery, Roger, and Jens Lerche (eds). 2003. *Social and Political Change in Uttar Pradesh: European Perspectives*. Delhi: Manohar.

Jeffrey, Craig. 1999. "Reproducing Difference: The Accumulation Strategies of Richer Jat Farmers in Western Uttar Pradesh, India," PhD dissertation, University of Cambridge.

———. 2000. "Democratisation without Representation? The Power and Political Strategies of a Rural Elite in North India," *Political Geography*, 19, pp. 1013–36.

———. 2001. "A Fist Is Stronger than Five Fingers: Caste and Dominance in Rural North India," *Transactions of the Institute of British Geographers*, 25, 2, pp. 1–30.

———. 2002. "Caste, Class and Clientelism: A Political Economy of Everyday Corruption in Rural North India," *Economic Geography*, 78, 1, pp. 21–42.

———. 2008. "Kicking Away the Ladder: Student Politics and the Making of an Indian Middle Class," *Environment and Planning D: Society and Space*, 26, 3, pp. 105–23.

Jeffrey, Craig, Patricia Jeffery and Roger Jeffery. 2008. *Degrees Without Freedom? Education, Masculinities and Unemployment in North India*. Stanford, CA: Stanford University Press.

Johnson-Hanks, Deborah. 2002. "On the Limits of Life Stages in Ethnography: Towards a Theory of Vital Conjunctures," *American Anthropologist*, 104, 3, pp. 865–80.

Joshi, E. B. (ed.). 1965. *Uttar Pradesh District Gazetteer, Meerut*, Department of Uttar Pradesh District Gazetteers, Lucknow.

Joshi, Sanjay. 2001. *Fractured Modernity: Making of a Middle Class in Colonial North India*. New Delhi: Oxford University Press.

Joshi, Vijay. 2009. "Economic Resurgence, Lop-sided Performance, Jobless Growth," in *Continuity and Change in Contemporary India: Politics, Economic, and Society*, ed. Anthony Heath and Roger Jeffery. Delhi: Oxford University Press, pp. 80–100.

Kalecki, Michael. 1972. *Selected Essays on the Economic Growth of the Socialist and Mixed Economy*. Cambridge: Cambridge University Press.

Kamat, Sangeeta. 2002. *Development Hegemony: NGOs and the State in India*. Delhi: Oxford University Press.

Kaplinsky, Raphael. 2005. *Globalization, Poverty and Inequality: Between a Rock and A Hard Place*. Cambridge, UK: Polity.

Keniston, Kenneth. 1971. *Youth and Dissent: The Rise of a New Opposition*. New York: Harcourt Brace Jovanovich.

Kermode, Frank. 1967. *The Sense of an Ending: Studies in the Theories of Fiction*. Oxford: Oxford University Press.

Kingdon, Geeta, and Mohammad Muzammil. 2003. *The Political Economy of Education in India: Teacher Politics in Uttar Pradesh*. Oxford: Oxford University Press.

Knox, Hannah, Mike Savage and Penny Harvey. 2006. "Social Networks and the Study of Relations: Networks as Method, Metaphor and Form," *Economy and Society* 35, 1, pp. 113–40.

Kracauer, Siegfried. 1995 [1963]. *The Mass Ornament: Weimar Essays* [translated and edited by Thomas Y. Levin]. Cambridge, MA: Harvard University Press.

Krishna, Anirudh. 2002. *Active Social Capital: Tracing the Roots of Development and Democracy*. New York: Columbia University Press.

Krishnan, Kavita. 2007. "Penalizing Progressive Student Activism," *Economic and Political Weekly*, 42, 3, pp. 3199–3202.

Kumar, Krishna. 1988. "Origins of India's 'Textbook Culture," *Comparative Education Review*, 32, 4, pp. 452–64.

———. 1994. *Democracy and Education in India*. London: Sangam Books.

Lanjouw, Peter, and Nicholas H. Stern. 1998. *Economic Development in Palanpur over Five Decades*. Oxford: Oxford University Press.

Leavitt, Stephen C. 1998. "The Bikhet Mystique: Masculine Identity and Patterns of Rebellion among Bumbts Adolescent Males," in *Adolescence in Pacific Island Societies*, ed. Gilbert Herdt and Stephen C. Leavitt. Pittsburgh: University of Pittsburgh Press, pp. 173–94.

Lerche, Jens. 1995. "Is Bonded Labour a Bound Category? Reconceptualising Agrarian Conflict in India," *Journal of Peasant Studies*, 22, pp. 484–515.

———. 1999. "Politics of the Poor: Agricultural Labourers and Political Transformations in Uttar Pradesh," in *Rural Labour Relations in India*, ed. Terence J. Byres, Karin Kapadia and Jens Lerche. London: Frank Cass, pp. 182–243.

Levinson, Bradley A. 1999. "Una Etapa Siempre Dificil: Concepts of Adolescence and Secondary Education in Mexico," *Comparative Education Review*, 43, 2, pp. 129–61.

Li, Tania. 2005. "Beyond the State and Failed Schemes," *American Anthropologist*, 107, 3, pp. 383–94.

————. 2007. *The Will to Improve: Governmentality, Development, and the Practice of Politics*. Durham, NC: Duke University Press.

Lieten, G. Kristoffel. 1996. "Panchayats in Western Uttar Pradesh: 'Namesake' Members," *Economic and Political Weekly*, 31, 39, pp. 2700–2705.

Lieten, G. Kristoffel, and Ravi Srivastava. 1999. *Unequal Partners: Power Relations, Devolution and Development in Uttar Pradesh*. Delhi: Sage.

Lipton, Michael. 1977. *Why Poor People Stay Poor: A Study of Urban Bias in World Development*. London: Temple Smith.

Lukose, Ritty. 2005. "Consuming Globalization: Youth and Gender in Kerala, India," *Journal of Social History*, 38, 4, pp. 915–35.

Lynch, Kathleen. 1990. "Reproduction: The Role of Cultural Factors and Educational Mediators," *British Journal of Sociology of Education*, 11, 1, pp. 3–20.

Madison, Soyini. 2005. *Critical Ethnography: Ethics, Methods and Performance*. London: Sage.

Madsen, Stig T. 1998. "The Decline of the BKU," paper presented at the European Conference of Modern Asian Studies, Charles University, Prague, September. Mimeo.

Madsen, Stig T., and Staffan Lindberg. 2003. "Modelling Institutional Fate: The Case of a Farmers' Movement in Uttar Pradesh," in *Social and Political Change in Uttar Pradesh. European Perspectives*, ed. Roger Jeffery and Jens Lerche. Delhi: Manohar, pp. 199–223.

Mains, Daniel. 2007. "Neoliberal Times: Progress, Boredom, and Shame among Young Men in Urban Ethiopia," *American Ethnologist*, 34, 4, pp. 659–73.

Mannheim, Karl. 1972. "The Problem of Generations," in *The New Pilgrims: Youth Protest in Transition*, ed. Philip Altbach and R. Laufer. New York: David McKay and Company, pp. 101–38.

Masani, Minoo. 1979. "Is JP the Answer?" Delhi: Macmillan.

Masquelier, Adeline, M. 2005. "The Scorpion's Sting: Youth, Marriage and the Struggle for Social Maturity in Niger," *Journal of the Royal Anthropological Institute*, 11, 1, pp. 59–83.

Mawdsley, Emma. 2004. "India's Middle Classes and the Environment," *Development and Change*, 35, pp. 79–103.

Mazumdar, Ranjani. 2007. *Bombay Cinema: An Archive of the City*. Minneapolis: Minnesota University Press.

Mbembe, Achille. 2004. "Aesthetics of Superfluity," *Public Culture*, 16, pp. 373–405.

McCartney, M., and Barbara Harriss-White. 2000. "The Intermediate Regime and Intermediate Classes Revisited: A Political Economy of Indian Development from c.1980 to Hindutva," Queen Elizabeth House, Working Paper Number 34.

McDowell, Linda. 2003. *Redundant Masculinities? Employment Change and White Working Class Youth*. Oxford: Blackwell.

McGregor, Robert S. 1993. *The Oxford Hindi-English Dictionary*. Oxford: Oxford University Press.

McKibbin, Ross. 1994. *The Ideologies of Class: Social Relations in Britain, 1880–1950*. Oxford: Clarendon Press.

Mendelsohn, Oliver, and Marieke Vicziany. 1998. *The Untouchables: Subordination, Poverty and the State in Modern India*. Cambridge: Cambridge University Press.

Michelutti, Lucia. 2007. "The Vernacularization of Democracy: Political Participation and Popular Politics in North India," *Journal of the Royal Anthropological Institute*, 13, 3, pp. 639–56.

Milanovic, Branko. 2005. *Worlds Apart: Measuring Global and International Inequality*. Princeton, NJ: Princeton University Press.

Miles, Ann. 1998. "Women's Bodies, Women's Selves: Illness Narratives and the 'Andean' Body," *Body and Society*, 4, 3, pp. 1–19.

Miles, Rebecca. 2002. "Employment and Unemployment in Jordan: The Importance of the Gender System," *World Development*, 30, 3, pp. 413–27.

Mishra, Pankaj. 2004. *The Romantics*. New York: Random House.

———. 2006. *Butter Chicken in Ludhiana: Travels in Small Town India*. London: Picador.

Mittal, K. 1978. "The Role of Meerut College in the Freedom Struggle of India," *Social Scientist*, 7, 76, pp. 35–54.

Mohanty, Chandra T. 2003. "'Under Western Eyes' Revisited: Feminist Solidarity through Anticapitalist Struggles," *Signs: Journal of Women in Culture and Society*, 28, 2, pp. 499–535.

Mooij, J., and S. M. Dev. 2002. "Social Sector Priorities: An Analysis of Budgets and Expenditures," Institute of Development Studies. *IDS Working Paper* 164, University of Sussex, Brighton, UK.

Moore, Donald. 2005. *Suffering for Territory: Race, Place, and Power in Zimbabwe*. Durham, NC: Duke University Press.

Moran, Joe. 2004. "November in Berlin: The End of the Everyday," *History Workshop Journal*, 57, 1, pp. 216–34.

Myrdal, Jan. 1967. *India Waits*. New York: Lake View Press.

Nandy, Ashis. 1998. "Indian Popular Cinema as a Slum's Eye View of Politics," in *The Secret Politics of Our Desires: Innocence, Culpability, and Indian Popular Cinema*, ed. Ashis Nandy. London: Palgrave MacMillan, pp. 1–18.

Nair, Neeti. 2009. "Bhagat Singh as Satyagrahi: The Limits to Non-Violence in Late Colonial India," *Modern Asian Studies*, 43: 649–81.

Nesfield, J. C. 1885. *Brief View of the Caste System of the North Western Provinces and Oudh.* Allahabad: Government Branch Press.

Nevill, H. H. 1922. *Meerut—A Gazetteer.* Lucknow: Government Branch Press.

Nijman, Jan. 2006. "Mumbai's Mysterious Middle Class," *International Journal of Urban and Regional Research*, 30, 4, pp. 758–75.

Nisbett, Nicholas. 2007. "Friendship, Consumption, Morality: Practising Identity Negotiating Hierarchy in Middle Class Bangalore," *Journal of the Royal Anthropological Institute*, 13, 4, pp. 935–50.

O'Dougherty, Maureen. 2002. *Consumption Intensified: The Politics of Daily Middle Class Life in Brazil.* Durham, NC: Duke University Press.

Øian, Hogne. 2004. "Time Out and Drop Out: On the Relationship between Linear Time and Individualism," *Time and Society*, 13, 2–3, pp. 173–95.

Osella, Caroline, and Filippo Osella. 2002. "Contextualising Sexuality: Young Men in Kerala, South India," in *Coming of Age in South and Southeast Asia : Youth, Courtship and Sexuality*, ed. L. Rice Pranee and L. Manderson, Richmond, UK: Curzon.

Osella, Filippo, and Caroline Osella. 2000. *Social Mobility in Kerala: Modernity and Identity in Conflict.* London: Pluto Press.

———. 2007. *Men and Masculinities in South India.* London: Anthem Press.

Pai, Sudha. 2000. "New Social and Political Movements of Dalits: A Study of Meerut District," *Contributions to Indian Sociology*, 34, 2, pp. 189–220.

———. 2002. *Dalit Assertion and the Unfinished Democratic Revolution: The Bahujan Samaj Party in Uttar Pradesh.* Delhi: Sage.

Pai, Sudha, and Jagpal Singh. 1997. "Politicisation of Dalits and Most Backward Castes: Study of Social Conflict and Political Preferences in Four Villages of Meerut District," *Economic and Political Weekly*, 32, 23, pp. 1356–61.

Parry, Jonathan P. 1996. "No Mother and Father Like It: Bhilai Steel Plant in Central India," Seminar presentation, Department of Anthropology, University of Cambridge.

———. 1999. "Two Cheers for Reservation: The Satnamis and the Steel Plant," in *Institutions and Inequalities*, ed. Ramachandran Guha and Jonathan P. Parry. Delhi: Oxford University Press, pp. 128–69.

Patnaik, Utsa. 1976. "Class Differentiation within the Peasantry: An Approach to the Analysis of Indian Agriculture," *Economic and Political Weekly*, 11, 39, pp. A82–A101.

Pinney, Christopher. 2002. "Photographic Portraiture in Central India in the 1980s and 1990s," in *The Material Culture Reader*, ed. Victor Buchli. Oxford: Berg, pp. 87–104.

Postone, Moishe. 1993. *Time, Labour and Social Domination: A Reconsideration of Marx's Critical Theory*. Cambridge: Cambridge University Press.

Prause, J., and D. Dooley. 1997. "Effects of Underemployment on School-leavers' Self-esteem," *Journal of Adolescence*, 20, pp. 243–60.

Raheja, Gloria G. 1988. *The Poison in the Gift: Ritual Prestation, and the Dominant Caste in a North Indian Village*. Chicago: University of Chicago Press.

Ralph, Michael. 2008. "Killing Time," *Social Text*, 26, pp. 1–29.

Rana, M. S. 1994. *Bharatiya Kisan Union and Ch. Tikait*. Meerut: Paragon Publications.

Reddy, G. Ram, and G. Haragopal. 1985. "The Pyraveekar: 'The Fixer' in Rural India," *Asian Survey* 25, 11, pp. 1148–62.

Registrar General and Census Commissioner of India. 2004. *Table C-14: Population in Five Year Age-group by Residence and Sex*. Delhi: Census Commissioner Tabulations made available in electronic format.

Robison, R., D., and S. G. Goodman (eds). 1996. *The New Rich in Asia: Mobile Phones, McDonald's and Middle-class Revolution*. London: Routledge.

Robinson, Marguerite. 1988. *Local Politics: The Law of the Fishes—Development Through Political Change in Medak District, Andhra Pradesh (South India)*. Delhi: Oxford University Press.

Rogers, Martyn. 2008. "Modernity, 'Authenticity,' and Ambivalence: Subaltern Masculinities on a South Indian Campus," *Journal of the Royal Anthropological Institute*, 14, pp. 79–95.

Roitman, Janet. 2004. *Fiscal Disobedience: An Anthropology of Economic Regulation in Central Africa*. Princeton, NJ: Princeton University Press.

Ross, Kristin. 2002. *May '68 and its Afterlives*. Chicago: Chicago University Press.

Rostow, Walter W. 2008 [1959]. "The Stages of Economic Growth," *The Economic History Review*, 12, 1, pp. 1–16.

Roulet, Margueruite. 1996. "Dowry and Prestige in North India," *Contributions to Indian Sociology*, 30, 1, pp. 89–107.

Ruddick, Susan. 2003. "The Politics of Aging: Globalization and the Restructuring of Youth and Childhood," *Antipode* 35, pp. 335–64.

Rudolph, Lloyd I., and Susanne Hoeber Rudolph. 1987. *In Pursuit of Lakshmi: The Political Economy of the Indian State*. Chicago: University of Chicago Press.

Rutten, Mario. 1995. *Farms and Factories*. Delhi: Sage.

Ruud, Arild. 2008. "To Create a Crowd: Student Leaders in Dhaka," Mimeo.

Samata Sanghatana. 1991. "Upper Caste Violence: Study of the Chunduru Carnage," *Economic and Political Weekly*, 26, 36, pp. 2079–84.

Sangtin Writers, and Richa Nagar. 2006. *Feminist Thought and Activism through Seven Lives in India*, Minneapolis: Minnesota University Press.

Savage, Mike. 2003. "A New Class Paradigm?" *British Journal of Sociology of Education*, 24, 4, pp. 535–41.

Savage, Mike, and Tim Butler. 1992. "Assets and the Middle Classes in Contemporary Britain," in *Property, Bureaucracy and Culture: Middle Class Formation in Contemporary Britain*, ed. Mike Savage, J. Barlow, P. Dickens and T. Fielding. London: Routledge, pp. 245–59.

Savage, Mike, Alan Warde and Fiona Devine. 2005. "Capitals, Assets and Resources: Some Critical Issues," *The British Journal of Sociology*, 56, 1, pp. 31–47.

Scheper-Hughes, Nancy. 1992. *Death Without Weeping: The Violence of Everyday Life in Brazil*. Berkeley: University of California Press.

————. 1995. "The Primacy of the Ethical: Propositions for a Militant Anthropology," *Current Anthropology*, 36, 3, pp. 409–40.

Scott, James. C. 1985. *Weapons of the Weak: Everyday Forms of Peasant Resistance*. New Haven, CT: Yale University Press.

Scrase, Timothy. 2006. "The 'New' Middle Class in India: A Re-assessment," Paper presented at the 16th Biennial Conference of the Asian Studies Association of Australia, University of Wollongong, Australia.

Scrase, Timothy J., and Ruchira Ganguly-Scrase. 2008. *Globalisation and the Middle Classes in India: The Social and Cultural Impact of Neoliberal Reforms*. London: Routledge.

Sen, A. 1999. *Development as Freedom*. New York: Knopf.

Shah, Alpa. 2006. "Markets of Protection," *Critique of Anthropology*, 26, 3, pp. 297–314.

Sharma, Rita, and Thomas T. Poleman. 1993. *The New Economics of India's Green Revolution: Income and Employment Diffusion in Uttar Pradesh*, Ithaca: Cornell University Press.

Sheth, D. L. 1999. "Secularization of Caste and the Making of a New Middle Class," *Economic and Political Weekly*, 34, 34, pp. 2502–10.

Shukla, Shrilal. 1992. *Raag Darbari* (translated by Gillian Wright). New Delhi: Penguin.

Siddiqui, Kalim. 1999. "New Technology and Processes of Differentiation: Two Sugarcane Cultivating Villages in Uttar Pradesh," *Economic and Political Weekly*, 34, 52, pp. A139–A151.

Silberschmidt, M. 2001. "Disempowerment of Men in Rural and Urban East Africa: Implications for Male Identity and Sexual Behaviour," *World Development*, 29, pp. 657–71.

Simone, Abdoumaliq. 2005. "Urban Circulation and the Everyday Politics of African

Urban Youth: The Case of Douala, Cameroon," *International Journal of Urban and Regional Research*, 29, pp. 516–32.

Singh, Ajit Kumar. 2007. "The Economy of Uttar Pradesh since the 1990s: Economic Stagnation and Fiscal Crisis," in *Political Process in Uttar Pradesh: Identity, Economic Reforms and Governance*, ed. Sudha Pai. London: Pearson Longman, pp. 273–294.

Singh, Jagpal. 1992. *Capitalism and Dependence: Agrarian Politics in Western Uttar Pradesh 1951–1991*. Delhi: Manohar.

———. 1995. "Political Economy of Unaided and Unrecognised Schools: A Study of Meerut District of Western Uttar Pradesh," unpublished Report, National Institute of Educational Planning and Administration, New Delhi.

Spivak, Gayatri. C. 1988. "Can the Subaltern Speak?" in *Marxism and the Interpretation of Culture*, ed. C. Nelson and Lawrence Grossberg. Chicago: Chicago University Press.

———. 2004. "Righting Wrongs," *The South Atlantic Quarterly*, 103, 2/3, pp. 523–81.

Srinivas, M. N. 1955. "The Social System of a Mysore Village," in *Village India*, ed. McKim Marriott. Chicago: Chicago University Press.

———. 1989. *The Cohesive Role of Sanskritization and Other Essays*. Oxford: Oxford University Press.

Srivastava, Ravi. 1995. "India's Uneven Development and its Implications for Political Processes: An Analysis of some Recent Trends," in *Industry and Agriculture in India Since Independence*, ed. T. V. Sathyamurthy. Delhi: Oxford University Press, pp. 190–221.

Stambach, Amy. 1998. "'Too Much Studying Makes me Crazy': School-related Illness on Mount Kilimanjaro," *Comparative Education Review*, 42, 4, pp. 497–512.

Stepputat, Finn. 1992. "Beyond Relief? Life in a Guatemalan Refugee Settlement in Mexico," PhD Dissertation, Institute of Cultural Sociology, University of Copenhagen.

———. 2002. "The Final Move? Displaced Livelihoods and Final Returns," in *Work and Migration. Life and Livelihoods in a Globalizing World*, ed. Karen F. and Ninna N. Sørensen. London: Routledge, pp. 202–24.

Stokes, Eric. 1986. *The Peasant Armed: The Indian Revolt of 1857*. Oxford: Clarendon Press.

Stone, Ian. 1984. *Canal Irrigation in British India: Perspectives on Technological Change in a Peasant Economy*. Cambridge: Cambridge University Press.

Superintendent of Printing and Stationery, Allahabad. 1931. *Census of India, The United Provinces of Agra and Oudh*.

Syed, Rashi Ali. 1997. *Culture of Student Politics*. Delhi: Inter-India Publications.

Tambiah, Stanley J. 1997. *Leveling Crowds: Ethno-nationalist Conflicts and Collective Violence in South Asia.* Berkeley: University of California Press.

Tarlo, Emma. 2003. *Unsettling Memories: Narratives of the Emergency in Delhi.* Delhi: Permanent Black.

Thrift, Nigel. 1996. "Owners' Time and Own Time: The Making of a Capitalist Time-consciousness 1300–1880," in *Human Geography: An Essential Anthology*, ed. John Agnew, David Livingstone, and Alisdair Rogers. Oxford: Blackwell, pp. 552–570.

Thompson, Edward P. 1963. *The Making of the English Working Class.* London: Victor Gollacz.

———. 1967. "Time, Work Discipline and Industrial Capitalism," *Past and Present*, 38, pp. 56–97.

Ul Haq, M. 2003. *Human Development in South Asia 2003: The Employment Challenge.* Delhi: Oxford University Press.

Upadhya, Carol B. 1988. "From Kulak to Capitalist: The Emergence of a New Business Community in Coastal Andhra Pradesh, India," PhD dissertation, Yale University.

Vale de Almeida, M. 1996. *The Hegemonic Male: Masculinity in a Portuguese Town.* Providence, RI: Berghahn.

Van Wessel, Margit. 2007. "Talking About Consumption," *Cultural Dynamics* 16 (1), 93–116.

Varma, Pavan K. 2006. *The Great Indian Middle Class.* Delhi: Viking.

Varshney, Ashutosh. 1995. *Democracy, Development and the Countryside: Urban-Rural Struggles in India.* Cambridge: Cambridge University Press.

Vatuk, Sylvia. 1972. *Kinship and Urbanization: White Collar Workers in North India.* Berkeley: University of California Press.

Verdery, Katherine. 1996. *What Was Socialism and What Comes Next?* Princeton, NJ: Princeton University Press.

Vigh, Henrik. 2006. *Navigating Terrains of War: Youth and Soldiering in Guinea-Bissau.* New York: Berghahn.

Visaria, Pravin. 2003. "Unemployment among Youth in India: Level, Nature and Policy Implications," Mimeo.

Wade, Robert. 1985. "The Market for Public Office: Why the Indian State Is Not Better at Development," *World Development*, 13, 4, pp. 467–97.

———. 1988. "Politics and Graft: Recruitment, Appointment and Promotions to Public Office in India," in *Corruption, Development and Inequality: Soft Touch or Hard Graft?* ed. Peter Ward. London: Routledge, pp. 73–110.

Wadley, Susan S. 1994. *Struggling with Destiny in Karimpur, 1925–1984.* Delhi: Vistaar Publications.

Weiss, Brad. 2002. "Thug Realism: Inhabiting Fantasy in Urban Tanzania," *Cultural Anthropology*, 17, 1, pp. 93–124.

Whyte, W. F. 1993. *Street Corner Society: The Social Structure of an Italian Slum*. Chicago: Chicago University Press.

Wiener, M. J. 1981. *English Culture and the Decline of the Industrial Spirit 1850–1980*. Cambridge: Cambridge University Press.

Williams, Raymond. 1977. *Marxism and Literature*. Oxford: Oxford University Press.

———. 1985. *Keywords: A Vocabulary of Culture and Society*. Oxford: Oxford University Press.

Willis, Paul. 1977. *Learning to Labour: How Working Class Kids Get Working Class Jobs*. Farnborough: Saxon House.

———. 1982. "Cultural Production and Theories of Reproduction," in *Race, Class and Education*, ed. L. Barton and S. Walker. London: Croome Helm, pp. 112–42.

Wong, Diana. 1991. "Asylum as a Relationship of Otherness: A Study of Asylum Holders in Nuremberg, Germany," *Journal of Refugee Studies*, 4, 2, pp. 150–63.

World Bank. 2006. "Monitoring Poverty in Uttar Pradesh: A Report on the Second Poverty and Social Monitoring Survey (PSM-II)." Available at worldbank.org, accessed 7 Sept. 2008.

Wright Mills, C. 1959. *The Sociological Imagination*. Oxford: Oxford University Press.

Yon, D. 2000. "Urban Portraits of Identity: On the Problem of Knowing Culture and Identity in Intercultural Studies," *Journal of Intercultural Studies*, 21, 2, pp. 143–57.

Zerubavel, E. 1985. *Hidden Rhythms: Schedules and Calendars in Social Life*. Berkeley: California University Press.

Index